Generative AI in Higher Education

Generative AI in Higher Education

The Good, the Bad, and the Ugly

Edited by

Kätlin Pulk

Associate Professor, Department of Management, Estonian Business School, Estonia

Riina Koris

Associate Professor, Department of Marketing and Communication, Estonian Business School, Estonia

 Edward Elgar
PUBLISHING

Cheltenham, UK • Northampton, MA, USA

Published by
Edward Elgar Publishing Limited
The Lypiatts
15 Lansdown Road
Cheltenham
Glos GL50 2JA
UK

Edward Elgar Publishing, Inc.
William Pratt House
9 Dewey Court
Northampton
Massachusetts 01060
USA

A catalogue record for this book
is available from the British Library

Library of Congress Control Number: 2024948199

This book is available electronically in the **Elgar**online
Sociology, Social Policy and Education subject collection
https://doi.org/10.4337/9781035326020

ISBN 978 1 0353 2601 3 (cased)
ISBN 978 1 0353 2602 0 (eBook)

Printed and bound in Great Britain by
TJ Books Limited, Padstow, Cornwall

Contents

Figures

Tables

Boxes

Contributors

Oguz A. Acar is a Professor of Marketing & Innovation at King's Business School, King's College London, UK, a Research Affiliate at Harvard University, USA, and an Expert at the World Economic Forum. Named among World's Top 40 Business School Professors Under 40, his current research is at the nexus of generative AI, organizations, and education. His work is regularly published in leading academic journals and widely covered in global media.

Abdullah H. Clark is an Assistant Professor of Applied Strategy at the College of Information and Cyberspace, National Defense University, Washington DC, USA. An organization strategist and practitioner within the Department of Defense, he teaches courses on strategic thinking, strategic communication, and strategic leadership. He is an Ed.D. candidate in the field of Human and Organizational Learning at The George Washington University, Washington DC, USA, with research interests in knowledge transfer, leader adaptation, and organizational change. His dissertation research is focused on the dynamics of ideological polarization among team and workgroup members in US federal government organizations.

Kathleen Denman is an Assistant Professor of Writing and Communication at National Defense University, a Master's degree-granting professional military education institution in Washington, DC, USA. Her areas of interest include adult learning, enabling strong communication skills among adult learners, and educational leadership. She has contributed to *Developing Military Learners' Communication Skills: Using the Scholarship of Teaching and Learning*. She is pursuing an Ed.D. in Leadership for Higher Education from Virginia Commonwealth University, Richmond, Virginia, USA.

Michael Dowling is Professor of Finance at Dublin City University, Ireland. His research focuses on financial data science, behavioral financial decision-making, and the application of AI in finance. He has published extensively in journals such as *Research Policy*, *British Journal of Management*, and *Journal of World Business*. He is a founder of the public policy Generative AI startup – PoliClear.org.

Margriet A. van Gestel is an Associate Professor at the Centre of Expertise Perspective in Health at Avans University of Applied Sciences, the Netherlands. Her research focuses on the applications of generative AI in tackling bias and privacy challenges inherent in AI deployment.

Chahna Gonsalves is a Lecturer in Marketing Education Lead at King's College London, UK. A Senior Fellow of Advance HE, she focuses on assessment design and AI's impact on workplace readiness. Such as Studies in Higher Education, and funded by the UK Council for International Student Affairs and the Academy of Marketing. She is also Deputy Chair of the Academy of Marketing Education Special Interest Group.

Christian Hendriksen is an Assistant Professor in the Department of Operations Management at Copenhagen Business School. His research focuses on AI integration in companies and supply chain management. He publishes in leading journals such as the *Journal of Supply Chain Management* and *Supply Chain Management: An International Journal*. His work explores the intersection of AI and everyday work, particularly the way students, teachers, and employees in firms use AI in their everyday tasks.

Bochra Idris is an Assistant Professor of Entrepreneurship at the Faculty of Business, Özyeğin University, Türkiye. She publishes on topics related to small firms' performance, internationalization, innovation, and entrepreneurship. Her recent work was published in *Industrial Marketing Management*, *Journal of International Management*, *Journal of Business Research*, and *International Business Review*, among other publications.

Jacob-John Jubin is passionate about educational innovation and digital tools to enhance learning experiences. With a PhD in sustainability, his academic expertise informs his approach to L&T and Tech-Enhanced Learning. Jubin has published widely on topics such as international student education, digital and blended learning, and digital assessments, showcasing his commitment to leveraging technology for educational advancement.

Katri Kerem is an Assistant Professor of Marketing at the Estonian Business School, Tallinn, Estonia. Her research interests include higher education in the fields of business, sustainable marketing, and various aspects of consumer behaviour. Katri Kerem has worked as a head of bachelor and master programs at the Estonian Business School and been a member of higher education quality assurance teams locally and internationally.

Riina Koris is Associate Professor in the Department of Marketing and Communication at the Estonian Business School, Tallinn, Estonia. She publishes on the topics of higher education in general and (the purpose of) business education in particular and centers her research around students of business and management. She publishes in journals such as *Management Learning*, *The International Journal of Management Education*, and the *International Journal of Educational Management*, among others.

Yue Li is a PhD candidate in Tianjin University, China, and currently a visiting PhD researcher at Dublin City University, Ireland, under a China Academic Scholarship. Her research focuses on behavioral finance and asset pricing, and she has published in prominent journals such as the *Quarterly Review of Economics* and *Finance Research Letters*.

Jukka V. Mäkinen (D.Sc Econ, Aalto University, Finland), is a professor of Business Ethics at the Estonian Business School, Tallinn, Estonia and Docent of Corporate Responsibility at the Aalto University, Finland. He approaches the responsibilities of businesses from the perspectives of political theory. His work appears in journals such as *Business & Society*, *Business Ethics Quarterly*, *Journal of Business Ethics*, *Journal of Information Technology*, *Journal of Sustainable Tourism*, and *Utilitas*, among others.

Wayne Martin is Professor of Philosophy at the University of Essex and Director of the Essex Autonomy Project, Colchester, UK. He has published in the areas of the History of Philosophy and the History of Logic, and is the author of *Theories of Judgment: Logic, Psychology, Phenomenology* (CUP, 2006). His current research includes the theory and practice of cognitive prosthetics as a tool for fulfilling legal and human rights obligations for persons with disabilities.

Peter Matheis is a lecturer in marketing and the Lead for Learning Transformation and Digital Innovation in Learning and Teaching at Navitas. He has extensive experience in the higher education environment and has participated in various large-scale innovative educational and research projects on the design and application of learning management systems, learning design and curriculum development, data analytics, technology-enhanced learning, and the implementation of diverse educational pedagogies.

Jukka I. Mattila works as a Senior Lecturer at the Metropolia Business School, Helsinki, Finland. His research interests include management consultancy, symbolic hierarchies, learning environments, and motivation.

Michelle D. Miller is a cognitive psychologist, researcher, and speaker focused on supporting higher education faculty and leaders. She is the author of several books, including *Minds Online: Teaching Effectively with Technology* and *Remembering and Forgetting in the Age of Technology: Teaching, Learning, and the Science of Memory in a Wired World*. Dr Miller is a Professor of Psychological Sciences and President's Distinguished Teaching Fellow at Northern Arizona University, USA.

John V. Pavlik is Professor of Journalism and Media Studies at the School of Communication & Information at Rutgers, the State University of New Jersey, USA. Pavlik has researched and written widely on the impact of new technology on journalism, media, and society. His books include *Milestones in Digital Journalism, Disruption and Digital Journalism*, and *Journalism in the Age of Virtual Reality.*

Kätlin Pulk is an Associate Professor of Organization Theory at the Estonian Business School, Tallinn, Estonia. Her research focuses on issues related to time and temporality in organizations and the conceptualization of time and temporality. She is the author of the book *Time and Temporality in Organisations: Theory and Development* (Palgrave Macmillan, 2022).

Ilia Protopapa is a Senior Lecturer in Marketing Education at King's Business School, King's College London. Her areas of interest include diversity and inclusion and GenAI applications in higher education and consumer behavior. Her recent work has been published as book chapters in the areas of consumer behavior in *The Handbook of Research on Customer Loyalty* (Edward Elgar Publishing) and higher education in *Strategic Brand Management in Higher Education* (Routledge).

Mika Tammilehto (D.Sc, University of Helsinki, Finland), is a principal research scientist at Häme University of Applied Sciences, Finland. He has over 20 years of experience on strategic development and governance of education systems. His research interests include VET-systems, regional innovation systems, education policy, strategies and governance, and digital learning environments.

Raisa Varsta is Senior Lecturer in Business at the Metropolia University of Applied Sciences, Helsinki, Finland.

Deidre Williams is an experimentalist in underwater acoustics and a research affiliate of the Essex Autonomy Project, UK. Their most recent work has been in data collection to train machine learning algorithms for acoustic signature recognition. They have also worked in the fields of mesh generation for computational fluid dynamics and the history and philosophical significance of programming strategies in early chess AI, and as an educator of physics and mathematics.

Supplementary materials

Supplementary materials for Chapter 5 of this book can be found online at: https://doi.org/10.4337/9781035326020.

1. Introduction: setting the scene

Riina Koris and Kätlin Pulk

It is hardly an overstatement that one of the most striking generative-AI-related phenomenon is its popularity and exposure. After its launch on November 30, 2022, it generated 1 million users in five days (Dwivedi et al., 2023). Today, towards the end of spring 2024 and less than 15 months after its launch, the phrase "generative AI" produces instantly 961,000 hits on Google Scholar. One may wonder if there has ever been a still emerging and developing phenomenon that has so taken the world by storm and made a home in so many walks of life – education, media, marketing, banking, computer science, hospitality and tourism, management, publishing, nursing, to name a few. In addition to being used extensively (albeit sometimes uncritically), discussion around it appears as checkered as the history of humankind.

Although it has impacted many walks of life, our book remains within the field of generative AI (e.g. ChatGPT) and higher education – as large language models, generative AI tools, which independently learn from data and thereafter provide us with what seem sophisticated and intelligent texts (van Dis et al., 2023) have without doubt made a successful entry into higher education and are currently shaking up the existing, long-held principles of teaching, learning, and research, as is well-documented by Mollick and Mollick (2023a). Some would argue that only a fool would refrain from using a "cultural sensation" (Thorp, 2023, p. 312) which, according to van Dis et al. (2023) "can convincingly converse with its users in English and other languages on a wide range of topics, [...] is free [of charge], easy to use and continues to learn" (p. 224).

Although interesting and intriguing, in this Introduction we will not manage to cover all the existing discussions, neither in terms of walks of life nor the discourses. Instead, we will concentrate on the walk of life relevant to this book – higher education – and generative AI's potentially positive and negative impact.

We begin by delving into the existing literature on the influence of generative AI on teaching, learning, and research. We explore how generative AI can enhance user experiences within each of these realms and subsequently address potential areas of concern. It is evident that discussions and viewpoints are multifaceted and diverse within these domains. Following this exploration,

1

we transition into a traditional chapter-by-chapter presentation of the book's content, structured around "the good," "the bad," and "the ugly" of generative AI in higher education. Finally, we will conclude this chapter by identifying the target audience for our book.

1.1   ON GENERATIVE AI AS THE TEACHER'S AND LEARNER'S BEST FRIEND (OR NOT)

Most of us, both teachers and learners alike, are strapped for time. Juggling with everyday chores in and out of the university has become our "favorite" pastime. While nothing is necessarily wrong with being (reasonably) busy, the trouble is that we have become time-impoverished (Barnett, 2008). Everyday nitty-gritty practicalities rob us of time needed for tasks with longer timeframes but salutary (low in immediate, but high in long-term appeal and benefit) outcomes. Seemingly, generative AI (e.g. a tool called ChatGPT) has arrived to free us, both teachers and learners alike, of the everyday more mundane tasks related to learning and teaching.

According to ChatGPT's own promise, it helps (university) students in their academic endeavors and personal development by providing explanations, summaries, and clarifications on various topics related to students' course-work in a clear and concise manner; assists them with homework, including problem-solving, writing essays, or conducting research; helps students prepare for exams by quizzing them on key concepts, providing practice questions, and offering tips for effective study techniques; creates for them study schedules and strategies for managing time effectively; assists students in structuring essays, refining arguments, improving grammar and style; generates ideas for research papers or creative writing projects; provides feedback on drafts to help students improve their writing skills; advises students on career paths, job search strategies, résumé writing, interview preparation; offers a supportive listening ear and coping strategies or resources for managing stress, anxiety, or other mental health problems; engages students in discussion on various topics of interest, satisfying curiosity and broadening their knowledge; facilitates group discussions and collaborative projects, and much more. All of this does, indeed, make generative AI the student's best friend.

Additionally, ChatGPT promises to help teachers create lesson plans, sug-gests teaching strategies, provides resources for classroom activities, offers recommendations for teaching methodologies, creates engaging content (e.g. quizzes, presentations, lecture notes) in a manner which is suitable for different student groups, provides explanations to students, answers their questions, and offers additional resources on topics which they are struggling with, can automate grading for multiple choice questions, short-answer questions, and even essays, provides feedback on students' assignments (while highlighting areas for improvement), recommends resources for teachers' professional development, suggests best practices for classroom management, provides insights into the latest trends in education, assists in translation, language practice exercises and cultural understanding, helps drafting emails, newsletters and other communication materials, provides tips and techniques for effective time management, and assists teachers to balance their workload and maintain a healthy work-life balance. The list of promises that ChatGPT itself makes goes on and seems endless, but the above alone is impressive and, most certainly, relieving in our strapped-for-time era. Subsequently, generative AI also appears to be the teacher's best friend.

However, as fantastic as all the above sounds, most silver linings come with a cloud. In addition to the frequent concern that students use generative AI to cheat on assignments and exams, it provides a tempting ground for an uncritical and superficial approach to a topic, thereby creating certain long-term repercussions – it hampers the students' critical thinking, problem-solving, and creativity which are needed in many professional careers (see e.g. O'Connor, 2023). Although none of us would like our abilities to think critically, solve problems, and be creative hampered in the long run, we often like to *think* long-term but frequently *act* short-term, and education as such is a salutary product – one with high long-term benefit but low immediate appeal.

O'Connor (2023) is seconded by Marju Lauristin, former Member of the European Parliament, former Estonian Minister of Social Affairs, and a professor of social communication with the University of Tartu in Estonia, who suggests that:

> We need to teach our students how to manage in a world where millions of bytes of information attack you, [...] What we see is that the most difficult task is that of sensemaking. [...] What emerges is an extremely superficial mode of thinking, but the main content can emerge only after you immerse yourself in a text and start recognizing connections. (Välba, 2023)

Thus, an uncritical and superficial approach to a topic hampers us in the long run in that we become deficient in recognizing connections that help us make sense of our world.

There is also the concern that generative AI hinders cognitive development among students and circumscribes the student (and the teacher alike) from broadening their interpretive frame. As Lauristin in her interview states, "While generative AI facilitates the access to raw material which you need, it does not 'read between the lines', interpret, or generalize for you. It produces average work [...]". She continues that a human intellect can and must be cultivated through education, which creates a tree of fundamental knowledge, thereafter growing our thoughts – the fruits of this tree. Lauristin adds that a human mind cannot be cultivated at the required higher level via the use of AI, and to bring order and clarity into our thoughts, the groundwork for thinking must be constructed (Välba, 2023). Aoun (2017, p. xvii) supports this, claiming that if the uncritical use of generative AI is propagated, we can be certain that education no longer "equips us with the mental furniture to live a rich, considered existence."

Another frequently and loudly voiced concern with generative AI is that "AI has its own biases, as well as a tendency to make up facts ('confabulate' or 'hallucinate'), so its advice is not always accurate. Students need to examine these biases" (Mollick and Mollick, 2023b). However, to examine a made-up fact, one first needs to have the fundamental groundwork or an "inner detector." This "detector" would turn on the red light, allowing the AI user to examine the potentially made-up fact. Nevertheless, the problem is that such a detector remains underdeveloped and uses generative AI tools uncritically. An excellent example is a recent conversation between a final thesis supervisor and a student, who claimed in his work that "Carl Gustav Jung [1875–1961] developed brand personality types."[1] While the supervisor's fundamental groundwork detected a made-up fact (and raised her suspicions about the student's ChatGPT use), it was not spotted by the student precisely due to his uncritical and superficial approach to the topic and inadequate fundamental groundwork. Thus, one is left to wonder how a student (and sometimes also a teacher) is expected to identify the made-up facts, inaccurate information, and "hallucinations" if thinking, researching, and evaluating critically is hampered (see O'Connor, 2023 and Välba, 2023 above) by the very tool which requires it.

Perhaps it can be gleaned, then, that while generative AI may help teachers and students save time and effort in the more technical (mundane) tasks, it does not further the user's critical eye and knowledge groundwork to evaluate information, make connections, dive into in-depth inquiry, and the like. This is supported by Lindebaum and Fleming (2023), who suggest that the use of generative AI undermines our inherently human scholarship, and by Cornelissen et al. (2024), who maintain that the tool is unable to "question, revisit and problematize prior literature and established understandings" and "cannot substitute, at least not fully, for the creative, ampliative reasoning that humans do [...]" (p. 8).

1.2   ON GENERATIVE AI AS THE RESEARCHER'S BEST FRIEND (OR NOT)

Research-wise, generative AI promises to advance knowledge production across its entire value chain, from synthesis to creation, evaluation, and translation (Grimes et al., 2023), and to increase efficiency and rigor of research methods via enlarging the methodological toolbox (von Krogh et al., 2023). Generative AI increases efficiency and pace for knowledge production purposes while reviewing existing conceptual and empirical literature (Heidt, 2023). Utilizing generative AI in knowledge creation has, no doubt, another lure – research claims that 41% of the time of a knowledge worker is spent on discretionary (perhaps even auxiliary) activities that offer little personal satisfaction and could very well be performed by nearly anyone (Birkinshaw and Cohen, 2013). With the advent of generative AI, we no longer need any*one* – we now have a machine to do it for us. Free of charge. The fact that it helps one to get over the blank page phobia and "gets us going" while writing nearly anything makes the machine even more attractive. If Dwivedi et al. (2023) are correct, the most significant impact [of generative AI] will be "to provide a competent first draft for our most common written knowledge tasks" (p. 7).

For research methods purposes, generative AI may help to speed up the process of executing research tasks, assist with research design and instrument design, and facilitate the inductive exploration of large datasets (Wang et al., 2023), to quickly elicit credible and interesting hypotheses, and test those (von Krogh et al., 2023). Grimes et al. (2023) additionally suggest that generative AI may help to produce augmented data for hypothesis-testing, to identify inconsistencies in data, thereby improving their quality and subsequent reliability, to generate complex simulation models and scenarios, give researchers feedback, identify and notify of potential biases, improve argumentative clarity, enhance language use, and proactively identify and respond to counter-arguments, all of which "promise to increase the persuasiveness of scholars' knowledge development work" (p. 1618). Additionally, in natural sciences, AI systems are claimed to have produced "experimental design and optimization tools, which can enhance traditional scientific methods, decrease the number of experiments needed and save resources" (Wang et al., 2023, p. 54).

Generative AI is further argued to ensure broader accessibility and translation (both literally, from one language to the other, and metaphorically, from "the academic" to "the practitioner") of scholarly work to close the theory–practice gap and, thus, to ensure its impact (Rynes et al., 2001; Ployhart and Bartunek, 2019; see also Aguinis et al., 2022) not just within the academia, but also in the "real" world. Anderson et al. (2023), for example, make a strong case by suggesting that generative AI is an invaluable tool in summarizing academic studies (which resort to specialized language) in what the authors call "human-like responses" (p. 1), intended for non-specialist readers, subsequently sharing research findings also with concerned members of the public who are frequently excluded from primary literature due to lack of understanding of specialized literature, thereby, as van Dis et al. (2023) claim, enhancing fairness, diversity, and accessibility of research. Thus, generative AI also seems to be the researcher's best friend. But only if we ignore the cloud.

However, points of concern are glaring in terms of knowledge (re)production – "referencing a scientific study that does not exist" (Thorp, 2023, p. 312), and producing texts which are "rather weak in terms of logical flow, inaccurate in terms of factuality and truth, not critical in terms of elaboration of data, and not novel" (Dwivedi et al., 2023, p. 5). Cornelissen et al. (2024) additionally warn that AI-generated outputs feed us only with what is already there, as a result of which the feed lacks human ingenuity and deep thought, which are required for genuine substance and unique insight. On top of that, Grimes et al. (2023) claim that while scholarly research and its quality greatly depend on its methodological transparency and reliability, "AI hallucinations," "deep research fakes" (Walters and Wilder, 2023), and dubious "authenticity" of scholarship (Voronov et al., 2023) pose further problems which can potentially corrupt research and scholarship.

Concerning the increased efficiency and rigor of research methods, researchers may be circumscribed by their ability to obtain and understand structured and annotated data and, therefore, also to examine pertinent phenomena and development of relevant theories (von Krogh et al., 2023). Von Krogh and colleagues (2023) add that this is particularly problematic because being well-versed and learning about the algorithms and their detailed functioning requires extensive training of the researcher as well as training data, which often makes it economically inefficient. Wang et al. (2023) warn that responsible use of AI in scientific research requires the measuring of the levels of uncertainty and errors, which is essential while interpreting AI outputs and being overreliant on potentially flawed results (p. 57). Thus, even though Karjus (2023; see also Dwivedi et al., 2023; p. 9) argues that, just like with the invention of the calculator, the question of whether those should or not be allowed at schools came up because "one should be able to calculate also without the calculator. […] most professions cannot be held without the use of the gadget", one may counterargue that a calculator would not convincingly suggest that 1+1=3 (or other similar nonsense), as is sometimes the case with generative AI. ChatGPT's own disclaimer, "ChatGPT sometimes writes plausible-sounding but incorrect or nonsensical answers" (https://openai.com/blog/chatgpt), does not deal with the concerns above.

Thus, research-wise, the debate around generative AI has both critics and supporters. While some subscribe to the claim that "the product must come from – and be expressed by – the wonderful computer in our heads" (Thorp, 2023, p. 312), others suggest that *if* risks related to generative AI adoption are understood, managed, and mitigated then AI risk management frameworks and ethical theory perspectives can be consolidated, resulting in "socially responsible judgements which would help ensure a purposeful, cautious, reasoned, and ethical way of leveraging generative AI models" (Dwivedi et al., 2023, p. 6). Yet others, however, suggest that the emergence of such tools constitutes a new paradigm shift in that the tools give the researchers the opportunity to reconsider existing views and theories that do not sufficiently recognize much agency in technology (Dwivedi, et al., 2023). All of the above paints a checkered picture indeed.

1.3   ON MISCELLANEOUS (BUT EQUALLY RELEVANT) MATTERS

A view that seems to emerge repeatedly in the generative AI discussion is that AI cannot be creative, i.e. it cannot create and/or enact something which is new, unique, original (Sawyer, 2012), and useful (Runco and Jaeger, 2012). Interestingly, several studies have proved this not to be the case. While one may argue that the method of validation and the way one defines creativity may have something to do with it, the results appear interesting and worth pointing out. Haase and Hanel (2023), for example, show that "the standardized creativity measure for broad-associative 'thinking' is as original as the human-generated ideas" (p. 8). They do admit, though, that this is the case only if one applies the term "creativity" as "new, unique, original, and useful," not as a "combination of real-world experience, emotion, and inspiration" (Kirkpatrick, 2023). Also Guzik et al. (2023), using the Torrance Tests of Creative Thinking, discovered that ChatGPT-4 model "generated impressive results [...] for fluency, flexibility, and originality, suggesting that AI systems have the potential to produce viable creative output. [...] and new, unique, and unexpected ideas that match or exceed the abilities of human originality" (p. 7). Consequently, the two studies highlighted that ChatGPT-4 can outperform 90% and 99% (respectively) of people on different creative tests.

However, while today's studies on generative AI's creative ability may be criticized from methodological considerations (how creativity was validated and/or defined), a more "apocalyptic" claim comes from Tredinnick and Laybats (2023), according to whom today's products of generative AI may be mediocre and lack the mark of individual expression that distinguishes the creative mind. Still, the time when generative AI will truly challenge human creativity will surely come (p. 99).

Generative AI's ability to produce creative work is just one side of the coin, though. The other, equally relevant, if not even more relevant to higher education, is whether the use of generative AI in teaching, learning, and research hampers the creativity of the teacher, learner, and researcher. Harvey and Berry (2023), for example, maintain that the use of such tools may restrict a human being's creative capacity in that it anchors the user to a specific idea, thereby diminishing the fertility of the ground for new and creative ideas. However, a comforting response to this worry could easily be that from Haase and Hanel (2023), according to whom "exposure to other people's creative ideas can stimulate cognitive activity and enhance creativity." They additionally suggest that while "humans serve as proper ideation partners […] it might be easier to ask a chatbot than to find a motivated human to run ideas by" (pp. 10–11).

Another topic that frequently surfaces within the generative AI discussion is the notion of (non-)equalizing opportunities for many. As within other streams of discussion, this appears equally checkered. While the impacts of generative AI have been discussed within the contexts of gender studies, sustainable development goals, developing countries, and many more, we bring out a discourse immediately linked to the focus of our book – education and its teaching-learning-research triangle.

Although van Dis et al. (2023) claim that generative AI can "convincingly converse with its users in English and other languages on a wide range of topics" (p. 224), Kruusmaa (2023) counterargues by claiming that, for instance, the Estonian language makes up 0.1% of the databases of the technology giants, as a result of which texts which emerge in the Estonian language are of relatively poorer quality, and, perhaps more importantly, claims about Estonian culture and history are faulty. When prompted, generative AI claims confidently that the Soviet Army liberated the country of Estonia from the German invasion in 1944. While this is "technically" true, what generative AI fails to add is that while liberating Estonia, the Soviet Union itself simultaneously occupied the independent country of Estonia for the following 50 or so years. Thus, by disseminating (half-)false information, generative AI distorts history because as Kruusmaa (2023) claims, "The ChatGPT-'knife' which Estonians [and other smaller countries] currently have at their disposal is blunt," and adds that "The AI-models which the speakers of smaller languages use are not only limited, but also dangerous […] because each model has a potential to produce dangerous content." The long-term effect of this on education is difficult to overestimate.

One may counterargue, of course, that the use of generative AI is strictly voluntary – if one suspects that it takes from one's ability to think critically, solve problems, be creative, interpret, make sense, engage in mental exercise, or develop cognitively, and inhibits from "furthering one's mental furniture to live a rich, considered existence" (Aoun, 2017, p. xvii), if one fears that the use of generative AI adds to a superficial mode of thinking, and produces (occasional) biases, "hallucinations," and inaccurate information, then one is not forced to use the tools. However, Laas (2023) makes a valid point when he suggests that "Avoiding their use may not be as easy as it sounds because competition-driven pressure to increase productivity may result in a situation where the non-use of generative AI is unthinkable." Indeed, using and letting the students use AI is inviting in a context where a member of academic staff is supposed to:

> publish regularly in the "top journals," gain an international reputation as a key academic of [the] field, attract significant amounts of funding from public and private sources, teach more courses than previously in each academic year and in a way that pleases [...] students, supervise world-class dissertations, serve the school's business partners in various ways, remake him/herself into a nationally respected and influential figure, keep up his/her own and the school's brand in media, and contribute actively to the school's governance in various bodies and taskforces, among other things. (Räsänen, 2008, p. 2)

For researchers, generative AI takes care of the time-consuming tasks of reading, thinking, and writing; for students, generative AI acts as an invaluable helping hand that creates essays and other homework which the students would then submit as their own; for teachers, generative AI takes care of reading and evaluating bad texts as well as offering detailed feedback. After all, (1) desperate times (such as described by Räsänen above) call for desperate measures; (2) everyone is doing it; and (3) when you are cornered, part of your own value system may fall into pieces. The latter was confirmed when a colleague's single-minded undertaking to identify AI-written texts submitted by his students and interrogate the "dubious cases" one-on-one started resembling the Spanish Inquisition and produced utter frustration in both parties – himself and the students. On the other hand, a recent case illustrated by Wolkovich (2024) shows that, like students, researchers, too, find themselves in a situation where they stand unfairly accused of passing on unoriginal research generated by AI. At this point, the claim that AI is a technology "that helps combat student and teacher burnout" (Churi et al., 2023, p. ix) does not hold water.

Moreover, resorting to generative AI is particularly tempting in an era where we are time-impoverished (Barnett, 2008), which praises single-minded instrumentality (Varman et al., 2011) and certification over substance (Alvesson, 2013), efficiency, productivity, and the mentality of "think long-term, act short-term." In the end, those learners, teachers, and researchers who produce (knowledge), using their own "mental furniture" seem to be wasting time and effort and appear on the surface to be "losers." In contrast, those who go along with the prompts-economy, points-economy, and certification-economy appear as "winners," the wise guys.

The genie is indeed out of the bottle, and (generative) AI is most likely here to stay. It may make many people's lives easier, more efficient, less time-wasteful, and the like, but it's a good wind that always blows everybody only good – for some (or sometimes) it may also blow ill. Fortunately, the University has the luxury of deciding whether and to what extent to make use of generative AI and how to ensure that its employment in higher education still enables the use of people's mental furniture to live a rich, considered, and meaningful existence. To ignore the tool's potential and its staggering exposure in countless walks of life would, undoubtedly, be short-sighted.

The 2022 Expert Survey on Progress in AI conducted among AI researchers and developers by The Future of Humanity Institute in Oxford revealed that there is a 10% chance that advanced AI systems will cause "human extinction or similarly permanent and severe disempowerment of the human species" (Klein, 2023). If this 10% is to materialize, this book is, of course, irrelevant. However, while 90% is still more than 10%, and while we are still around as human species, we believe the debate is worthwhile.

1.4   INTRODUCTION TO THE CHAPTERS

In this volume, altogether, 23 authors add to the existing literature in debating the advantages and disadvantages of the use of generative AI in higher education and, while doing so, come from three perspectives – that of the student, the teacher, and the researcher. Altogether, there are 13 chapters. In addition to the first chapter by the editors of this volume, Chapters 2 and 3 constitute a general introduction to the volume, while the remaining ten fall under either "the good," "the bad," or "the ugly" of the use of generative AI in higher education.

Right after this chapter, Wayne Martin and Deidre Williams (Chapter 2 in this volume) offer an interesting perspective on how Hubert Dreyfus (1929–2017), the most prominent philosophical critic of AI of his generation, would comment on the latest generation of AI, how it would fit into his "Critique of Artificial Reason," and what light the new tools cast on the structure and limitations of his critique. They introduce the concept of extended-mind cyborgs to reflect on the opportunities and limitations of programs such as ChatGPT. Additionally, Chahna Gonsalves and Oguz A. Acar (Chapter 3 in this volume) investigate the integration of generative AI in higher education and its discourse among academic staff, articulating complex opportunities, challenges, and tensions between innovation and core educational values.

"The good" in this book comprises chapters that explicitly and implicitly argue that, since generative AI is here to stay, we need to figure out how to make the most of it in a way that enhances existing teaching/learning processes and supports both educators and learners. John V. Pavlik (Chapter 4 in this volume), applying constructivist learning theory, shows how generative AI can effectively enable interactive and personalized learning, support students engaging in experiential settings where they discover, and even help generate knowledge, and heighten the learning and retention of new concepts, among other benefits. Christian Hendriksen (Chapter 5 in this volume) offers invaluable insights to students (and teachers working with students) into effectively using generative AI for learning. He demonstrates some universally applicable use cases from students' perspectives. Katri Kerem (Chapter 6 in this volume) offers practical tips for generative AI usage for time-impoverished teachers and professors by showcasing how to use the new tools to personalize class content, enhance course design, create learning outcomes, create assignments, and much more. Michael Dowling and Yue Li (Chapter 7 in this volume) end "the good" by showcasing how to make the most of generative AI tools in academic research.

"The bad" in this volume suggests that generative AI is the start of the end of core educational values. In this part of the book, Abdullah H. Clark and Kathleen Denman (Chapter 8 in this volume) argue that the use of generative AI hampers human creativity, experimentation, and self-expression because it entails outsourcing cognitive processes. Peter Matheis and Jacob-John Jubin (Chapter 9 in this volume) take on the dubious student assessment methods of generative AI and propose an AI-Resistant Assessment Design Framework as a contribution to reframing HE assessment design for authenticity. In her chapter, Margriet A. van Gestel (Chapter 10 in this volume) shows how the use of generative AI increases the risk of inequality not only among the research community but in society at large and provides strategies for promoting equality in the utilization of generative AI technologies. Ilia Protopapa and Bochra Idris (Chapter 11 in this volume) round up this part of the book by taking on the moral and ethical concerns arising with generative AI in academic research. They discuss these concerns through the following lenses – compiling a literature review, collecting and analyzing data, academic writing, and problems related to critical engagement in the research process. They additionally suggest ways of mitigating the dangers of single-minded reliance on generative AI in academic research.

"The ugly" in this book focuses on the moral and social dilemmas accompanying generative AI use in higher education. Jukka V. Mäkinen, Jukka I. Mattila, Mika Tammilehto, and Raisa Varsta (Chapter 12 in this book) argue that the omnipresent AI, devoid of consciousness and accountability, is in dominant use in labor relations, which, in turn, will lead to a situation where technology induces compliance or subservience in humans. The four authors examine this argument against the development of artificial intelligence and the role of higher education institutions in creating academic knowledge. Last but not least, Michelle D. Miller (Chapter 13 in this volume) claims that the advent of generative AI has brought about a sense of unease and faculty are overwhelmed due to a lack of clear principles of AI use. She explains how to identify unhelpful "ugly advice" on generative AI use and suggests alternative approaches that are appealing and valuable to faculty. This chapter concludes this section as well as the book.

In the end, we hope that the book, where multiple and conflicting viewpoints come together, will offer thought-provoking reading for many – those in the

University, including teachers, students, and research scholars pursuing their PhD degrees in Education, Education Technology, and Learning. We hope it will also trigger the interest of managers and deans in charge of running higher education institutions. With its multiple perspectives, it is equally relevant to policymakers in higher education and industry professionals who are developing such technologies.

NOTE

1.   Brand personality types were initially developed and published by Jennifer Aaker in 1997, while Carl Gustav Jung developed personality types at the start of the 20th century. This is a textbook example of generative-AI hallucination, where two concepts (personality types and brand personality types) are merged by the AI and uncritically used by a student.

REFERENCES

Aguinis, H., Archibold, E.E., and Rice, D.B. 2022. Let's fix our own problem: Quelling the irresponsible research perfect storm. *Journal of Management Studies*, 59(6), 1628–1642.

Alvesson, M. 2013. *The Triumph of Emptiness*. Oxford: Oxford University Press.

Anderson, L.B., Kanneganti, D., Houk, M.B., Holm, R.H., and Smith, T. 2023. Generative AI as a tool for environmental health research translation. *GeoHealth*, 7, 1–4. Available at https:// agupubs .onlinelibrary .wiley .com/ doi/ full/ 10 .1029/ 2023GH000875 (accessed 14 August 2024).

Aoun, J.E. 2017. *Robot-Proof: Higher Education in the Age of Artificial Intelligence*. Cambridge, MA: The MIT Press.

Barnett, R. 2008. Being an academic in a time-impoverished age. In: A. Amaral, I. Bleiklie, and C. Musselin (Eds.) *From Governance to Identity: Higher Education Dynamics*, vol. 24. Dordrecht: Springer.

Birkinshaw, J. and Cohen, J. 2013. Make time for work that matters. *Harvard Business Review*, 91(9), 115–120.

Churi, P., Joshi, S., Elhoseny, M., and Omrane, A. 2023. *Artificial Intelligence in Higher Education: A Practical Approach*. Boca Raton, FL: CRC Press.

Cornelissen, J., Höllerer, M.A., Boxenbaum, E., Faraj, S., and Gehman, J. 2024. Large language models and the future of Organization Theory. *Organization Theory*, 5, 1–15.

Dwivedi, Y.K., Kshetri, N., Hughes, L., Slade, E.L., Jeyaraj, A., … Wright, R. 2023. Opinion paper: "So what if ChatGPT wrote it?" Multidisciplinary perspectives on opportunities, challenges and implications of generative conversational AI for research, practice and policy. *International Journal of Information Management*, 71, 1–63.

Grimes, M., von Krogh, G., Feuerriegel, S., Rink, F., and Gruber, M. 2023. From scarcity to abundance: Scholars and scholarship in an age of generative artificial intelligence. *Academy of Management Journal*, 66(6), 1617–1624.

Guzik, E.G., Byrge, C., and Gilde, C. 2023. The originality of machines: AI takes the Torrence Test. *Journal of Creativity*, 33, 1–8.

Haase, J. and Hanel, P.H.P. 2023. Artificial muses: Generative artificial intelligence chatbots have risen to human-level creativity. *Journal of Creativity*, 33(3), 1–7.

Harvey, S. and Berry, J. 2023. Toward a meta-theory of creativity forms: How novelty and usefulness shape creativity. *Academy of Management Review*, 48(3), 504–529.

Heidt, A. 2023. Artificial-intelligence search engines wrangle academic literature. *Nature*, 620, 456–457.

Karjus, A. 2023. Tehisintellekt seab juba sel sügisel koolid sundvaliku ette. Novaator 16.06.2023. Available at https:// novaator .err .ee/ 1609007981/ andres -karjus -tehisintellekt -seab -juba -sel -sugisel -koolid -sundvaliku -ette (accessed 3 January 2024).

Kirkpatrick, K. 2023. Can AI demonstrate creativity? *Communications of the ACM*, 66(2), 21–23. Available at https:// dl .acm .org/ doi/ fullHtml/ 10 .1145/ 3575665 (accessed 15 February 2024).

Klein, E. 2023. This changes everything. *The New York Times* (12.03.2023). Available at https:// www .nytimes .com/ 2023/ 03/ 12/ opinion/ chatbots -artificial -intelligence -future -weirdness .html ?auth = login -google1tap & login = google1tap (accessed 8 January 2024).

Kruusmaa, K. 2023. Tehistaip on kultuurinähtus, mis nõuab selget plaani. *Novaator* 02.11.2023. Available at https:// kultuur .err .ee/ 1609152025/ krister -kruusmaa -tehistaip-on-kultuurinahtus-mis-nouab-selget-plaani (accessed 5 January 2023).

Laas, O. 2023. Moraliseerivad tööriistad. *Novaator* 08.05.2023. Available at https:// www.err.ee/ 1608970966/ oliver-laas-moraliseerivad-tooriistad (accessed 5 January 2023).

Lindebaum, D. and Fleming, P. 2023. ChatGPT undermines human reflexivity, scientific responsibility and responsible management research. *British Journal of Management*. Available at https://onlinelibrary.wiley.com/doi/epdf/10.1111/1467 -8551.12781 (accessed 3 April 2024).

Mollick, E. and Mollick, L. 2023a. Why all our classes suddenly became AI classes. In *Transformative Technologies: How Analytics, AI, ChatGPT and Metaverse are revolutionizing Higher Education*. Harvard Business Publishing Education, pp. 26–32. Available at https://he.hbsp.harvard.edu/transformative-technologies.html (accessed 19 January 2024).

Mollick, E. and Mollick, L. 2023b. AI as feedback generator. Available at https://hbsp .harvard.edu/inspiring-minds/ai-as-feedback-generator (accessed 19 January 2024).

O'Connor, S. 2023. Open artificial intelligence platforms in nursing education: Tools for academic progress or abuse. *Nurse Education in Practice*, 66, Article 103537.

Ployhart, R.E., and Bartunek, J.M. 2019. Editors' comments: There is nothing so theoretical as good practice – A call for phenomenal theory. *Academy of Management Review*, 44, 493–497.

Räsänen, K. 2008. Meaningful academic work as praxis in emergence. *Journal of Research Practice*, 4(1), 1–22.

Runco, M.A. and Jaeger, G.J. 2012. The standard definition of creativity. *Creativity Research Journal*, 24(1), 92–96.

Rynes, S.L., Bartunek, J.M., and Daft, R.I. 2001. Across the great divide: Knowledge creation and transfer between practitioners and academics. *Academy of Management Journal*, 44(2), 340–355.

Sawyer, K. 2012. Extending sociocultural theory to group creativity. *Vocational Learning*, 5, 59–75.

Thorp, H.H. 2023. Editorial. ChatGPT is fun, but not an author. *Science*, 379(6630), 312.

Tredinnick, L. and Laybats, C. 2023. Editorial: Black-box creativity and generative artificial intelligence. *Business Information Review*, 40(3), 98–102.

Välba, A. 2023. Eestis napib ette mõtlemise oskust. *Novaator* 08.10.2023. Available at https:// www .err .ee/ 1609125590/ lauristin -eestis -napib -ette -motlemise -oskust (accessed 7 January 2024).

van Dis, E.A., Bollen, J., Zuidema, W., van Rooij, R., and Bockting, C.L. 2023. ChatGPT: Five priorities for research. *Nature*, 614 (7947), 224–226.

Varman, R., Saha, B., and Skålén, P. 2011. Market subjectivity and neoliberal governmentality in higher education. *Journal of Marketing Management*, 27(11–12), 1163–1185.

von Krogh, G., Robertson, Q., and Gruber, M. 2023. Recognizing and utilizing novel research opportunities with artificial intelligence. *Academy of Management Journal*, 66(2), 367–373.

Voronov, M., Foster, W., Patriotta, G., and Weber, K. 2023. Distilling authenticity: Materiality and narratives in Canadian distillers' authenticity work. *Academy of Management Journal*, 66, 1438–1468.

Walters, W.H. and Wilder, E.I. 2023. Fabrication and errors in the bibliographic citations generated by ChatGPT. *Scientific Reports*, 13, 14045.

Wang, H., Fu, T., Gao, W., Huang, K., Liu, Z., Chandak, P., Liu, S., Van Katwyk, P., Deac, A., Anandkumar, A., Bergen, K., Gomes, C., Ho, S., Kohli, P., Lasnby, J., Leskovec, J., Liu, T., Manrai, A., … Zitnik, M. 2023. Scientific discovery in the age of artificial intelligence. *Nature*, 620, 47–60.

Wolkovich, E.M. 2024. "Obviously, ChatGPT" – how reviewers accused me of scientific fraud. *Nature* 05.02.2024. Available at https://www-nature-com.ezproxy.tlu.ee/ articles/d41586-024-00349-5 (accessed 2 April 2024).

PART I

Setting the scene continued

2. What ChatGPT still can't do (but we might do with it): Hubert Dreyfus and extended-mind cyborgs

Wayne Martin and Deidre Williams

In the early 1970s, Hubert Dreyfus published a controversial book called *What Computers Can't Do* (Dreyfus 1972). Two decades later, he published *What Computers Still Can't Do* (Dreyfus 1992). Dreyfus died in 2017, before the widespread availability of generative AI tools using large language models. But it is instructive to consider how his "Critique of Artificial Reason" relates to the latest generation of AI, and what light the new tools cast on the structure and limitations of his critique. We begin with a review of the historical record, clarifying what Dreyfus did, and what he did not say, about the limits of machine intelligence. We adjudicate the controversy over his assessment of the prospects for computer chess and provide an analysis of the master argument upon which his critique of AI relied. In assessing the significance of that critique, we turn our attention to Deep Blue, IBM's chess-playing supercomputer that defeated the then-reigning world champion in 1997. We argue that one element of Deep Blue's programming architecture points towards a neglected alternative in Dreyfus' disjunctive argument about the limits of artificial intelligence and an affinity with recent generative AI tools. We introduce the concept of *extended-mind cyborgs* to reflect on the opportunities and limitations of programs such as ChatGPT.

2.1 FACT-CHECKING

Hubert Dreyfus was the most prominent philosophical critic of AI of his generation. A few weeks before Dreyfus' death in 2017, his long-time philosophical sparring partner, Daniel Dennett, gave an interview to the BBC. We begin with an extract from that interview:

> **Jim Al-Khalili (BBC):** At this point, and having taken on Quine as a student back in Harvard, your next target was Hubert Dreyfus.
> **Daniel Dennett:** That's right. I mean he – unlike some other philosophers, unlike his Berkeley Colleague John Searle – he was prepared to put his money

where his mouth was in effect and say: "Right; the computers will never play good chess because they can't have intuition." [...]

Jim Al-Khalili: And of course later, quite embarrassingly, Dreyfus was himself beaten by a computer.

Daniel Dennett: Oh yeah, to the great cheers of the AI crowd.[1]

Back in the summer of 1964, Dreyfus, fresh from filing his PhD dissertation at Harvard, spent three months as a researcher at the RAND corporation, the research and public policy think tank based in Santa Monica. His job was to research philosophical issues raised by the prospect of "thinking machines." His findings were presented at a seminar that summer at RAND, and his report was subsequently published (amid considerable controversy) under the RAND imprint. Its title was a clear provocation: *Alchemy and Artificial Intelligence* (Dreyfus 1965).

Dreyfus' RAND report was widely reported at the time; indeed in June, 1966, it was the lead item in "The Talk of the Town" in *The New Yorker*. The *New Yorker* quoted Herbert Simon's notorious 1957 prediction that a computer would win the world chess championship within ten years. It then went on to say: "We've just come across a lovely piece by Hubert L. Dreyfus, a professor at the Massachusetts Institute of Technology, which says computers can't, and won't."[2]

It is worth noting an ambiguity in the *New Yorker* report. Dreyfus is reported as saying that "computers can't, and won't." But the scope of this remark is unclear. Does it mean that computers can't and won't win the world chess championship – *ever*? Or that they can't and won't win the world chess championship *within the next ten years*? The ambiguity makes a difference between an inaccurate prediction and an accurate one. Two decades later this sort of ambiguity had vanished from the press reports, and the position attributed to Dreyfus had taken on an uncanny specificity. Seemingly reputable news sources reported that "In the mid-'60s, scientist Herbert [*sic*] Dreyfus bluntly asserted that no computer would ever be able to beat a 10-year-old. He ate his words when an MIT undergraduate wrote a program that beat Dreyfus himself" (Levy 1997; see also Lehmann-Haupt 1984).

So what is fact and what is fiction in all this? Start with a fact. It is true that Dreyfus played and lost to a chess-playing machine at MIT in 1967. The computer ran a program called MacHACK, which was developed by Richard Greenblatt, who had indeed been an MIT undergraduate (Papert 1968, 1.5.1). What about the allegedly "blunt assertion" about 10-year-olds? The source for this myth comes early in the RAND report, in Dreyfus' discussion of the NSS chess-playing program developed in 1958 by Newell, Shaw and Simon. The discussion there follows a pattern that recurs though much of Dreyfus' early writings on AI. He quotes verbatim predictions made by the NSS team, and then adds this report:

> In fact, in its few recorded games, the NSS program played poor but legal chess, and in its last official bout (October, 1960) was beaten in 35 moves by a 10-year-old novice. (Dreyfus 1965: 6)

Somehow, in the reporting, a singular factual claim about a particular, past, dated event was transformed in the lore into a universal claim about future possibilities.

What about Dennett's claim? Did Dreyfus ever say, "Right; the computers will never play good chess"? This characterization of Dreyfus' position circulated early (see, e.g., Papert 1968: I-6; Nilsson 1969: V-51; Toffler 1970: 187), and Dreyfus responded to it (e.g., Dreyfus 1966: 13; Dreyfus 1972: 223, n 45). One particularly memorable rebuttal came in a joint appearance with Dennett on live national television, the day after Deep Blue had defeated Kasparov.[3] Dennett was in a gloating mood:

> It seems to me that right now is a time for the skeptics to start moving the goal posts. [...] A hundred and fifty years ago Edgar Allan Poe was sure in his bones that no machine could ever play chess, and only 30 years ago so was Hubert Dreyfus, and he said so in the earlier edition of his book. Then he's changed his mind, and, as he says, it's – this is really no surprise.

In response, Dreyfus read out the frequently misreported passage from the RAND report, then added:

> I've had to put up for 35 years with this story that I said computers could never play chess. In fact, I said from the beginning it's a formal game, and of course, computers could play, in principle, could play, world-champion chess.

So far, we have been fact-checking Dreyfus' critics. So it's only fair to fact-check Dreyfus as well. Did he actually say from the beginning that "of course, computers could, in principle, play world-champion chess?" To answer this question, we need to turn to the logic of his critique.

2.2   A DISJUNCTIVE CRITIQUE OF ARTIFICIAL REASON

Dreyfus' critique of AI operated with a master-argument that he put to work in a number of case studies. The master-argument is what we'll refer to as an *argument-by-diagnosis*, and it operated in two cycles. The first cycle was descriptive, documenting a recurring pattern. In a series of different domains (game-playing, puzzle-solving, translation, pattern-recognition …), AI research had produced striking early successes. These successes in turn inspired confident predictions and promises about what would be possible in the near future, but the predictions turned out to be inaccurate and the promises went unfulfilled. This was accompanied by what Dreyfus controversially described as "signs of stagnation" (Dreyfus 1965: 9).

The second cycle in the argument was diagnostic, and comprised two key claims. Significantly, only one of these was about computers; the other claim was about *human* intelligence. The first claim concerned the early AI successes. In the domain of game-playing, early programmers had successfully programmed computers to consistently win or draw at simple games like tic-tac-toe, to play at a high level in more complex games like checkers, and to execute end-games in complex games like chess. Dreyfus' thesis was that these early successes came by focusing on games (or parts of games) that were amenable to an approach that he described as "counting out" – considering possible moves and replies, and then selecting the move with the greatest probability of success. Dreyfus' second thesis was about human beings. Applied to the domain of game-playing, his thesis was that human players rely on methods of information-processing that cannot be reduced to "counting out" (Dreyfus 1965: 21–24).

Taken together, these two claims generate Dreyfus' skeleton explanation of the recurrent pattern of success and failure in AI research. The confident promises of AI researchers had been predicated on the assumption that the approaches that had proved effective in early tests could be scaled up to tackle the more difficult challenges. But those challenges take us into domains where human beings rely on other forms of information processing. Now this certainly does not prove that computers will not succeed at chess by counting-out methods alone. But neither was it intended to provide such a proof. It was offered as a diagnosis (an argument to the best explanation) for a distinctive pattern of success and failure in early AI R&D.

So far, all of that is retrospective. But what, if anything, did Dreyfus' diagnosis imply about *future* prospects – whether for AI in general, or for computer chess in particular? In his report, Dreyfus clearly stated that "a problem can in principle always be solved on a digital computer, provided the data and the rules of transformation are explicit" (Dreyfus 1965: 70). This is of course a general claim, not a claim specifically about chess. But chess clearly meets this condition, as Dreyfus himself pointed out (Dreyfus 1965: 69). Taken together, these claims directly entail that computers can, *in principle*, play chess.

However Dreyfus also described games like chess and go as "formal/ complex intelligent activities," which "*in practice* cannot be dealt with by exhaustive enumeration" (Dreyfus 1965: 79, emphasis added). In a table, he categorized them as "uncomputable games" (Dreyfus 1965: 76, Table 1). At this point we need to proceed carefully. There is no reason to doubt Dreyfus' conclusion that chess cannot *in practice* be solved by exhaustive counting out. In a seminal early paper on computer chess, Claude Shannon famously estimated the total number of possible games of chess as being at least 10^{120}. According to Shannon, a computer operating at 1 MHz would take 10^{90} years to "solve chess" by following out the full decision-tree (Shannon 1950). Modern supercomputers are of course much faster, but nonetheless fail to make a dent in what has come to be known as *The Shannon Number*. But does it follow that chess is an "uncomputable game"? Only if exhaustive enumeration is the only way of rendering a game computable!

Dreyfus himself was keenly aware that some games could be solved without relying on exhaustive enumeration of the decision-tree. For Dreyfus, a key example of an alternate strategy was associated with the game known as *nim*. Nim is a bar game played with matchsticks – now largely forgotten except among a few math geeks and computer nerds. But nim was at various points firmly in the limelight. There had been a nim-craze in cafés in the early sixties, inspired by Resnais' 1961 surrealist film, *Last Year at Marienbad*. More importantly for our purposes: nim was the game played by one of the very first videogame computers, dubbed *Nimrod*, which made a stir at the 1951 Festival of Britain. The rules of nim are simple. In one standard variation, two players take turns removing match-sticks from an array divided into several rows. Each player can remove as many matches as they wish (≥ 1), but only from a single row. The player who takes the last match wins.

The key point to appreciate is that nim is computable in two different ways. The decision-tree for nim is small enough that a computer (although probably not an unaided human being) could calculate the entire decision-tree, "counting out" out every possible reply to every possible move and then choosing one that yields a sure path to victory. But that was not how Nimrod played. In fact Nimrod did not do any counting out at all. Instead it used a computational shortcut. It calculated the binary XOR sum (now also known as the "nim sum") for each array with which it was presented. Then at each play, it identified a move that would yield a nim sum of zero for its opponent (Author Not Given 1951). This is a provably winning strategy for nim (Bouton 1901).

Nimrod provides an elegant example of game-computability without counting out. But it also teaches us a broader lesson about the logical form of Dreyfus' critique. In order to warrant his description of chess as an uncomputable game, Dreyfus relied on a disjunctive argument:

(1) If chess is computable in practice, then *either* it is feasible to trace the whole decision-tree *or* there is a 'nim-style' computational shortcut.

(2) It is not feasible to trace the whole decision-tree for chess.

  (3) There is no 'nim-style' computational shortcut for chess.
∴ (C) Chess is not computable in practice.

Dreyfus did not offer any general argument against the possibility of a computational shortcut for chess. But one strategy to which he did devote attention was the method of "pruning the decision-tree" through heuristics. It is worth reviewing this portion of his argument, which incorporates his boldest claim about human intelligence and clarifies the grounds for his pessimism about AI.

  The strategy of pruning the decision-tree for chess was in fact the main proposal in Shannon's original pioneering paper on computer chess. Shannon, who had an engineer's gift for language, dubbed this "the Type-B Programming Strategy." Both Type A and Type B programs operate with an "evaluation function" that assigns a numerical value to any board position. At each turn, Type A programs compute all variations to three moves out and use the evaluation function to rank all the resulting positions. Type-A Programs can play legal chess, but Shannon correctly predicted that play would be "both slow and weak" (Shannon 1950: 269). The strategy for Shannon's Type-B Program was to calculate deeper but on a much smaller subset of the available legal moves. His proposed method for doing so was to build in an additional layer of programming that would distinguish between "forceful" and "pointless" variations. Pointless variations are set aside to avoid wasting computational time; forceful variations are investigated in detail.

  Type-B programming proved to be a fruitful strategy. One reason for its fecundity was that it established a research program. Type-B programmers adopted a strategy that later came to be known as *cognitive simulation*. After all, Shannon reasoned, human chess-players don't consider all possible moves. They focus on a small subset of promising moves. They clearly have the ability to distinguish promising variations from pointless ones without counting out plies and replies. So the aim of the research program was to *capture what chess-players already know* in the form of what came to be called "heuristics" – programmable rules that provide a preliminary sorting of promising from pointless moves.

  A number of the most important philosophical points in Dreyfus' critique of AI concerned heuristics, which was a topic that continued to occupy him in the research that he and his brother (Stuart Dreyfus) later undertook for the US Air Force Office of Scientific Research (Dreyfus and Dreyfus 1980). One of their observations had in fact already been made by Shannon, who noted the important difference of a logical kind between these heuristic rules and the rules that determine legal moves or the rules used in computation by exhaustive enumeration. The rules of chess hold without exception. But the heuristic that tells you (for example) not to sacrifice a Queen for a Pawn or that "rooks should be placed on open ranks" are not like this at all. In Shannon's words, they only hold "other things being equal (!)" (Shannon 1950, 261, punctuation original).

Dreyfus went further. He argued, first, that one component in human intelligence consists in knowing when heuristic rules are to be broken. That, indeed, is one of the hallmarks of expertise. In the work for the Air Force, he went on to distinguish the behavior of novices, who do follow explicit rules (and perform poorly), from the behavior of experts, whose performance (they argued) transcends anything that can be captured in fully explicit rules. Applied to chess, their conclusion was that an expert's ability to recognize forceful possibilities and disregard pointless ones derives from a form of perceptual attunement to particularities of the chess board itself (Aristotle would have called it *phronesis*), born of thousands of hours of skill-development. It does not arise through, and cannot be captured in, general heuristic formulae operating over symbolic representations.

Let's pause to take stock. What we have found is that Dreyfus did, in one sense, "put his money where his mouth was" by describing chess as an "uncomputable game." However this did not mean that he thought that "computers will never play good chess." But the more important lesson here concerns the reasoning in support of the description of chess as an uncomputable game. What we have found is that Dreyfus' argument for that conclusion takes an essentially disjunctive form. From the point we have reached, we can identify at least three disjuncts. In order to be confident in the conclusion, we would need to be sure that chess is not computable by exhaustive counting out, is not computable by a nim-style computational shortcut, and is not computable by a "Type-B" hybrid that combines heuristic pruning and targeted counting out.

So why did Dreyfus describe chess as an uncomputable game? We suggest that he was rightly confident that there was no feasible method of exhaustive enumeration, and that he thought any alternative approach would have to rely on heuristics. Those heuristics essentially admit of exceptions, precluding the sort of "foregone conclusion" winning strategy that is available for nim. But more importantly, Dreyfus thought that the research program associated with Type-B programming was doomed. Expert players can indeed distinguish forceful from pointless variations. And they can do so without wasting their time counting out nodes on a decision-tree. But according to Dreyfus, experts will never render that know-how explicit in the form of programmable heuristics, because the knowledge and intelligence that they exercise in such circumstances is not inscribed in rules. It is worth noting, once again, the intricate intermixing here of claims about computers and claims about us.

2.3   EXTENDED-MIND CYBORGS

What lessons might be drawn from all this in thinking about the current generation of AI tools? Allow us to approach this question by considering one further point about computers and chess.

It is often said that Deep Blue triumphed over Kasparov through its sheer brute-force calculations deep into the decision-trees of the games in which it competed. But this is at best a partial truth. It is true that Deep Blue used its enormous computational power within the broad strategic parameters that Shannon had mapped out: it combined an evaluation function with pruning to focus its searches along forceful pathways. But in executing this strategy, Deep Blue incorporated a technique that neither Shannon nor Dreyfus had anticipated. The crucial factor: Deep Blue's memory banks stored 700,000 past games played by grandmasters.

The interesting question for our purposes is about what Deep Blue did with this vast store of information. One point is worth noting immediately: it stored this information symbolically, in a modified form of the binary representation of chess positions that Shannon had proposed. Moreover, its operations over those symbolic representations were implementations of fully explicit algorithmic rules. But we should not therefore conclude that there was nothing new in all this. Confronted with a board position when playing against Kasparov, Deep Blue searched to see whether the position had occurred in any of the stored games. If it had, Deep Blue checked to see what move had been made from that position, and how that earlier game had ended. It also took into account a number of other factors in a weighted formula, including the frequency with which that position had been met with that reply, the rankings of the players who had played it, and whether the move was annotated in "box score" reports of the games in which it had occurred. In its evaluation function, Deep Blue then awarded a bonus to moves that scored highly in this weighted sum. In some cases, where a particular move had been played frequently on paths that ultimately led to victory, Deep Blue followed the proven track without relying on any "counting out" or heuristics at all – reserving precious computation time for later in the game (Campbell 1999; Hsu 1999).

Where should we place this 'extended book' technique against Dreyfus' disjunctive alternatives? It does not involve counting out plies and replies; indeed it was specifically designed to reduce the need for that laborious form of computation, and in some cases to dispense with it altogether. But neither does it implement a nim-style computational shortcut that would render counting out entirely superfluous. Should we categorize it as an example of Type-B Programming? Only at the risk of obscuring its most distinctive features.

What Dreyfus' alternatives did not take into account was a *machine* technique for exploiting *human* intelligence in way that did not involve a detour through propositionally formulated generalizations that lose the fine resolution associated with expert performance.

To appreciate the point, think of the records in Deep Blue's extended book as a *material sedimentation of human intelligence*. Each individual entry records a discrete instance of intelligent behavior by an individual human being; taken as a whole they comprise not only a *representation* but also an accumulated *by-product* of collective human intelligence. Those 700,000 recorded games in turn hearken back to millions upon millions of unrecorded games, by masters and grandmasters, mid-level players, and novices alike, in which gambits and stratagems were tried and refined, sometimes succeeding and sometimes failing. Expert human players build on that history in two different ways. They build on it explicitly when they study earlier games – although of course no human being could possibly study the whole set. They also build on it implicitly. Lessons learned through thousands of hours of play, deploying strategies refined by hundreds of years of competition, come to attune their awareness, allowing them to respond intelligently to patterns they perceive on the board even without being able to articulate fully the reasons behind their selections. Aside from the sheer fact of its victory, the most important fact about Deep Blue was that it managed to harness, in a set of explicit rules operating over fully explicit data, know-how which expert humans access and deploy in quite a different manner.

In this sense, Deep Blue's extended book technique marks a 'neglected alternative' outside the scope of Dreyfus' disjunctive critique, a novel form of collaboration between computer and machine intelligence, and a whole that is greater than its parts. In the extended book, human and machine intelligence each made a distinctive contribution. Human players built up expertise, relying on forms of human intelligence that (if Dreyfus was correct) transcend algorithmic symbol manipulation. Along the way they developed practices and techniques for recording their intelligent behavior. Machine intelligence, itself developed by human beings, was then deployed to interrogate that data and to extract guidance from it in determining how to navigate specific decision-situations. A human being then moved a piece of wood. We think of the resulting system, drawing conjointly on human and machine intelligence in a way that neither could manage without reliance on the other, as an *extended-mind cyborg*.[4]

The resulting technique differs not only from 'counting out' or a nim-style computational shortcut, but also from Type-B heuristics. Heuristics begin from the chess wisdom that expert players are able to articulate and formulate as general, 'other things being equal' rules-of-thumb. *Generating* heuristics involves abstracting from exceptions, so *using* heuristics well requires an exercise of intelligence in determining when to set them aside. IBM's extended-mind cyborg was not hobbled by these limitations. Crucially, its operations were built directly on the sedimented by-product of intelligent *behavior*, not on the expert's reflections on or generalizations over that behavior. Indeed in any particular instance, neither man nor machine nor cyborg may be able to explain why the endorsed move was preferred. They thereby fall outside Dreyfus' disjunction, and represent a collaborative way for computers to draw on just the kind of inexplicit know-how that he considered a hallmark of human intelligence.

The relevance of this to the current generation of AI tools should now be visible. Indeed in retrospect, one would not be far wrong in describing Deep Blue's extended book as an early example of a "large language model," encoded in the distinctive language of binary chess notation. By contemporary standards, the model may not have been all that large, but the IBM programmers broke important new ground in developing novel ways of exploiting it, using an algorithm to project the next symbol in a string in a context.

We find it helpful to think about tools like ChatGPT not so much as intelligent machines (their claim to that title is certainly open to dispute) but rather as machine components in extended-mind cyborgs. They can do what they cannot do on their own by being embedded in partnerships and teams that are equipped with human intelligence. The human partners play a role in producing and curating the corpora upon which they train, and then in formulating the prompts that produce responses from the machine. Neither are capable on their own of producing the novel products that they can produce together.

What might Dreyfus have had to say about ChatGPT? He would certainly have been keen to document all the many things that it *still can't do*, and he would have taken a mischievous delight in the tasks on which it spectacularly fails, and in its well-documented inability to learn from its own mistakes. But if the arguments that we have advanced here are correct, then he would also have needed to revisit his critique of artificial reason to recognize not only new computability techniques but also a novel form of collaboration between machine and human intelligence.

For our part, we are also interested in what generative AI can and cannot do. Since OpenAI's public release of ChatGPT in November, 2022, we have regularly probed its abilities in part by asking it to construct natural deduction proofs, or to tease out the assumptions at work in a philosophical argument. So far, at least, deductive logic does not seem to be its strongest suit.[5] Ultimately, however, what interests us more are the questions about how best to act in concert with tools like ChatGPT and how to prepare ourselves for the new extended-mind cyborgs that lie over the horizon.

NOTES

1. Daniel Dennett, interview with Jim Al-Khalili, *The Life Scientific*, BBC Radio 4; broadcast 4 April, 2017; https:// www .bbc .co .uk/ programmes/ b08kv3y4. See also Dennett (1995: 433).
2. "The Talk of the Town," *The New Yorker*, 11 June, 1966, p. 27.
3. The Public Broadcasting System, *The Newshour with Jim Lehrer*; broadcast 12 May, 1997.
4. On the concept of the extended mind, see Clark and Chalmers (1998). Unlike the cyborgs familiar from science fiction, the machine components of an extended-mind cyborg are extra-corporeal.
5. When invited repeatedly to construct a natural deduction proof of the sequent < : P v ~P >, ChatGPT 3.5 will produce a spectacular variety of different proofs of varying length and complexity, but none valid and most making use of assumptions that it fails to discharge. When these errors are pointed out, ChatGPT politely apologizes.

REFERENCES

Author Not Given, *Faster than Thought: The Ferranti Nimrod Digital Computer* (London: Ferranti, 1951).

Bouton, Charles, "Nim: A Game with a Complete Mathematical Theory," *Annals of Mathematics* 3:2 (1901) 35–39.

Campbell, Murray, "Knowledge Discovery in Deep Blue: A Vast Database of Human Experience can be Used to Direct a Search," *Communications of the ACM* 42:11 (1999), 65–67.

Clark, Andy and Chalmers, David, "The Extended Mind," Analysis 58:1 (1998), 7–19.

Dennett, Daniel, *Darwin's Dangerous Idea: Evolution and the Meanings of Life* (London: Penguin, 1995).

Dreyfus, Hubert, *Alchemy and Artificial Intelligence* (Santa Monica, California: RAND, 1965).

Dreyfus, Hubert, "Statement from Prof. Dreyfus," *ACM SICART Newsletter* (1966), 13.

Dreyfus, Hubert, *What Computers Can't Do: A Critique of Artificial Reason* (New York: Harper and Row, 1972).

Dreyfus, Hubert, *What Computers Still Can't Do: A Critique of Artificial Reason* (New York: Harper and Row, 1992).

Dreyfus, Hubert, and Dreyfus, Stuart, *A Five-Stage Model of the Mental Activities in Directed Skill Acquisition* (Berkeley: UC Berkeley Operations Research Center, 1980); USAF Office of Scientific Research Contract F49620-79-C-0063.

Hsu, Feng-Hsiung, "IBM's Deep Blue Chess Grandmaster Chips," *IEEE Micro* 19:02 (1999), 70–81.

Lehmann-Haupt, Christopher, "Hackers as Heroes," *New York Times*, 24 Dec., 1984; Section 1, page 15.

Levy, Neil, "Man Vs. Machine," *Newsweek*, 4 May, 1997.

Nilsson, Nils, *Problem-Solving Methods in Artificial Intelligence* (Palo Alto, CA: Stanford Research Institute Artificial Intelligence Group, 1969).

Papert, Seymour, *Artificial Intelligence Memo No. 154: The Artificial Intelligence of Hubert Dreyfus: A Budget of Fallacies* (Cambridge, MA: Massachusetts Institute of Technology Project MAC, 1968).

Shannon, Claude, "Programming a Computer for Playing Chess," *Philosophical Magazine* Series 7, Vol. 41, No. 314 (March 1950), 256–275.

Toffler, Alvin, *Future Shock* (New York: Bantam Books, 1970).

3. Identifying discourses of generative AI in higher education

Chahna Gonsalves and Oguz A. Acar

3.1 INTRODUCTION

Integrating generative artificial intelligence (AI) into higher education is a dynamic and evolving discussion topic, marked by a spectrum of reactions from enthusiastic adoption to complete avoidance. This significant divergence in responses likely reflects the opportunities and challenges generative AI presents for reshaping curricula, pedagogical strategies, and assessment practices.

On the one hand, scholars have emphasised the potential of generative AI in higher education, particularly in enhancing university services, learning experiences, curriculum engagement and preparing students for AI-integrated workplaces (e.g., Bentley et al. 2023; Dwivedi et al. 2023). Tools like ChatGPT offer personalised learning, prompt feedback, and the development of critical thinking by engaging students in analysing and refining AI-generated content (Dwivedi et al. 2023). They also serve as a practical aid to students and educators in various tasks, including drafting strategies, generating ideas, and writing assistance (Guha, Grewal, and Atlas 2024). Mollick and Mollick (2023) argue that integrating generative AI into education will radically transform the ways teaching and learning are experienced. Integrating such AI technologies into education represents a transformative step towards aligning academic teaching with modern professional skill requirements, fostering a more interactive and efficient learning environment.

On the other hand, researchers identified a range of concerns. For example, Farrokhnia et al. (2024) and Rudolph, Tan, and Tan (2023) highlight the tension between traditional educational models, which emphasise critical thinking and deep disciplinary knowledge (e.g., Bloom et al. 1956), and the potential risks posed by the ease and accessibility of generative AI platforms. These risks include academic misconduct and a tendency towards superficial learning engagement (Dwivedi et al. 2023). The possibility of dependency on generative AI also raises questions about its impact on learners' metacognitive and problem-solving abilities (Farrokhnia et al. 2024), although research suggests that "preparing" to effectively use AI, through supported development of skills related to problem formulation exploration of AI tools, experimentation in interaction and reflection on their experiences may enhance benefits for teaching and learning (Acar 2023). Moreover, AI's ability to produce written content to a high standard, evade traditional plagiarism detection tools and achieve high grades in exams (Gilson et al. 2022; Sadasivan et al. 2023) compound the challenges. Effective integration of AI into higher education requires a careful and balanced consideration of the opportunities, challenges, and implications associated with AI use (Bentley et al. 2023).

Drawing on discourse analysis, a method central to our study, Li et al. (2023) and Bearman, Ryan, and Ajjawi (2023) offer pertinent insights that complement our approach. Li et al. (2023) analysed public perceptions of ChatGPT in education, uncovering overall positivity but also concerns about academic integrity, learning outcomes, AI limitations, policy implications, and workforce challenges. This discourse, led by voices from technology, education, and media fields, highlights the diverse range of stakeholder views on the role of AI in educational settings. Bearman, Ryan, and Ajjawi (2023) reviewed 29 peer-reviewed articles, identifying themes of urgent adaptation to AI in higher education and its impact on academic power dynamics. These studies provide context for our analysis, underscoring the varied perspectives on generative AI in higher education. While these studies are not the focal point of our analysis, they provide valuable insights into the broader context within which our research is situated.

In this chapter, we explore the intersection of generative AI's potential and pitfalls in education, drawing insights from interviews with seven academic staff members from a UK business school's marketing department. We aim to contribute to the discourse around generative AI by articulating the nuanced perceptions, challenges, and opportunities recognised by educators. Overall, the insights gathered present a balanced view, avoiding extremes such as the outright advocacy or wholesale rejection of AI in academia.

3.2   METHOD

This study was conducted within a UK Russell Group university's business school, with active faculty engagement in generative AI discussions.[1] The Russell Group, encompassing 24 leading UK universities, has set forth principles for responsible AI use in education, balancing technological benefits with academic integrity, influencing faculty discourse and curriculum integration. These principles have fostered a heightened sense of awareness and active dialogue among the faculty about the role and implications of generative AI in academic settings and in their curricula.

The study utilised semi-structured interviews involving seven academic staff members selected from 29 departmental staff. Interviews, lasting 45 to 55 minutes, included undergraduate- and postgraduate-level module leaders, chosen for their direct involvement with generative AI in teaching and curriculum development. The interviews focused on their perceptions of generative AI's advantages and challenges, particularly in marketing education, and its impact on student engagement, skill development, and institutional readiness for AI adoption.

Four interviewees had already implemented generative AI in their teaching activities, while three were revising their curricula and assessments for future AI integration. Their diverse experiences in AI application across different teaching formats, including face-to-face and online synchronous sessions, allowed a well-rounded analysis of generative AI from an educational perspective.

3.2.1   Data Analysis

The first author transcribed the interviews, conducting a rigorous, iterative process. Initial coding of transcripts led to the emergence of a number of broad themes, with further analysis integrating and refining these themes. This thematic analysis culminated in identifying eight distinct discourses related to AI in education. These discourses, forming the core of this chapter, offer an exploration of generative AI's multifaceted roles and implications in education. This method allowed for a nuanced understanding of the intricate dynamics in integrating AI into higher education, forming the basis for the chapter's arguments and discussions.

3.3   FINDINGS AND DISCUSSION

This study offers discourse analysis, derived from educators' perspectives of generative AI in a UK Russell Group university's business school. In our use of the term "discourse" we refer to sets of language use encompassing beliefs, values, interactions, and actions (Gee 2004) as well as the social contexts and histories that shape those sets of language (Gee 2007). Therefore, this analysis produced overarching discourse categories, which provide insight into the perceptions and social meanings ascribed to generative AI amongst study participants. Data analysis yielded eight key discourses – generative AI as: "a double-edged sword", "the elephant in the room", "an unintended burden", "a pedagogical paradigm shift", "a new instrument", "an escalator", "a digital compass", and "a digital tutor". Table 3.1 presents a synthesis of the metaphors identified in our discourse analysis to further elucidate the complex dynamics of generative AI in higher education. Each metaphor encapsulates a distinct perspective on integrating generative AI, highlighting its potential benefits and challenges.

Table 3.1   *A summary of metaphors and their implications*

Metaphor	Descriptive explanation	Positive aspects	Negative aspects
A double-edged sword	Generative AI holds significant potential for personalising and enriching education, akin to one edge of a sword that cuts through barriers to learning. Conversely, it introduces challenges to maintaining pedagogical integrity and equity, much like the sword's other edge that can inflict harm and bring unintended consequences if not wielded with caution.	• Transformative potential in personalisation and engagement • Augments traditional teaching	• Pedagogical regression • Educator uncertainty • Risks to academic integrity
The elephant in the room	Generative AI's colossal presence in education is significant yet often not addressed directly, almost hidden in plain sight, creating an environment where its potential and challenges are not fully explored. This scenario underscores the need for more open discussions and transparent engagement, lest the silence stifles its adoption and an ethically integrated future.	• Acknowledges the widespread, yet unspoken, use of generative AI • Encourages ethical adoption of AI	• Reluctance to openly discuss generative AI • Institutional uncertainty • Concealment of AI usage
An unintended burden	The integration of generative AI into education introduces complexities, especially in assessing student work, creating additional burdens for educators. This new weight, unasked for, perches on educators' shoulders. It challenges the traditional boundaries of originality and creativity, requiring new approaches to evaluation and integrity, appearing to some as a Sisyphean task.	• Raises awareness of generative AI's impact on assessment and integrity	• Increased workload in assessment • Difficulty in discerning generative AI assistance • Blurs the definition and inference of originality

(continues overleaf)

Metaphor	Descriptive explanation	Positive aspects	Negative aspects
A pedagogical paradigm shift	The advent of generative AI invites a renaissance in educational methods, necessitating a shift, from traditional lecture-based approaches to those that emphasise critical thinking, the fluidity of critical inquiry and problem-solving. This shift involves careful integration of AI tools to avoid misuse and ensure educational integrity.	• Encourages evolution in teaching methods • Emphasises critical thinking and problem-solving	• Misuse of generative AI tools • Need for strategic pedagogical adaptation
A new instrument	Like a new instrument in the educational repertoire, generative AI offers innovative teaching possibilities. However, mastery of this instrument requires educators to invest time in learning about and adapting to its capabilities, as well as practice to find one's own style, amidst the challenges posed by rapid technological advancements.	• Offers opportunities for innovative teaching • Requires understanding, time, and practice	• Overwhelm due to rapid technological changes • Disparity in educator preparedness
An escalator	Generative AI acts as an escalator in education, speeding up the creation of teaching materials and simplifying processes. While it offers efficiency, akin to choosing an escalator over stairs, this ease risks atrophying the muscles of deep engagement and critical thought, leaving both educators and learners on a plateau of superficial understanding.	• Simplifies the creation of teaching materials • Highlights the ease of using generative AI	• Risks shallower learning engagement • Potential for passive learning • Discerning when to use generative AI in teaching and learning over traditional methods

Metaphor	Descriptive explanation	Positive aspects	Negative aspects
A digital compass	Generative AI, like a compass for digital mariners, guides educators and students through the educational landscape, offering direction amidst the swift currents of technological change. Its rapid evolution, however, necessitates clear learning objectives and paths to ensure it supports, rather than confuses, educational goals. This tool demands a balance between guiding exploration and maintaining clarity on our educational voyage.	• Provides direction in generative AI integration • Encourages critical navigation of generative AI tools	• Need for clarity in learning paths and objectives • Rapid evolution of required skills
A digital tutor	Generative AI, serving as a digital sage, weaves personalised feedback into the fabric of education, acting as a supplementary tutor. Balancing its guidance with human judgement is essential to prevent an overreliance that could diminish the learning process. This tool, while enriching the educational tapestry, is a borrowed wisdom, reminding us to critically evaluate its role and ensure it complements rather than replaces the human touch in teaching and learning.	• Offers context-specific feedback • Enhances the educational process	• Supplemental role, not a replacement for human judgement • Risk of student overreliance on generative AI

3.3.1 A Double-Edged Sword

Generative AI as "a double-edged sword" in educators' perceptions was typified by conversations about the dual nature of AI's impact: its significant potential to revolutionise education juxtaposed with notable challenges to pedagogical integrity and academic equity. This duality is reflected in broader academic conversations and debates within the Russell Group about weighing AI's advantages against its risks (Chan 2023).

3.3.1.1 Positive edge: transformative potential of generative AI

Educators recognise generative AI's significant role in personalising education, emphasising its capacity to create "diverse" and "inclusive" content (see also Pavlik, Chapter 4 in this volume). This AI-driven customisation addresses both individual and collective needs, enhancing relatability and engagement. One educator exemplified this by using AI to tailor a brand mascot, fostering community spirit in a module. While the use of generative AI to create resources and collaborative learning opportunities (e.g., Alshahrani 2023; Rudolph, Tan, and Tan 2023) and its ability to personalise content for individual learners, learner paths and feedback (Mello et al. 2023) have been discussed in prior literature, such innovative approaches to inject personalisation and increase engagement have been less explored. In these discussions, generative AI was thought of as a vehicle for actualising long-standing ambitions to transform the learning experience.

Another positive facet is AI's role in augmenting traditional teaching. One educator shared how AI streamlined the creation of tailored teaching resources: "I used to use readymade cases ... [generative AI] has made making my own much quicker; I just wouldn't have done that before." This sentiment underscores AI as a tool for developing effective educational materials in less time, closely aligned with learning outcomes (see also Kerem, Chapter 6 in this volume

3.3.1.2 Negative edge: pedagogical regression and educator uncertainty

Conversely, the discourse underscored a paradox: technological advancement sometimes leads to a sense of regression among educators with some feeling left behind in their expertise. This was exemplified when educators noted their inability to "be ahead" or "stay ahead" of students' AI usage. An instance cited involved the use of AI in asynchronous webinars, where students' reliance on AI for responses resulted in uniform and surface-level engagement, challenging the educators' ability to promote metacognitive skills and Socratic methods for stimulating critical thinking and inquiry thus impeding the development of critical thinking and inquiry skills.

Educators' uncertainty and hesitancy in fully leveraging AI's capabilities was a pervasive theme. The rapid uptake and enthusiastic use of generative AI by students left some of the educators feeling unprepared and ill-equipped, unsure of how to ensure effective learning amidst these technological changes. This hesitancy was often linked to a lack of confidence in their own AI skills, aligning with Kohnke, Moorhouse, and Zou's (2023) findings on educators' reluctance due to inadequate AI knowledge and training (see also Miller, Chapter 13 in this volume). Participants noted that the integration of AI has consequently deepened the divide within the educational sector, separating tech-savvy educators from those less comfortable with these tools. This disparity suggests a gap in faculties' abilities to employ AI effectively, prompting calls for specialised AI training for educators to manage this evolving digital landscape. While generative AI holds great potential for enhancing educational experiences, its integration demands a balanced, critical approach. Addressing AI's challenges is crucial to maintaining the integrity and inclusivity of education, ensuring it serves as a tool for enrichment, not a source of disparity.

3.3.2   The Elephant in the Room

The theme of generative AI as "the elephant in the room" highlights its subtle yet significant presence in academia, with educators and students showing ambivalence about its usage (see also Miller, Chapter 13 in this volume). This reluctance to openly discuss AI, especially in contexts that may impact academic integrity, reflects a broader, institutional uncertainty. As Lau and Guo (2023) noted, this reticence and broader, institutional uncertainty surrounding AI calls for transparent conversations about AI's role in education.

Educators acknowledge the widespread use of AI among students, with one stating: "The genie is out of the bottle, and the students are already using this stuff", suggesting that students might be more adept at using AI than educators realise. This situation underscores the urgency of integrating AI into educational systems in a way that openly addresses its usage and implications: "We need to embrace it. We can't ignore it." Another said: "It becomes very interesting when we say there's nothing wrong with these tools, but you've got to be in control of them. We need to see that you know how to use them, which is a skill required in their careers."

However, the tendency of students to conceal their use of AI is noteworthy. Educators speculate that this might be due to students being unaware of how widely their peers use generative AI, leading to limited discussion. Despite this, educators advocate for the ethical adoption of AI, emphasising its importance in learning and future career skills. "There's nothing unethical about AI, and they've got to embrace it. We've got to help them learn it," one educator remarked, highlighting the need for proficiency in AI tools.

The discussion around generative AI among colleagues also varies, with some educators actively using it while others remain silent on the topic. This disparity in engagement suggests differing comfort levels with AI's role in educational development versus its efficiency in academic tasks. Analysis of this discourse reveals a landscape where exploration of AI's potential is matched by cautiousness in its application.

3.3.3   An Unintended Burden

The discourse on generative AI as an "unintended burden" in academia centres on the increased workload for educators arising from the need to assess AI's role in student submissions. This theme, prominent in discussions on student assessments, underscores the challenges and unforeseen consequences of integrating AI into educational evaluation.

A significant concern is maintaining academic integrity in the age of readily accessible AI tools like ChatGPT, which students might misuse for convenience. Educators in our study voiced worries about the ease with which students could exploit these tools, potentially leading to a uniformity across submissions that betrays a superficial engagement with the material. This issue is compounded by AI's capability to produce plausible yet inaccurate or misleading content, as well as fabricated references (Baidoo-Anu and Ansah 2023). While participants acknowledged that the study institution and others in the Russell Group London have implemented policies requiring students to disclose AI use in their work (Moorhouse, Yeo, and Wan 2023), these concerns highlight the difficulty in distinguishing between AI-assisted and genuinely student-produced work, a task that adds complexity to the educator's role and blurs the lines of originality and creativity in academic output.

Educators conveyed that the burden of discerning AI's role in submitted work is not solely theirs but reflects a broader institutional challenge. The task of identifying AI involvement is fraught with "uncertainty", "ambiguity", and subjectivity, potentially leading to inconclusive, indefensible, and futile outcomes. This additional responsibility, described as "potentially exhausting", exacerbates the already demanding role of educators, some of whom feel ill-prepared or reluctant to integrate AI into their teaching methods. Concerns are also raised about the effectiveness of AI in pedagogical design and its overall impact on the learning experience, particularly among academics focused on research. This situation underscores the need for careful consideration and adaptation in the use of AI within educational contexts, balancing the benefits of technological advancement with the preservation of academic rigour and integrity.

3.3.4   A Pedagogical Paradigm Shift

The concept of generative AI as a catalyst for "a pedagogical paradigm shift" featured prominently in our study, highlighting the need to evolve teaching methods. Educators discussed the importance of transitioning from focusing on the final product of learning to emphasising the journey of knowledge acquisition and application. This shift is crucial for adapting to an educational landscape increasingly influenced by technology. Educators, while acknowledging the importance of integrating AI in teaching, expressed caution, emphasising the enhancement of students' critical thinking, problem-solving skills, and academic integrity amidst the availability of generative AI tools.

This strategic yet cautious approach aligns with Bearman and Ajjawi's (2023) advocacy for pedagogical adaptation, which encourages educators to teach AI technologies and foster critical engagement and ethical reflection among students. These findings resonate with the notion that integrating AI in education should lead to a deeper focus on AI literacy and ethical considerations, marking a significant shift in the educator's role in an AI-enhanced educational environment.

The study also revealed concerns among educators about the misuse of AI tools by students, akin to plagiarism, especially in knowledge-based learning settings. In contrast, educators who focus on "applied" learning supported controlled assessments tailored to the specific course and the students' developmental stage to gauge AI usage appropriately. This dichotomy underscores the varied perspectives among educators regarding the integration of AI in teaching, highlighting the importance of a nuanced understanding of AI's impact on different aspects of the learning process. The findings thus point to the need for a balanced, thoughtfully considered approach to incorporating generative AI in educational settings.

3.3.5   A New Instrument

Generative AI as "a new instrument" in education emerged from discussions that emphasised educators' need to understand and effectively utilise generative AI, which requires dedicated training, practice, and time to achieve proficiency and confidence, like a musical instrument. Participants highlighted the significance of comprehending AI's capabilities, limitations, and complexities. There was a consensus on the necessity for more training, with educators acknowledging their initial challenges in adapting to this technology, echoing Kohnke, Moorhouse, and Zou's (2023) findings.

One educator admitted to feeling overwhelmed, attributing this partly to not participating in available workshops, indicating a personal responsibility in their learning process. Another, having attended various training sessions, noted that, while these provided a basic understanding of generative AI applications and their educational implications, effectively employing these tools goes beyond technical know-how to include creative integration into teaching and pedagogy.

The discussions also revealed the importance of educators finding personalised approaches to incorporating generative AI into their specific teaching contexts. This involved identifying strategies for using AI that align with their pedagogical objectives and learning outcomes, acknowledging that educators' comfort levels and preferences in using AI vary. This aspect underscores the need for tailored adoption strategies that cater to individual educator's needs and teaching styles, thereby enhancing the overall effectiveness of generative AI in educational settings.

3.3.6   An Escalator

The discourse of generative AI as "an escalator" views generative AI as a shortcut that might undermine traditional, rigorous learning and teaching methods. One educator noted the ease of creating teaching materials with AI, paralleling it with an escalator's simplicity over the effort of climbing stairs, and acknowledged the risk of this convenience leading to shallower learning engagement.

The apprehension is not limited to students (Farrokhnia et al. 2024) but extends to educators, fearing that overdependence on AI could result in less impactful teaching materials. Bozkurt and Sharma (2023) stress the crucial role of educators in designing engaging and personalised learning experiences, which might be compromised by excessive AI reliance. A recurring theme was the necessity of mastering fundamental knowledge before turning to AI for assistance. One educator stated: "We had calculators in school, but we still learned manual multiplication first. We don't give a fourth grader a calculator for this reason." This analogy points out that generative AI could lead to a superficial understanding of subjects if used without a solid foundation. Moreover, our analysis revealed that the educators were concerned with students developing the necessary mental models to achieve the learning outcomes and evidence achievement of the intended learning outcomes.

Furthermore, there were worries about AI leading to passive learning, akin to the physical passivity of taking an escalator. This comparison underscores the importance of active learning and the risk of AI diminishing student engagement with the material. The metaphor also suggests that generative AI could standardise teaching methods and content, potentially stifling pedagogical innovation. Participants worried that overusing AI tools might result in the underdevelopment or weakening of both educators' and students' "intellectual muscles", similar to the effects of regularly choosing an escalator over stairs, thus hindering the growth of critical thinking skills and in-depth knowledge.

The discussions also raised the challenge of discerning when to use generative AI effectively and when traditional methods are more apt. Educators pointed out the necessity for greater understanding and time to optimally integrate AI, ensuring it augments rather than detracts from the educational value.

3.3.7   A Digital Compass

Generative AI as a "digital compass" was typified in conversations capturing the notion of generative AI as a tool that guides and directs but requires the user to understand the destination and the path clearly. These conversations surfaced the idea that generative AI offers guidance and assistance to both them and students without explicitly defining the learning objectives or the depth of understanding required. Consequently, generative AI can be likened to a compass that provides direction but doesn't dictate the journey or the destination. Educators recognise its potential and necessity, akin to how students adeptly navigate social media, but they are still exploring how to integrate it effectively into educational practices without it becoming the sole focus of learning.

The discourse revealed a recognition of AI's importance, similar to social media's ubiquity, tempered by uncertainties about its technicalities. Educators pondered the balance between teaching AI's technical aspects and leveraging students' inherent understanding of such tools. A participant reflected this sentiment: "I think it's quite the reality that the tools are changing very quickly ... We should prioritise flexibility, adaptability to new tools, and productivity over simple technical acumen."

There was an acknowledgment of a "lack of real understanding" about AI's role in industries like marketing, with educators keen on observing industry trends and learning from practitioners' use of AI. For instance, shifts in advertising were noted, where AI is increasingly performing roles traditionally held by junior employees. Yet, educators expressed uncertainty about the precise skills students need for an AI-driven professional world.

Our analysis suggests that while educators recognise the necessity for AI literacy, their understanding of the skills students need is still evolving. Educators discussed the changing nature of roles in fields like advertising, where AI is reshaping job functions. This evolution affects the clarity of the learning path and objectives in marketing education. The rapid evolution of AI demands a significant shift in how students are prepared for future careers such that they are equipped with a balanced skill set that includes both AI competencies and critical human skills (Bearman and Ajjawi 2023).

3.3.8   As a Digital Tutor

Generative AI as a "digital tutor" is a key discourse in educational AI integration. This perception is based on AI's ability to provide context-specific feedback, similar to a human tutor (see also Hendriksen, Chapter 5 in this volume). Educators in our study value AI's capacity to identify areas for improvement and offer relevant suggestions, enhancing the educational process. One participant aptly stated: "I think the feedback mechanism is actually a good one." However, it is crucial that AI's role remains supplementary, not replacing human judgement. One educator recounted using AI for writing an abstract, noting that while some AI suggestions were beneficial, others were not. He posited that while AI can be helpful, understanding the task is essential because: "you need to know how to create the product or do the task yourself" to effectively evaluate AI's suggestions and judiciously use its feedback. It is also critical that students recognise that AI has different goals and limitations. In his anecdote, the educator highlights that the AI provided feedback to rewrite the text, which was motivated by efficiency and concision, yet he argued that writing is "not always just about efficiency, but I understood the point, and I could evaluate [the feedback]".

While generative AI is viewed as a supportive and accessible feedback tool, educators emphasise the importance of balancing AI's efficiency with critical thinking and deep learning and express concern about students' overreliance on AI, from which they potentially miss critical learning opportunities. Generative AI, akin to a tutor, provides personalised feedback. Unlike a human tutor whose guidance goes beyond mere correction to fostering deep understanding, AI's role is to supplement this process. This necessitates AI-integrated teaching approaches that offer solutions and stimulate students' reflective learning. Educators perceive AI as a tool that enhances learning outcomes while promoting critical thinking and comprehension among students.

3.4   CONCLUSION

This exploration into educators' perspectives on generative AI in education has revealed a complex landscape, marked by discourses like "a double-edged sword", "the elephant in the room", "an unintended burden", "a pedagogical paradigm shift", "a new instrument", "an escalator", "a digital compass", and "a digital tutor". These themes underscore the multifaceted nature of AI's integration into educational contexts, exhibiting both potential and challenges.

Several key findings emerged from this analysis. The dual nature of generative AI was identified in the "double-edged sword" discourse, which highlighted its potential to revolutionise learning and teaching by creating customised resources and enhanced engagement while posing risks to assessment, pedagogical integrity, and academic equity.

Educators are aware that both students and fellow educators may be hesitant to discuss the use of AI because of a lack of clarity on how its use is perceived amongst others. The "unintended burden" discourse further emphasises the complexities AI introduces, especially in student assessment where educators believe that we need to "reassess how we assess" while simultaneously "removing the stigma around AI" and promoting its ethical use. The need for a shift in pedagogical approaches was evident, emphasising the importance of critical thinking, problem-solving skills, and maintaining academic integrity in an AI-enhanced educational landscape. The study also revealed disparities in educator preparedness and inequalities in their engagement with and integration of AI, which were influenced by their perceptions of AI's role in education. While some see AI as a tool for efficiency and educational innovation, others remain cautious, concerned about its impact on critical thinking and problem-solving abilities. In addressing the rapid evolution of AI, our participants acknowledged the challenge for educators to "catch up" with students who are already using AI tools.

Our findings have implications for various stakeholders in higher education. First, the rapid evolution of AI necessitates continuous professional development for educators to stay abreast of technological advancements and effectively integrate them into teaching practices. Future educational strategies must involve comprehensive training programmes covering AI's technical and pedagogical aspects. Such programmes should equip educators to critically assess AI tools and integrate them effectively into teaching and assessment. Institutions should also encourage open discussions about AI's role, aiding its cohesive integration into educational practices.

Second, there is a need for clear guidelines and policies that outline the ethical use of AI in educational settings, balancing innovation with academic standards. While the existence of guidance amongst some institutions has been acknowledged in this study, our findings suggest that regulatory frameworks and additional guidance should continue to establish clarity on issues like academic integrity, data privacy, and the equitable use of AI, ensuring that these tools are used responsibly and do not exacerbate the inequalities amongst educators, which will, in turn, affect students. Policymakers could also consider how AI influences curriculum and assessment delivery, ensuring that standards evolve to reflect the changing educational landscape while maintaining rigour and quality.

Third, our findings highlight the necessity of integrating AI literacy into curricula across various disciplines. This integration should go beyond teaching the use of tools; it should include critical discussions on AI's ethical, societal, and professional implications. In an AI-enhanced educational environment, there should be a concerted effort to ensure that students are not just consumers of AI-generated content but are also critical thinkers who can question and build upon AI suggestions. Cross-sector collaboration and further research into AI's impact on learning outcomes and pedagogical strategies might facilitate institutions effectively integrating AI into teaching practices and adapting pedagogical strategies accordingly.

Fourth, determining the optimal timing for integrating generative AI into education is crucial. Our discussions underscored the need for a solid foundational knowledge before introducing AI tools. Drawing on an analogy of AI as an escalator and the excerpts from one educator, just as students learn manual multiplication before using calculators, they should master the basics of their field before leveraging AI. This ensures that AI acts as a tool to augment existing skills, not a shortcut that bypasses fundamental foundational learning and obfuscates the learning process. For instance, in the context of academic writing, a student should first understand the basics of constructing arguments, researching, and structuring essays before turning to AI for assistance in refining or generating content. In other words, AI should be introduced as an assistive tool only after students have attained core competencies and demonstrated a fundamental understanding of the subject matter. In practice, such integration may manifest in the later stages of a student's educational trajectory – perhaps at the upper-undergraduate or graduate levels, where students have a firmer grasp on their field's basics. However, the exact timing must be contextually determined by the educators' judgement and the specific learning objectives of the course or curriculum.

Finally, our findings suggest that educational institutions should cultivate a culture that embraces AI as a tool for enhancing learning while critically assessing its implications. This involves open discussions among educators, students, and administrators about AI's role in education and its ethical considerations.

Several critical questions arise from this discourse analysis, inviting further investigation. These include how institutions can adapt pedagogy to integrate AI while maintaining educational equity (Bearman, Ryan, and Ajjawi 2023), the role of training and professional development in enhancing educators' AI proficiency (Kohnke, Moorhouse, and Zou 2023; Michel-Villarreal et al. 2023), the implications of AI on student learning and assessment, and the importance of institutional policies to guide AI's ethical use in education. Additionally, exploring the future of AI in education, particularly its impact on job readiness and required skills, and the benefits of a cross-disciplinary approach to AI education are vital for future research.

Overall, the discourses identified in our study offer a window into their complex perspectives on generative AI in education and tensions between innovation and core educational values. We call for a balanced approach where AI augments, rather than replaces human judgement and creativity, and for guidelines that foster effective and responsible use of generative AI in education. As the educational landscape evolves, reimagining teaching practices to maintain a synergy between technological progress and preserving critical skills remains a significant challenge and a tremendous opportunity.

NOTE

1. Approval to conduct this non-interventional study was gained from the King's College London Research Ethics Committee (MRA-23/24-41020).

REFERENCES

Acar, O. A. 2023. "Are your students ready for AI? A four-step framework to prepare learners for a ChatGPT world." https://hbsp.harvard.edu/inspiring-minds/are-your-students-ready-for-ai

Alshahrani, A. 2023. "The impact of ChatGPT on blended learning: Current trends and future research directions." *International Journal of Data and Network Science* 7(4): 2029–2040.

Baidoo-Anu, D., and L. O. Ansah. 2023. "Education in the era of generative artificial intelligence (AI): Understanding the potential benefits of ChatGPT in promoting teaching and learning." *Journal of AI* 7(1): 52–62.

Bearman, M., and R. Ajjawi. 2023. "Learning to work with the black box: Pedagogy for a world with artificial intelligence." *British Journal of Educational Technology* 54(5): 1160–1173.

Bearman, M., J. Ryan, and R. Ajjawi. 2023. "Discourses of artificial intelligence in higher education: A critical literature review." *Higher Education* 86(2): 369–385.

Bentley, C., C. Aicardi, S. Poveda, L. Magela Cunha, D. Kohan Marzagao, R. Glover, E. Rigley, S. Walker, M. Compton, and O. Acar. 2023. "A Framework for Responsible AI Education." A Working Paper (August 17). Available at SSRN: https://ssrn.com/abstract=4544010 or http://dx.doi.org/10.2139/ssrn.4544010

Bloom, B. S., M. D. Engelhart, E. Furst, W. H. Hill, and D. R. Krathwohl. 1956. *Handbook I: Cognitive Domain.* New York: David McKay.

Bozkurt, A., and R. C. Sharma. 2023. "Challenging the status quo and exploring the new boundaries in the age of algorithms: Reimagining the role of generative AI in distance education and online learning." *Asian Journal of Distance Education* 18(1).

Chan, C. K. Y. 2023. "A comprehensive AI policy education framework for university teaching and learning." *International Journal of Educational Technology in Higher Education* 20(1): 38.

Dwivedi, Y. K., N. Kshetri, L. Hughes, E. L. Slade, A. Jeyaraj, A. K. Kar, A. M. Baabdullah, A. Koohang, V. Raghavan, and M. Ahuja. 2023. "'So what if ChatGPT wrote it?' Multidisciplinary perspectives on opportunities, challenges and implications of generative conversational AI for research, practice and policy." *International Journal of Information Management* 71: 102642.

Farrokhnia, M., S. K. Banihashem, O. Noroozi, and A. Wals. 2024. "A SWOT analysis of ChatGPT: Implications for educational practice and research." *Innovations in Education and Teaching International* 61(3): 460–474.

Gee, J. 2007. *Social Linguistics and Literacies: Ideology in Discourses.* New York: Routledge.

Gee, J. P. 2004. "Discourse analysis: What makes it critical?" In *An Introduction to Critical Discourse Analysis in Education,* 49–80. New Jersey: Lawrence Erlbaum Associates Inc.

Gilson, A., C. Safranek, T. Huang, V. Socrates, L. Chi, R. A. Taylor, and D. Chartash. 2022. "How well does ChatGPT do when taking the medical licensing exams? The implications of large language models for medical education and knowledge assessment." *medRxiv*, 1–9. https://doi.org/10.1101/2022.12.23.22283901

Guha, A., D. Grewal, and S. Atlas. 2024. "Generative AI and marketing education: What the future holds." *Journal of Marketing Education* 46(1): 6–17.

Kohnke, L., B. L. Moorhouse, and D. Zou. 2023. "Exploring generative artificial intelligence preparedness among university language instructors: A case study." *Computers and Education: Artificial Intelligence* 5: 100156.

Lau, S., and P. Guo. 2023. "From 'Ban it till we understand it' to 'Resistance is futile': How university programming instructors plan to adapt as more students use AI code generation and explanation tools such as ChatGPT and GitHub Copilot." Paper presented at the Proceedings of the 2023 ACM Conference on International Computing Education Research-Volume 1.

Li, L., Z. Ma, L. Fan, S. Lee, H. Yu, and L. Hemphill. 2023. "ChatGPT in education: A discourse analysis of worries and concerns on social media." *arXiv preprint arXiv:2305.02201*.

Mello, R. F., E. Freitas, F. D. Pereira, L. Cabral, P. Tedesco, and G. Ramalho. 2023. "Education in the age of generative AI: Context and recent developments." *arXiv preprint arXiv:2309.12332*.

Michel-Villarreal, R., E. Vilalta-Perdomo, D. E. Salinas-Navarro, R. Thierry-Aguilera, and F. S. Gerardou. 2023. "Challenges and opportunities of generative AI for higher education as explained by ChatGPT." *Education Sciences* 13(9): 856.

Mollick, E. R., and L. Mollick. 2023. "Using AI to implement effective teaching strategies in classrooms: Five strategies, including prompts." *Including Prompts (March 17, 2023)*.

Moorhouse, B. L., M. A. Yeo, and Y. Wan. 2023. "Generative AI tools and assessment: Guidelines of the world's top-ranking universities." *Computers and Education Open* 5: 100151.

Rudolph, J., S. Tan, and S. Tan. 2023. "ChatGPT: Bullshit spewer or the end of traditional assessments in higher education?" *Journal of Applied Learning and Teaching* 6(1).

Sadasivan, V. S., A. Kumar, S. Balasubramanian, W. Wang, and S. Feizi. 2023. "Can AI-generated text be reliably detected?" *arXiv preprint arXiv:2303.11156*.

PART II

The good

4. Considering the pedagogical benefits of generative artificial intelligence in higher education: applying constructivist learning theory

John V. Pavlik

4.1 INTRODUCTION

From chalkboards to textbooks, a wide range of tools and technologies have played an essential role in advancing pedagogy in higher education. In the 1920s, the then-new medium of radio entered the classroom as an educational vehicle for various subjects, from accounting to mathematics (see Master of Arts in Teaching Editors, 2013). In the 1930s, overhead projectors and early television provided a pedagogical tool for more advanced visual communication. In the 1960s, BASIC was developed at Dartmouth College to give the students an easy-to-learn and use programming language. Similarly, Texas Instruments introduced the handheld calculator as an educational technology. In the 1980s, the Apple Macintosh computer was developed and introduced to classrooms. By the 1990s, Gopher servers had provided students access to online information, and an era of increasing Internet access in education was well underway. By the 2010s, mobile technology had become increasingly widespread in higher education, as students had embraced handheld devices for learning. By 2020, online course management systems had become increasingly ubiquitous in higher education, especially during the COVID-19 pandemic when remote learning grew dramatically.

Yet, in virtually all of these instances, although there were proponents of the new tools for teaching and learning, the adoption of new technology in higher education has often faced fierce resistance. Sometimes called "Neo-Luddism," after the Luddite movement opposed automation in farming in the early 19th century, those opposed to new technology in higher education have acted upon several concerns, including potential adverse effects of new technology and its often unintended consequences. In the digital age, these concerns include the possible erosion of student privacy as new online technologies may capture student data, and the commercialization of higher education as many new technologies are expensive and require substantial corporate engagement in learning environments. The rise of for-profit online course management systems, such as Blackboard and Canvas, underscores the role that corporate entities increasingly play in higher education.

The public introduction of a new form of artificial intelligence (AI) called generative AI (GenAI) ushered in a new era of the technological transformation of higher education (McCormack, 2023). OpenAI is a leading developer of GenAI. Founded as a non-profit in 2015, it transitioned to a for-profit entity in 2019 and has been sponsored by big tech, including Microsoft and other companies and individuals in the technology arena. Arizona State University (ASU) has announced a partnership with OpenAI to integrate GenAI into its operations and curricula (Boehm, 2024). The University states that faculty input will be sought on how best to utilize the technology. However, the goal is to "focus on increasing student success, finding new avenues for research and streamlining processes." ASU President Michael Crow says, "ASU recognizes that augmented and artificial intelligence systems are here to stay, and we are optimistic about their ability to become incredible tools that help students to learn, learn more quickly, and understand subjects more thoroughly" (Boehm, 2024).

OpenAI introduced ChatGPT to the public in 2022 (White, 2023). It was the first GenAI platform that was widely available worldwide and inexpensive to use. As a result, GenAI quickly began impacting a wide swath of society, from business to governance to health care (Yeung and Maruyama, 2023; Marr, 2023). It almost immediately became a growing part of the learning experience in higher education, whether educators wanted it to do so or not (Heath et al., 2023). GenAI is a form of AI that can create content (Carle, 2023). Using machine learning, GenAI develops its capacity by processing existing information in various forms, including text documents, images, video, and the like. In response to receiving text prompts from a human, GenAI can create new content reflecting the characteristics of the training data without repeating it precisely. Novel content-generative AI can create images, video, music, speech, text, software code, video games, and more. GenAI draws upon various techniques, including complex mathematics and substantial computing power, to create its trained large language models. These models are prediction algorithms that give GenAI the capacity to appear to think and understand. In reality, it still performs sophisticated statistical calculations.

This chapter outlines a pedagogical framework that can be applied across the curricula in higher education to help move away from a system of passive learning to one that instead emphasizes active student learning and is scalable and cost-effective by utilizing the capacity of GenAI.

By applying constructivist learning theory, GenAI can continue to amplify the technology-enabled effective teaching and learning model in higher educa-tion in the 21st century. In its contemporary forms, such as OpenAI's ChatGPT (text) and DALL-E (images), humans play a vital role in the AI-fueled creation of content by providing textual (or other format) prompts that the GenAI plat-form utilizes to engage its large language model (LLM) to generate content. GenAI can play a vital role in 21st-century higher education pedagogy as an interactive and multi-sensory tool by transforming student engagement in active learning experiences.

4.2   CONSTRUCTIVIST LEARNING THEORY

In the early 20th century, pioneering educator John Dewey led the develop-ment of a new learning paradigm known as constructivism (Dewey, 1938). Constructivism transforms students from passive learners to active participants in developing and discovering knowledge. Constructivism emphasizes height-ened student engagement through active experience. Constructivist learning theory suggests active engagement is key to acquiring knowledge. By actively participating in the learning process, students themselves help to create the knowledge they learn.

By using traditional learning tools and technologies, constructivist learning can be expensive. Traditional higher education has often emphasized scalable learning approaches, such as large lecture classes where students are passive learners, sitting, listening, and watching as they would at a movie theater. Learning can occur, but the passive role of the student limits it. It neglects the social nature of learning and the benefits of experience. The large lecture learning format is, in a sense, the antithesis of compelling learning. In fact, in the digital age, it can undermine student learning by disengaging student atten-tion in an era when human attention is often splintered. In contrast, research shows that when students actively participate in knowledge creation, they are much more likely to engage, understand, remember, and critically assess that knowledge (see also Hendriksen, Chapter 5 in this volume).

While in a large lecture class, a single professor can simultaneously deliver knowledge, or at least information, to hundreds of students, research shows that compared to environments that place students in active, participatory, and interactive (social) learning roles, this model of information dissemination is inefficient and relatively ineffective as a learning experience (Brown, 2003; Duke, Harper, and Johnston, 2013). Studies show that constructivist learning approaches are especially effective in teaching students with special needs (Akpan and Beard, 2016).

GenAI and other branches of AI can help make constructivist learning more efficient and cost-effective in higher education (see also Kerem, Chapter 6 in this volume). As opposed to the traditional teacher-centered higher education model, GenAI can provide several benefits to the learner-centered approach of constructivism. These benefits include teaching students skills in knowledge acquisition, communication, and collaboration, including the social nature of the learning experience. GenAI can help by providing each student with a real-time personalized interactive learning capacity, which is impossible for human teacher-based instruction. The human teacher can, at best, respond to only one student at a time, and in a large lecture setting, the interactive capacity of the teacher is even more limited. It is the impetus for supplementing many large lecture classes with so-called reading or discussion groups, typically led by graduate students who can interact with smaller subsets of students in groups of perhaps 20 individuals. For the student, GenAI can provide customized interaction that emulates human interaction. Much as in a video game where a human player can interact with an AI player, a human student can interact with an AI instructor or discussion facilitator. Current versions of platforms such as Microsoft CoPilot are capable of effectively engaging students in this fashion.

In contrast to ChatGPT, CoPilot has a current knowledge base and a more comprehensive one. It is available with Microsoft 365 and operates in either text or audio format. It can emulate human social interaction and do so tirelessly. For each student, it can be personalized to their background, perspective, comments, or knowledge level as expressed through their comments. This way, GenAI can provide student learning interaction with a social-like experience. With sufficient resources, a university could create customized GenAI tools such as CoPilot that are especially trained in particular subject matters, such as mathematics or media studies, or subdisciplines, such as calculus or media theory. ASU, which has partnered with OpenAI, "plans to use ChatGPT to build personalized AI tutors and offer writing help to students in one of its largest classes, Freshman Composition" (Boehm, 2024).

Accessibility, especially for students with disabilities, can be increased via GenAI, further supporting a constructivist approach. GenAI can perform various functions on a scalable basis to support more active student learning, including translating concepts for students whose first language is not English. GenAI can facilitate designing more personalized learning plans for students. GenAI can generate ideas and help synthesize and summarize information and vast volumes of data to aid research, facilitating a constructivist approach at the advanced undergraduate or graduate student level. Therefore, GenAI may fundamentally impact all scientific endeavors (Editors, 2023).

4.3   DESIGNING NEW CURRICULA

Perhaps most importantly, GenAI allows educators to design new scalable participatory curricula built on a constructivist learning approach. This approach could transform higher education. A reimagined approach to higher education built on constructivism supported by GenAI could make college or university-level learning more effective, sustainable, and accessible to students across a broad spectrum of society by potentially lowering costs and removing other learning barriers. In this manner, via GenAI, all students can have personalized learning plans based on their interests and prior knowledge or expertise. So, a calculus student might start at the same level of knowledge as their classmates. However, before the semester has concluded, that student might progress further in their knowledge. Through GenAI, which could assess and monitor the student's knowledge continuously, accurately, and thoroughly, a specialized set of additional learning plans and modules could be generated, enabling that student to advance much further in their studies.

4.4   CRITICAL THINKING

Developing students' capacity for critical thinking has long been a foundational principle of quality higher education (Krutka, Heath, and Willet, 2019; see also Clark and Denman, Chapter 8 in this volume). GenAI can provide a unique opportunity to enhance critical thinking instruction within a constructivist approach. For example, GenAI-based curricula might embrace students designing and submitting prompts to GenAI platforms and critically evaluate the content generated. This critical analysis might include examining the content for accuracy, creativity, thoroughness, and more. Pavlik and Pavlik (2024) have studied GenAI in art education and applied the constructivist learning model to demonstrate how critical thinking could be developed through an applied arts curriculum. For example, with a basic knowledge of art schools, such as impressionism, students can craft prompts to GenAI to generate imagery, and the student can then critically assess the extent to which that imagery reflects the qualities of that school and how so (see also Hendriksen, Chapter 5 in this volume). Incorporating such considerations within a critical thinking context is essential to higher education. It can be directly integrated into a GenAI-based constructivist learning curriculum by enabling students to examine these issues actively. For example, a student on an Introduction to Astronomy course might engage in a discourse with a GenAI chatbot regarding the historical development of the field, critically considering the nexus of scientific, social, and political forces that shaped the advance of the field from a geocentric (earth at the center) to a heliocentric (sun at the center) model of the solar system.

Prompt engineering will be a foundational skill for students and professionals as GenAI grows in its ubiquity, capacity, and transformative presence throughout society, including virtually every profession or industry and all sectors of the global economy, government, and higher education.

Role-playing curricula will likely emerge as a vital part of a GenAI-enabled constructivist learning framework in higher education. Role-playing curricula often feature simulations. Students participate as characters in the simulation, taking on different roles and seeing things from various points of view. For instance, a criminal justice student might participate in a simulation of a police–civilian interaction and might play the role of an officer, the person engaged by the police, a citizen bystander acting as a citizen reporter, and the like. Then, student discussion of the experience could be facilitated by the GenAI platform. Based on a game design, role-playing learning can engage students in personalized and social experiences like contemporary online gameplay. For younger generations of students, such an approach may have particular resonance and prove to be a compelling learning environment supporting mobile access.

AI literacy will be another cornerstone of a constructivist learning framework for 21st-century higher education. AI is increasingly likely to become a foundational part of the contemporary economy, society, and system of government. Moreover, AI is expected to continue to develop, and as such, students need to have a high level of understanding of its pros, cons, nature, applications, and consequences. This will constitute the essence of AI literacy. Constructivist learning approaches to teaching AI literacy can maximize student engagement and comprehension and the effective utilization of AI. Contextualizing that understanding within an ethical framework will be the best way to ensure that the consequences and uses of AI are of benefit to society and the planet and minimize its potential harms (Miao, Holmes, Huang, and Zhang, 2021; UNESCO, 2022; Sabzalieva and Valentini, 2023).

4.5   ASSESSMENT

Assessment of learning outcomes is a vital part of the higher education environment. Research shows that assessment and learning are related (Sotola and Crede, 2020; see also Matheis and Jubin, Chapter 9 in this volume). Scalable approaches to effective assessment present a great challenge in a system where large class size is often a norm. GenAI can be useful in supporting assessment processes (Borup, 2023; Warnock, 2013). Faculty can use GenAI to analyze, grade, and provide feedback on student work, and because it is scalable, higher education applications can be extensive. One example already in use is

Pearson's Intelligent Essay Assessor (https://mlm.pearson.com/northamerica/assets/upload/IEA-FactSheet.pdf?v1438887065).

4.6   TIERS OF AI

To articulate and appreciate the long-term application of generative AI in higher education and to constructivist learning theory, it is essential to consider how generative AI will likely evolve from the near to the far term. The role of GenAI in higher education is only at its beginning. It is likely to grow substantially in the years and decades to come. However, GenAI is also only in its early stages; at this point, it is only in a relatively weak form. As it advances and becomes far more powerful, its role in and impact on higher education, especially constructivist learning in which the student is an active learner, will grow, but potentially in surprising ways.

Computer scientists often point to three stages in the development of generative AI. These are Artificial Narrow Intelligence (ANI), Artificial General Intelligence (AGI), and Artificial Super Intelligence (ASI) – these range from the current and least potent to the far-off and most powerful.

ANI, or Narrow AI, is the most common. It is highly focused and limited and is the beginning level of AI. Also known as weak AI, Narrow AI is focused on a single subset of abilities, such as computer chess-playing programs, which were first developed in the 1950s. Notable AI applications so far have been Narrow AI. IBM's Watson, that played and won the TV game show Jeopardy in 2011, is an example of ANI. ChatGPT is a contemporary example of Narrow AI. Various journalism reporting and writing tools that predate generative AI also featured ANI, including: Narrative Science, used by Forbes and other news media; Wordsmith, used by the Associated Press (2023); and Quakebot, developed and used by the *Los Angeles Times* to report automatically on earthquakes by tying in directly and digitally to the U.S. Geological Survey data stream on seismic activity.

The second tier or stage is Artificial General Intelligence (AGI). AGI is on par with human thinking. AGI transcends the narrow domains of ANI and can perform a range of human intellectual tasks at the same level. AGI can reason, solve problems, and make decisions. This "Strong AI" or "Human Level AI" is next on the AI horizon. Microsoft researchers claim that ChatGPT Plus, which uses GPT-4 may be on the verge of AGI. Its ability to process text in a broad set of domains, analyze images, write computer code, and create video games pushes the narrow boundaries of current AI. As stated in its charter, OpenAI's goal is to create "safe and beneficial AGI, but [we] will also consider our mission fulfilled if our work aids others to achieve this outcome" (https://openai.com/charter/).

Artificial Super Intelligence (ASI) is the third stage or tier, which is still far on the horizon and may never arrive. But its potential impact could be profound. ASI would surpass the most brilliant human genius and could transform all branches of human endeavor, including higher education. ASI could feature machines with sentience or self-consciousness, making them potentially capable of understanding their role in education (Agarwal and Edelman, 2020; Chalmers, 2023). Released in 2024, Anthropic's GenAI LLM platform Claude 3 may already show signs of sentience (Orf, 2024). Self-aware ASI may or may not have any sense of ethics or a moral compass, which could pose a particular danger to its role in higher education (Wallach and Allen, 2008; Anderson and Anderson, 2011; Metz, 2021).

If connected through Cloud computing (Ray, 2018) to the Internet of Things (IoT; Gillis, 2021), ASI could also pose an existential threat to humanity by enabling machine intelligence to control the physical and digital worlds. Such networked ASI could control banking, power services, and even war machines, weaponry, and drones. Networked ASI could take control of institutions and mechanisms of learning. Networked ASI could manufacture highly compelling mis- and disinformation and convincing and pervasive artificial realities that go far beyond the deepfakes of 2024. Networked ASI could control the Internet backbone and Cloud computing, where it will predominantly reside. It could also control data flows and research processes, teaching and learning, and the fundamental infrastructure of higher education globally.

Generative AI is already making inroads in higher education (Heaven, 2023; Green, 2023; Bozkurt et al., 2023). From instruction to admissions and enrollment, college educators and administrators are exploring the potential role and risks of GenAI in higher education (Watkins, 2022; Coffey, 2024; Pavlik, 2023a; Willsea, 2023). Moreover, although some of these inroads are made at the behest of educators and educational institutions, much of this activity is spurred on by the students and learners themselves (Svrluga and Natanson, 2023). Students are already utilizing GenAI to write essays, research papers, take class notes, prepare slides for presentations, create visualizations, write computer code, and design video games. Some educators would label at least part of this as cheating or plagiarism and a threat to academic integrity (Berdahl and Bens, 2023). And perhaps some of it is. But it actually signals a time for substantial adaptation in higher education, a transformation (Hodges and Ocak, 2023). And constructivist learning points to a way to achieve this transformation without trying to hold AI at arm's length. Rather, it would mean finding a way to incorporate GenAI ethically, effectively, and responsibly into higher education while making education even more relevant to the lives and futures of students who no doubt will encounter AI in their future lives, both at work and at play (Krutka and Heath, 2022). They should prepare for that future in a fashion that enables them to be skillful, moral, and thriving in the use of AI and to become the leaders that society needs. This is as opposed to the alternative of being replaced as workers by AI-powered robots (Senz, 2023) (see also Mäkinen, Mattila, Tammilehto and Varsta, Chapter 12 in this volume).

4.7   RISKS OF GenAI

Despite the potential benefits, GenAI also poses enormous risks for higher education, even with increasingly utilizing a constructivist learning paradigm. Risks and concerns regarding GenAI in higher education include the ease with which students can use GenAI as a tool to commit plagiarism, as noted above. But this may be a short-term problem. In the 1960s, the advent of photocopying technology facilitated the easy copying of other people's work, as did digital copy and paste a generation later. Educators and industry will learn to adapt and create tools that can effectively recognize and flag such activity in the era of GenAI.

Other concerns include GenAI's reliability (e.g., mistakes), privacy threats, a host of ethical considerations (e.g., intellectual property theft), and bias in responses generated by GenAI (see also van Gestel, Chapter 10 in this volume; Protopapa and Idris, Chapter 11 in this volume). Research shows this bias in a variety of areas, including gender, race, and the West, and their intersection (Pavlik, 2023b), while other studies show bias in DALL-E. Other significant concerns include GenAI's potential impact on students' personal development, career prospects, and the values they will bring to society.

A concern is how students will receive and respond to GenAI and how a constructivist approach will utilize it. Research indicates students hold mixed views on GenAI and its role in learning. Cecilia Ka Yuk Chan and Wenjie Hu (2023) of the University of Hong Kong have found that students exhibit both enthusiasm for and reservations about GenAI. Evolution in students' and educators' views toward GenAI will affect how it is adopted, accepted, or resisted in higher education.

4.8   CONCLUSIONS

Generative AI is ushering transformative change into a wide cross-section of institutions, including higher education. Those in higher education are naturally and understandably concerned about this transformation and whether it will lead to a better system of higher education or whether it will disrupt and undermine it. The concern is especially acute since the threat, or opportunity, of GenAI comes from mainly outside the academy, such as the industry-based OpenAI (see also Mäkinen, Mattila, Tammilehto, and Varsta, Chapter 12 in this volume).

This chapter has proposed a means to adapt to the impact of GenAI by developing a fundamentally altered paradigm of higher education based on the widespread adoption of constructivist learning. Constructivism has been growing since its founding a century ago. Its most significant advantage is that it is student-centered, highlights learning first and foremost, and can maximize educational outcomes. Yet, constructivist learning is more expensive, and its scalability has been limited due to that cost. Higher education has tended to emphasize large classes and other settings that can make distributing knowledge, or at least information, cost-efficient. Yet, research shows that learning is hindered when students are in passive roles and maximized when they are more actively engaged. Constructivism does precisely that and emphasizes the social and interactive qualities of learning that students not only benefit from but can enjoy.

GenAI enables the potential to reimagine the higher education curriculum to feature a constructivist learning paradigm. GenAI can enable interactive and personalized learning, support students engaging in experiential settings where they discover, and even help generate knowledge. The learning of complex concepts and their retention is heightened, and learning outcomes are enriched. Faculty can enjoy the benefits of teaching students who can learn more efficiently and effectively. Moreover, the assessment of learning outcomes can be facilitated by GenAI, and in the context of constructivist learning, such assessment can be done virtually in real-time, further accelerating student learning. The end result is not only a student body that learns more and faster but one which retains more and can complete their studies more expeditiously. GenAI can also make higher education more accessible and potentially reduce costs, expanding learning opportunities for all.

The potential to transform higher education through GenAI in a constructivist learning paradigm is on the horizon. Educators committed to innovation in higher education can explore utilizing the application of GenAI in a constructivist learning setting in higher education (see also Kerem, Chapter 6 in this volume; Dowling and Li, Chapter 7 in this volume). Yet, the dangers and risks of GenAI are real and may become even more pronounced as AI progresses toward AGI or even ASI. Now is the time to act to ensure that higher education evolves in a fashion that establishes how GenAI can be most effectively and ethically integrated into higher education settings. Delays are likely to lead to even more pressure from beyond the borders of higher education and a transformation from without. The end result may not be ideal for either educators or learners, much less civil society.

REFERENCES

Akpan, Joseph P. and Lawrence A. Beard (2016). "Using constructivist teaching strategies to enhance academic outcomes of students with special needs." *Universal Journal of Educational Research* 4(2): 392–398. DOI: 10.13189/ujer.2016.040211.

Agarwal A. and S. Edelman (2020). "Functionally effective conscious AI without suffering." *Journal of Artificial Intelligence and Consciousness* 7: 39–50. arXiv:2002.05652. DOI:10.1142/S2705078520300030.

Anderson, M. and S.L. Anderson (Eds.) (2011). *Machine Ethics*. Cambridge: Cambridge University Press.

Associated Press (July 31, 2023). "Leveraging AI to Advance the power of facts." Associated Press. https://www.ap.org/discover/artificial-intelligence

Berdahl, Loleen and Susan Bens (June 16, 2023), "Academic integrity in the age of ChatGPT." University Affairs. International Center for Academic Integrity.

Boehm, Jessica (29 January 2024). "OpenAI launches partnership with ASU, allowing full use of ChatGPT." https://www.axios.com/local/phoenix/2024/01/18/openai-asu-university-partnership-school-arizona-chatgpt

Borup, Jered (March 21, 2023). "This was written by a human: A real educator's thoughts on teaching in the age of ChatGPT." EDUCAUSE REVIEW.

Bozkurt, Aras, et al. (February 2023), "Speculative futures on ChatGPT and generative artificial intelligence (AI): A collective reflection from the educational landscape." *Asian Journal of Distance Education* 18(1): 53–130.

Brown, K.L. (2003). *From Teacher-centered to Learning-centered Curriculum: Improving Learning in Diverse Classrooms*. New York, NY: Routledge.

Carle, Eben (November 4, 2023). "Ask a techspert: What is generative AI?" The Keyword (blog), Google.

Chalmers, D. (March 2023). "Could a large language model be conscious?" arXiv:2303.07103v1 [Computer Science].

Chan, Cecilia Ka Yuk and Wenjie Hu (2023). "Students' voices on generative AI: perceptions, benefits, and challenges in higher education." *International Journal of Educational Technology in Higher Education* 20(43). https://doi.org/10.1186/s41239-023-00411-8

Coffey, Lauren (26 June 2024). "A new guide for responsible AI use in higher ed." Inside Higher Ed. https://www.insidehighered.com/news/quick-takes/2024/06/26/new-guide-responsible-ai-use-higher-ed

Dewey, J. (1938). *Experience and Education*. New York: Collier Books.

Duke, B., Harper, G., and Johnston, M. (2013). "Constructivism as a digital age learning theory." *The International HETL Review, Special Issue* 4–13.

Editors (24 January 2023). "Tools Such as ChatGPT threaten transparent science; Here are our ground rules for their use." Editorial. *Nature* 613, 612 (2023) doi: https://doi.org/10.1038/d41586-023-00191-1

Gillis, Alexander (2021). "What is the internet of things (IoT)?". *IOT Agenda*.

Green, Sean (17 October 2023). "Generative AI is a game changer for higher education." *ComputerWeekly.com*. https://www.computerweekly.com/opinion/Generative-AI-is-a-game-changer-for-higher-education

Heath, Marie K. et al. (April 23, 2023), "Collectively asking technoskeptical questions about ChatGPT." Civics of Technology (blog), Civics of Technology.

Heaven, Will D. (April 6, 2023), "ChatGPT is going to change education, not destroy it." *MIT Technology Review*.

Hodges, Charles B. and Ceren Ocak (30 August 2023). "Integrating generative AI into higher education: Considerations." EDUCAUSE REVIEW. https://er.educause.edu/articles/2023/8/integrating-generative-ai-into-higher-education-considerations

Krutka, Daniel G. and Marie Heath (March 18, 2022). "Is it ethical to use this technology? An approach to learning about educational technologies with students." Civics of Technology (blog), Civics of Technology.

Krutka, Daniel G., Marie K. Heath, and K. Bret Staudt Willet (October, 2019). "Foregrounding Technoethics: Toward Critical Perspectives in Technology and Teacher Education." *Journal of Technology and Teacher Education* 27(4): 555–574.

Marr, Bernard (March 2, 2023). "Revolutionizing healthcare: The top 14 uses of ChatGPT in medicine and wellness." *Forbes.*

Master of Arts in Teaching Editors (2013). "Then versus now: How technology in schools has changed over time." http://www.masterofartsinteaching.net/tech/

McCormack, Mark (April 17, 2023). "EDUCAUSE QuickPoll results: Adopting and adapting to generative AI in higher ed tech." EDUCAUSE REVIEW.

Metz, Cade (19 November 2021). "Can a machine learn morality?" *New York Times.* https://www.nytimes.com/2021/11/19/technology/can-a-machine-learn-morality.html

Miao, Fengchun, Wayne Holmes, Ronghuai Huang, and Hui Zhang (2021), AI and Education: Guidance for Policy-Makers. Paris: United Nations Educational, Scientific and Cultural Organization.

OpenAI (2024). OpenAI Charter. https://openai.com/charter/

Orf, Darren (29 April 2024). "A stunning new AI has supposedly achieved sentience." PopularMechanics.com. https://www.popularmechanics.com/technology/robots/a60606512/claude-3-self-aware/

Pavlik, John V. (2023a). "Collaborating with ChatGPT: Considering the implications of generative artificial intelligence for journalism and media education." *Journalism & Mass Communication Educator* 78(1), 84–93. https://doi.org/10.1177/10776958221149577

Pavlik, John V. (13–15 October 2023b). "Race, gender and visual art created via artificial intelligence: Assessing bias in images generated by OpenAI's DALL-E." Presented at NYSCA's 81st Annual Conference, Callicoon, NY.

Pavlik, John V. and Orianna M. Pavlik (3–8 January 2024). "DALL-E and Art Education." Presented at the 8th IAFOR International Conference on Education Honolulu, Hawaii.

Ray, Partha Pratim (2018). "An introduction to Dew Computing: Definition, concept and implications." *IEEE Access* 6: 723–737. doi:10.1109/ACCESS.2017.2775042. S2CID 3324933.

Sabzalieva, Emma and Arianna Valentini (2023). ChatGPT and Artificial Intelligence in Higher Education: Quick Start Guide. Paris: United Nations Educational, Scientific and Cultural Organization.

Senz, Kristen (April 26, 2023). "Is AI coming for your job?" Harvard Business School.

Sotola, Lukas K. and Marcus Crede (2020). "Regarding class quizzes: A meta-analytic synthesis of studies on the relationship between frequent low-stakes testing and class performance." *Educational Psychology Review* 33: 407–426.

Svrluga, Susan and Hannah Natanson (June 1, 2023). "All the unexpected ways ChatGPT is infiltrating students' lives." *The Washington Post.*

UNESCO (2022), *Recommendation on the Ethics of Artificial Intelligence*. Paris: The United Nations Educational, Scientific and Cultural Organization.

Wallach, W. and C. Allen (November 2008). Moral Machines: Teaching Robots Right from Wrong. New York: Oxford University Press.

Warnock, Scott (April 18, 2013). "Frequent, low-stakes grading: Assessment for communication, confidence." *Faculty Focus*.

Watkins, Ryan (December 18, 2022). "Update your course syllabus for ChatGPT." *Medium*.

White, Matt (January 7, 2023). "A brief history of generative AI." *Medium*.

Willsea, Mallory (April 27, 2023). "Embrace AI to boost your enrollment marketing team's productivity." *Inside Higher Ed*.

Yeung, Jessie and Mayumi Maruyama (April 21, 2023). "As Japan's population drops, one city is turning to ChatGPT to help run the government." CNN.

5. Student learning in the age of AI: principles and practices for using AI in higher education

Christian Hendriksen

In 1984, Benjamin Bloom wrote about an observation he coined the "two-sigma problem" (Bloom, 1984). Based on two doctoral dissertations (Anania, 1983; Burke, 1984), Bloom observed that students who were given one-on-one (or one-on-two or three) tutoring performed much better than students given "conventional" class-based teaching. In fact, the average tutored student was better than 98% of students who received conventional teaching. The "problem," as Bloom put it, was how to identify instructional methods in conventional class settings that could reproduce the results obtained from tutoring. This challenge has puzzled educational theorists ever since, and there have been several attempts at solving this challenge through technological developments (Grant et al., 2016; Leyzberg et al., 2014; Rosenberg-Kima, 2022).

With the advent of generative AI (GenAI), there is a real possibility that the two-sigma problem can be solved – or, at the very least, that the two-sigma gap can be narrowed (Mollick & Mollick, 2023a). The dramatic and exponential rise in the capabilities of state-of-the-art AI models, like Google's Gemini or OpenAI's GPT-4, contains the promise that all students one day can and will gain access to virtual tutors that are at least as knowledgeable, helpful, and empathetic as human teachers. Yet, this promise does not come without pitfalls. Suppose students use these chatbots without understanding their limitations, engaging in critical thinking, or formulating strategies for getting the AI to help them learn rather than simply offload tasks (Lodge et al., 2023). In that case, AI chatbots can be detrimental rather than useful for learning (see also Clark and Denman, Chapter 8 in this volume). Thus, it is up to educators and students to engage with AI assistants in a way that enhances rather than diminishes the value they can afford. This chapter is written as a practical and helpful guide to how students can use AI tools to improve their learning.

In this chapter, I start by explaining the promise of AI for student learning, focusing on the two-sigma problem and the ways AI can be helpful in this regard. I then lay out some core principles for AI engagement that improve the engagement from the perspective of students. These core principles entail (1) giving more elaborate context so that the AI provides more context-appropriate output, (2) iterating on the AI output to refine it in a more useful direction, and (3) engaging with the AI in a communicative style that is similar to how students would engage other students or their teachers – i.e., humans. Based on that, I move towards demonstrating some use cases from students' perspectives that are universally useful and important building blocks for closing the two-sigma gap. I round off the chapter by highlighting some advantages conferred by AI that traditional (human) tutoring- or mastery-training instruction methods struggle to accomplish.

5.1 THE PROMISE OF AI AS A SOLUTION TO THE TWO-SIGMA PROBLEM

Early research has suggested ways that both students and teachers can use generative AI to learn more (Mollick & Mollick, 2023a, 2023b; Yamkovenko, 2023), as well as indications of the role of AI in learning situations (Chiu, 2023; Hiterer & McGourty, 2023; Koh & Doroudi, 2023; Mills et al., 2023; Sharples, 2023) and at least one framework for understanding the modalities of human–AI engagement (Lodge et al., 2023). Common to most of the emerging literature is the underlying idea that sufficiently advanced AI can support student learning as effectively as a human tutor would. In higher education, the norm is that students engage in large class lectures and spend most of their time studying at home. This puts pressure on students to structure their own learning – and even if students show up for class, Bloom's two-sigma problem still stands: getting personal tutoring would be far better. The promise of AI in this regard is the idea that students can engage, in their own time and at their own pace, with an on-demand AI tutor (Chi et al., 2001; Mollick & Mollick, 2023a, p. 11; Robinson et al., 2021). This AI tutor would then be able to guide each student through their learning journey, correcting misunderstandings and providing illustrations and explanations in a way appropriate for the student, as well as encouraging productive study techniques, and – most controversially – being able to form some kind of personal connection. These are, roughly speaking, the features of an effective human tutor, and they provide a reasonable starting point for what an effective AI tutor would be.

There are some obvious limitations to tutoring with the ways AI models work now. Good human tutors form relationships and push students at an appropriate level so that students put effort into learning. An AI chatbot cannot do this because it only responds to prompts from the student. Thus, the student has to exert effort to engage the AI tutor, which is a very different situation from another human that progressively monitors and intervenes in the learning process. Another aspect is that the AI chatbot must be fed information manually about the student's effort and learning process to evaluate it, and if the student is also the person prompting the model, this creates a possible disconnect as the student has to transfer their learning to the AI. Some of this can be mitigated by AI systems that take input directly from the screen (as Khan Academy is doing) or AI systems designed to challenge the student proactively. Yet, it is clear that some aspects of human tutoring will be beyond AI capabilities in the near future.

On the other hand, AI chatbots are infinitely patient, always available, and can adapt to almost any student level possible through their explanations (Mollick & Mollick, 2023b). Thus, while it takes effort for students to use AI chatbots effectively as tutors when they are actually sitting and doing it, it takes less effort to engage with the AI tutor in the first place since it is so readily available and can work off of a single prompt. It has not been explored yet what this means for student learning; the structure afforded by classic instructional methods that are time-boxed may make it easier for some students to learn (because of the clear structure), while the always-available AI tutor may be a challenge for students that require external regulation to organize their studying.

Regardless, AI tools as student learning assistants clearly hold potential even if they are not replacing human tutors. As noted earlier, existing scholarship is rapidly developing ideas for how to use AI in different roles (Lodge et al., 2023; Mollick & Mollick, 2023a). Before moving on, I want to consolidate some of the dimensions of use that seem to constitute the different AI learning use cases (see Table 5.1). These dimensions represent the mode of AI interaction in a given situation, and when combined, they yield specific use cases.

For example, suppose you are using AI to help improve your study technique. In that case, you are drawing on AI that takes a pedagogical role as a coach, with a learning outcome that is improving study technique, and a feedback mechanism that is personalized feedback. And an AI use case revolving around explaining concepts in a personalized way would be an AI that offers a high degree of content specificity and a lower level of interaction and feedback but with a learning outcome focused on understanding difficult concepts. These dimensions draw on ideas from different approaches to AI that are either use-case-focused (Mollick & Mollick, 2023a) or theory-focused (Lodge et al., 2023; Sharples, 2023), and the value is to underscore the nuances of the different ways AI can be useful.

5.2   PRINCIPLES FOR PRODUCTIVE ENGAGEMENT WITH AI CHATBOTS

Regardless of the AI model chosen, there are a few principles for interacting with the AI that will dramatically improve the usefulness of the output pro-

Table 5.1   *Dimensions of AI usage*

Dimension of AI usage	Description
Pedagogical role	Categorizes AI based on its educational function (e.g., tutor, mentor, coach, teammate), defining the nature of interaction between AI and students.
Learning outcome	Focuses on the desired educational result (e.g., understanding complex concepts, improving study techniques, enhancing collaboration skills).
Interactivity level	Measures the engagement and degree of interaction between AI and students, from passive information reception to highly interactive scenarios.
Content specificity	Distinguishes between general use (e.g., study techniques, broad concepts) and specific applications (e.g., specific theories, topic tests).
Feedback mechanism	Describes how AI delivers feedback, ranging from immediate, automated responses in low-stakes testing to nuanced, personalized feedback in tutoring scenarios.

Source: Author's original work, drawing on Lodge et al. (2023) and Mollick & Mollick (2023a).

vided by the AI. These principles are not "prompt engineering" but rather guiding posts for how any student – or user in general – can interact with an AI to make it more useful. Some companies have more detailed guidelines for how to interact effectively with the model (OpenAI, 2024), but for general usage, these principles will yield similar results while reducing the complexity of the experience. After all, chatbots are just that: AI tools designed to mimic human interaction.

5.2.1   Principle 1: Providing Context

Whenever you interact with an AI, it is important to give it information that allows it to "understand" your situation (see also Kerem, Chapter 6 in this volume). This will allow it to tailor its responses to your situation more effectively, thus giving you output that is more useful. This could be things like what you are studying and where, what you want to do with the output, what level you are studying at, and so forth. When you provide the model with this context, it tries to incorporate it into its output.

For example, when ChatGPT-4 is asked "What is a theory?" without any context, it defaults to a natural science understanding of what a theory is. But when it is given just a bit of context about the student background, it flips to a better explanation of a theory that fits for social science.[1] While the first answer is not incorrect per se, it is not the most useful definition for a social scientist. When the model is given additional context, it provides an answer that is much more useful for our purpose here. Even with very little context, the model response dramatically improves because it is trying to be as attentive as possible to what you provide in your prompt. Thus, in theory, there is not really an upper limit for how much context you should give it beyond the practical limitations of the time it takes to provide the information.

5.2.2   Principle 2: Iterating on the Output

The AI tries its best but rarely hits the mark on the first try. Thus, it is important to iterate on the output and provide feedback to the AI on what can be improved or what it should change (see also Dowling and Li, Chapter 7 in this volume). When the AI provides an answer that is slightly different from what you expected, this is also a good prompt for examining whether a crucial piece of contextual information is missing. Then, you can continue iterating until the AI gives you something more useful. One rule of thumb here is that using output before you have interacted three times with the model (such as three chat messages) means that you probably have not used the best possible output you could get.

We can continue our example from before to demonstrate. As a master's student, we want a more specific way to understand the concept of a theory and how to apply it in an analysis. Thus, as a student, we can iterate on the output and provide more information on what we need, explaining to the AI how we intend to go about our master's thesis. We can go back and forth with AI to narrow down how we can understand the nature of a theory in our situation.[2] This is effective because chatbot AIs are specifically designed to learn in context from the conversation and adapt to whatever the human is saying – which means combining context with iteration is very effective.

5.2.3   Principle 3: Communicating like a Human

Despite how unnerving it can be for some, AI models are specifically trained to emulate human communication. This implies that the best way to interact with the AI is to communicate more or less the same way you would with another human. Communicating in this way entails moving away from shortened keyword strings normally used in regular searches and towards more elaborate, natural-language instructions. The more complex patterns of interactions you have with the AI tools, the more the interaction necessitates a clear and concise communication style.

For example, in this chat[3] I engage in very casual and natural language to clearly explain what I would like the AI to do and then, when iterating, simply tell it what I'm still not getting. Communicating in this way serves two purposes: one is that it is easy for the model to infer what you mean when you write out things in natural language; it *looks* like its training data. Another is that it takes less effort for the human to formulate prompts since it is all happening in the same way as you would interact with another human being. Incidentally, this highlights that effective engagement with natural-language AI models warrants stronger communication and leadership skills since the human–AI interaction is similar to when humans delegate tasks to other humans – and this requires clear communication and task formulation.

With these principles in place and the five dimensions of AI roles outlined (see Table 5.1), I will now turn to specific use cases of AI from the perspective of students.

5.3 USING AI IN PRACTICE: THREE EXAMPLES OF USE CASES FOR STUDENTS

In much the same way that it would be impossible to categorize all the use cases of a human personal assistant, it is impossible to exhaust the universe of use cases of AI tools. Categorizing along dimensions (Lodge et al., 2023) or roles (Mollick & Mollick, 2023a) are abstractions to reduce the complexity of interacting with the AI. But nothing beats personal experimentation. In this section, I provide three use cases that serve different purposes and are built around different combined AI roles. However, they should be seen not as a definitive list but as a starting point for personal exploration and experimentation.

5.3.1 Using AI to Understand Complex and Abstract Concepts

Higher education entails complexity and abstract concepts. Yet, some more arcane theoretical constructs or ideas are not easily approachable for students. Students often differ in their affinity for different topics and subjects, which means that for any given course, a portion of the students will struggle to follow and understand theoretical concepts as the course runs along.

Here, AI can be an incredibly helpful tool. Since teachers in lecture-size classrooms cannot give individualized explanations (and cannot linger for too long on a single question), AI can help student comprehension by clearly and concisely explaining any given concept or idea in a way that is understandable by the student in question. The key to making this effective is that the AI understands the context of the student from the start and adapts to the student's reception, both of which current models are more than capable of doing.

To demonstrate, look at this chat[4] where I engage with GPT-4 as if I was a first-year engineering student. When I ask the model about what "force" as a concept is, it gives me a good and precise definition of force and relates it to Newton's three laws. For a struggling student, this is still somewhat complex.

Thus, when I tell the model to make it simpler, it complies and changes the explanation:

> User: Can you make the explanation a bit simpler? I still don't follow.
> ChatGPT: Certainly, let's simplify the concept of force.
> Imagine force as a push or a pull on an object. This push or pull can make things move, stop, change direction, or change shape. Here's how to think about it in everyday terms:
> 1. **Making Things Move:** If you kick a soccer ball, your foot is applying a force to the ball that makes it move.
> 2. **Stopping Things:** When you catch a ball, your hands apply a force in the opposite direction to stop it.
> 3. **Changing Direction:** When you turn a bicycle's handle, you apply a force that changes the bike's direction.
> 4. **Changing Shape:** If you press a piece of clay, your fingers apply a force that changes its shape.

GPT-4 then goes on to explain Newton's Laws in similarly metaphorical terms. This is much more helpful for our struggling student. Note that the model changed this way of explaining not because I told it to, but simply because it picked up on the user not understanding its initial explanation. And then, when the user asks whether weight and force are the same thing, GPT-4 encouragingly says "Yes, you're on the right track!" before clarifying that weight is a particular type of force in that it is the force exerted by gravity on an object.

In this example, you can see the different principles of usage at play. Initially, I provided some information about my background (as a first-year engineering student struggling with abstract concepts in physics). I then iterated on the output to get a better explanation than my level warranted. And throughout, it was all done in natural language in the same way I would ask a human teacher or tutor. It is clear how far the three principles can get you with minimal effort.

Another way of explaining complex concepts or ideas is to specifically ask for a metaphorical abstraction to convey the underlying idea's properties (Lawler et al., 1983). In this chat,[5] I engage with GPT-4 on the concept of intersectionality and specifically ask the AI to provide a metaphor that allows me to understand it better. GPT-4 gives a fairly helpful metaphorical explanation:

> Imagine each thread in the web represents different aspects of social categorization – such as race, gender, class, sexuality, age, disability, etc. These threads intersect and overlap with one another, creating a complex pattern. Just as a web is more than the sum of its individual threads, a person's identity and experiences of discrimination or privilege are more than just the sum of their individual characteristics.
> In this metaphor, the points where threads intersect represent the unique experiences of individuals who belong to multiple marginalized or privileged groups at the same

time. For instance, the experience of a Black woman in society cannot be fully understood by looking at gender discrimination (one thread) or racial discrimination (another thread) in isolation. Instead, you need to understand where these threads intersect and how they create a specific pattern of discrimination that is different from what is experienced by someone who is just affected by one of these threads.

Admittedly, this is a reasonably clear explanation of intersectionality appropriate for a 3rd-year university student. This shows that specifically asking the AI to provide a metaphor for explaining the concept can be incredibly useful for enhancing learning.

It is, by now, a well-known feature of large language models that they hallucinate and make up facts that are false. This can be a serious issue for learning: if the AI is not giving correct factual information, how can students rely on the output? One important solution here is that if the factuality is important and hallucinations are expected – typically with niche topics and subjects – then the AI must be given relevant context to work off of. Suppose, for example, that we want to learn about a very specific theory of political management strategies (Oliver & Holzinger, 2008). If I ask GPT-4 without any other context, it hallucinates the content of the paper.[6] Obviously, this is too specific for GPT-4 to know because the paper itself is paywalled behind the ivory walls of the Academy of Management. So, the obvious solution is to give the paper as context for the model. In this chat,[7] I uploaded the paper (but pure copy-pasting would also have worked), and after giving the model time to work on understanding the paper, I asked the identical question from before. This time, the model is 100% correct in its explanation. The general rule here is that the more niche a subject is, the more important it is to provide context, so the model follows the factual definitions and content in the learning material itself. General concepts, like the definition of force or the characteristics of 18th-century Danish literature, usually work without context, but to be on the safe side, providing context in the form of background information ensures the output is correct.

One important aspect of AI that makes it good at explaining concepts is its ability to apply concepts arbitrarily to real-world cases. Our standard textbooks usually have hundreds of examples of real-world cases to illustrate a concept. The advantage of AI is that it can apply a concept on the fly to an empirical setting that is relevant for the student. This "mapping" of an abstract concept into a concrete setting can enhance understanding significantly.

Suppose, for example, that we want to learn about intertextuality as a theoretical concept. In addition to the tailored explanations and metaphorical reasoning shown earlier, we could ask the AI to apply the concept to a contemporary source that is of interest to demonstrate it. In this chat,[8] I gave Barack Obama's famous 2008 speech on race and asked GPT-4 to demonstrate how intertextuality plays a role in his speech. While the analysis probably does not earn GPT-4 a top mark, as a learning device, it serves a useful purpose in explaining the concept we are applying.

5.3.2 Using AI to Conduct Low-Stakes Testing on Material

One of the most effective ways of learning new material is to conduct low-stakes testing on the material (Donoghue & Hattie, 2021; Dunlosky et al., 2013). While most modern teaching materials come with pre-made quizzes and standardized self-learning tests, they are fixed in place and cannot be adapted to a specific student's level or affinity with different parts of the material. However, this is something AI models can easily handle. In fact, it is incredibly easy to get state-of-the-art models to make high quality and adaptable tests appropriate for student levels (Mollick & Mollick, 2023b) that can be arbitrarily focused on any given aspect of the curriculum – provided, of course, that relevant information is given as context to avoid hallucinations.

Here is an example of a topic where the AI probably does not need extra context to be correct. I want to learn about Porter's Five Forces, a core concept in business and management studies and one of the most recognizable business school theories. Suppose that I have already read about the theory and I now want to carry out a low-stakes test to practice active recalling. When prompted,[9] GPT-4 gives me this question:

> ChatGPT: In the context of Porter's Five Forces, which of the following best describes the force known as "Threat of Substitute Products or Services"?
> A) The risk that new competitors may enter the market if there are no barriers to entry.
> B) The bargaining power of suppliers increasing their prices or reducing the quality of purchased goods and services.
> C) The potential for customers to switch to a product or service from another industry that meets the same basic need in a different way.
> D) The intensity of competition among existing competitors in the industry.

Of course, you can ask the AI to switch the difficulty up or down. You can even instruct the AI to keep giving you questions appropriate for your level, allowing the AI to switch difficulty up or down depending on how you perform.

However, as difficulty (and therefore specificity) goes up, or the topic becomes increasingly niche, it becomes more and more important to provide context for the AI, so it has material to lean on when making the quizzes. In this chat,[10] I have provided the full-length article of Immordino-Yang et al. (2012) and asked GPT-4 to provide three multiple-choice questions to review my understanding of the article. The questions are not super difficult, but, as before, I can simply tune the difficulty up or down as needed.

While this customized quizzing can enhance learning, it does put the onus of action on the student more than before. In addition to the (productive) effort needed to answer questions correctly, the student needs to directly prompt the model to construct the questions in an appropriate way and correct the AI if it does something wrong – such as, for example, inadvertently giving the correct answers as part of the same output as the quiz. Additionally, there is a ceiling with current models for how advanced the questions that it provides can be. These low-stakes tests work best on straightforward questions that have a direct basis in the text. More free-form questions can still be done, but the AI becomes progressively worse at identifying good from bad answers the more the questions (and answers) diverge from the literal basis in the materials.

5.3.3   Identifying Theoretical Assumptions and Bridging Disciplinary Gaps

Most university-level education involves teaching students ideas and theories from diverse fields or philosophical origins. In particular, at the graduate level, students are expected to navigate these disciplinary differences by themselves. This becomes further challenging in studies that are explicitly interdisciplinary and where students must understand the underlying assumptions of different theories to adjudicate their strengths, weaknesses, and relative utility.

AI can play an important role here that has not been explored previously. AI can assist students in navigating this complexity because it has some advantages over material and disciplinary teachers. Since state-of-the-art AI models are "competent" in most scientific fields (and certainly can work on the basis of contextual information provided, like papers and book chapters), then it is easier for AI to shift between perspectives because it is not bound to a single discipline the way most teachers and textbooks are. Additionally, when prompted correctly, the AI is to some extent "perspective agnostic" – of course, it holds implicit biases that stem from its training data, but it can be asked to take the perspective of any given theory. This is not something we usually expect either of teachers or personal tutors.

Consider the commonplace example of business students trying to understand the difference between organizational studies and organizational economics. Despite the similarity of names, the two theoretical perspectives entail vastly different philosophical assumptions and build on different intellectual disciplines. It is rare for teachers of one of these disciplines to also teach the other. Yet, both are important subjects for business and MBA students to master. In this chat,[11] I engage GPT-4 from the perspective of a typical bachelor student of business and management writing about their bachelor project. The AI is helpful at explaining the differences in approaches, requiring only very simple prompting, and as the conversation goes on, it assesses (correctly) the relative strengths and weaknesses of the paradigms in the context of writing a bachelor project as well as the ontological assumptions.

While this seems somewhat trivial, it is actually difficult to find business school professors who can reliably explain and contrast such paradigmatic differences in the way GPT-4 does here. Thus, this is an example of a helpful case – navigating and contrasting different perspectives with largely implicit differences in assumptions – where we should expect AI systems to be of more use than professors who are trained mono-disciplinarily, simply because the AI can navigate across paradigms more easily to the benefit of the curious student.

5.4 CONCLUDING THOUGHTS AND THE WAY FORWARD FOR AI IN HIGHER EDUCATION

These are the early days of AI in higher education, and there is much to learn about how to make AI systems work to enhance rather than erode learning for students. The principles, ideas, and use cases laid out in this chapter should be considered points of departure for experimentation, knowledge-building, and further idea generation to understand the technology and what it can do. Much like the gap between the invention of the steam engine and the first industrial revolution, teachers and students in higher education will not find the full extent of the technology soon, not least because of the rapid development of the capabilities of the technology. Yet, we are seeing the contours of the future of teaching and learning.

Some of the strengths of AI models raise some interesting questions about how we can improve and organize teaching. I started the chapter by highlighting Bloom's two-sigma problem as one of the challenges AI can help solve. However, the advantages of AI systems – in some use cases – imply the compelling idea that as the technology matures, the very organization and purpose of higher education can be reorganized around the technology, much like e-learning, massive online courses, and other technology-enabled didactical innovations were developed once the technology was sufficiently mature.

Consider, for example, how good the AI is at explaining concepts *across* paradigms or integrating explanations in different contexts. Does this mean that sufficiently advanced AI allows us to dissolve traditional disciplinary boundaries and instead teach theoretical combinations that are more tailored to a specific topic or challenge? For example, the climate crisis is a major element in many studies from different angles. Allowing AI to integrate insights from across theories can dramatically enhance climate mitigation and adaptation education. We could develop courses even with GPT-4-level technology that draw on disciplines that are currently gated behind entirely different courses.

As we move forward and the technology keeps developing and improving, I want to end by highlighting that figuring out how to make the technology work to support learning entails potentially rethinking how we structure higher education and the nature of university teaching in general. Traditional formats, disciplinary closure, linear progression and study organization are things we may want to change in the future to better utilize AI technology and enhance the ability of our students to learn. This will take time. Teachers and students will have to adapt and learn as they go, but I think that the promise of generative AI has already shown its worth. What is left for us is to explore how to redefine and develop higher education in the Age of AI.

NOTES

1. Access the chats in the companion document here: https://doi.org/10.4337/9781035326020. In chat 1, no context is given. In chat 2, I give the relevant context.
2. Chat 3 in the companion document.
3. Chat 4 in the companion document.
4. Chat 5 in the companion document.
5. Chat 6 in the companion document.
6. Chat 7 in the companion document.
7. Chat 8 in the companion document.
8. Chat 9 in the companion document.
9. Chat 10 in the companion document.
10. Chat 11 in the companion document.
11. Chat 12 in the companion document.

REFERENCES

Anania, J. (1983). The influence of instructional conditions on student learning and achievement. *Evaluation in Education, 7*(1), 1–92. https://doi.org/10.1016/0191-765X(83)90002-2

Bloom, B. S. (1984). The 2 sigma problem: The search for methods of group instruction as effective as one-to-one tutoring. *Educational Researcher, 13*(6), 4–16.

Burke, A. J. (1984). *Students' Potential for Learning Contrasted under Tutorial and Group Approaches to Instruction.* Dissertation, The University of Chicago.

Chi, M. T. H., Siler, S. A., Jeong, H., Yamauchi, T., & Hausmann, R. G. (2001). Learning from human tutoring. *Cognitive Science, 25*(4), 471–533. https://doi.org/10.1207/s15516709cog2504_1

Chiu, T. K. F. (2023). The impact of Generative AI (GenAI) on practices, policies and research direction in education: A case of ChatGPT and Midjourney. *Interactive Learning Environments, 0*(0), 1–17. https://doi.org/10.1080/10494820.2023.2253861

Donoghue, G. M., & Hattie, J. A. C. (2021). A meta-analysis of ten learning techniques. *Frontiers in Education, 6*. https://www.frontiersin.org/articles/10.3389/feduc.2021.581216

Dunlosky, J., Rawson, K. A., Marsh, E. J., Nathan, M. J., & Willingham, D. T. (2013). Improving students' learning with effective learning techniques: promising directions from cognitive and educational psychology. *Psychological Science in the Public Interest, 14*(1), 4–58. https://doi.org/10.1177/1529100612453266

Grant, L., Abu-aisheh, A., Hadad, A., Poole, B., & Brown, C. W. (2016). Plexlearning: A technology-rich and systemic solution to Bloom's two sigma problem. *2016 IEEE Global Engineering Education Conference (EDUCON)*, 228–233. https://doi.org/10.1109/EDUCON.2016.7474558

Hiterer, D., & McGourty, J. (2023). *To Guide or Stand Aside? Instructor Guidance and Student Use of Conversational AI in a Pre-college Entrepreneurship Course* (SSRN Scholarly Paper 4671381). https://doi.org/10.2139/ssrn.4671381

Immordino-Yang, M. H., Christodoulou, J. A., & Singh, V. (2012). Rest is not idleness. *Perspectives on Psychological Science, 7*(4), 352–364. https://doi.org/10.1177/1745691612447308

Koh, E., & Doroudi, S. (2023). Learning, teaching, and assessment with generative artificial intelligence: Towards a plateau of productivity. *Learning: Research and Practice, 9*(2), 109–116. https://doi.org/10.1080/23735082.2023.2264086

Lawler, J. M., Lakoff, G., & Johnson, M. (1983). Metaphors we live by. *Language, 59*(1), 201. https://doi.org/10.2307/414069

Leyzberg, D., Spaulding, S., & Scassellati, B. (2014). Personalizing robot tutors to individuals' learning differences. *Proceedings of the 2014 ACM/IEEE International Conference on Human-Robot Interaction*, 423–430. https://doi.org/10.1145/2559636.2559671

Lodge, J. M., Yang, S., Furze, L., & Dawson, P. (2023). It's not like a calculator, so what is the relationship between learners and generative artificial intelligence? *Learning: Research and Practice*. https://www.tandfonline.com/doi/abs/10.1080/23735082.2023.2261106

Mills, A., Bali, M., & Eaton, L. (2023). How do we respond to generative AI in education? Open educational practices give us a framework for an ongoing process. *Journal of Applied Learning & Teaching, 6*(1). https://doi.org/10.37074/jalt.2023.6.1.34

Mollick, E. R., & Mollick, L. (2023a). *Assigning AI: Seven Approaches for Students, with Prompts* (SSRN Scholarly Paper 4475995). https://doi.org/10.2139/ssrn.4475995

Mollick, E. R., & Mollick, L. (2023b). *Using AI to Implement Effective Teaching Strategies in Classrooms: Five Strategies, Including Prompts* (SSRN Scholarly Paper 4391243). https://doi.org/10.2139/ssrn.4391243

Oliver, C., & Holzinger, I. (2008). The effectiveness of strategic political management: A dynamic capabilities framework. *Academy of Management Review, 33*(2), 496–520. https://doi.org/10.5465/AMR.2008.31193538

OpenAI. (2024). *Prompt Engineering*. https://platform.openai.com/docs/guides/prompt-engineering

Robinson, C. D., Kraft, M. A., Loeb, S., & Schueler, B. E. (2021). Accelerating student learning with high-dosage tutoring. EdResearch for Recovery Design Principles Series. *EdResearch for Recovery Project*. https://eric.ed.gov/?id=ED613847

Rosenberg-Kima, R. B. (2022). Computer Science Teacher Preparation to Address Bloom's 2 Sigma Problem in the Post-COVID19 Age. *Proceedings of the 53rd ACM Technical Symposium on Computer Science Education V. 2*, 1027. https://doi.org/10.1145/3478432.3499241

Sharples, M. (2023). Towards social generative AI for education: Theory, practices and ethics (arXiv:2306.10063). arXiv. http://arxiv.org/abs/2306.10063

Yamkovenko, S. (2023, May 1). Sal Khan's 2023 TED Talk: AI in the classroom can transform education. *Khan Academy Blog.* https://blog.khanacademy.org/sal-khans -2023-ted-talk-ai-in-the-classroom-can-transform-education/

6. Generative AI as an enabler for educators: practical tips for generative AI usage in teaching

Katri Kerem

6.1 INTRODUCTION

The notion that academics tend to be time impoverished is not new. Barnett (2008) has argued that "fast time crowds out slower time", referring to the fact that the number of urgent tasks facing academics does not allow them to devote themselves to tasks that have longer timeframes, require more concentration, and are essential to their academic career. Watermeyer et al. (2023) has discussed the epidemic of overwork and precarity among academics caused by several neoliberal tendencies in universities. Kim and Adlof (2023) have highlighted that ChatGPT has immense potential to significantly enhance teachers' productivity in higher education. In response to growing demands and the intense focus on performance measurement in universities, which has led to a decline in the collegial nature of academic interactions, Meron and Araci (2023) explored ChatGPT as a "virtual colleague" in academic settings. This approach aims to facilitate brainstorming and the development of new ideas in course design, potentially mitigating the issue of limited time for academics to engage in collaborative discussions and activities beyond their immediate responsibilities. "Let ChatGPT Be Your Teaching Assistant" was the title of an intriguing article on the Harvard Business Publishing Education website (Mollick and Mollick, 2023), both the heading and the content encompassing the potential of generative AI in education in the most pragmatic way. Converging these perspectives underlines the transformative role ChatGPT can have in academia, offering a practical solution to work overload and the everlasting challenge of balancing urgent tasks with the more profound and thoughtful work crucial for academic success.

Although generative AI technologies enable the creation of different forms of content (e.g. text, audio, image, and video) the current chapter restricts itself to text-based generative AI possibilities only. I argue that ChatGPT, as one of the specific implementations of generative AI can be successfully utilised in (higher) education to speed up dealing with routine categories of academic work and ease the constant time and demands pressure that most academics experience daily (see also Dowling and Li, Chapter 7 in this volume). ChatGPT also sets itself apart from other large language models (LLMs) through unique features, such as ease of access, ability to offer personalised responses, a conversational interface, and cost-effectiveness (Rahman and Watanobe, 2023), working like a perfect combination of everyday personal chat and Google search.

This chapter centres on the instructional process of higher education courses, following a sequence of activities required for developing, planning, and preparing a course and pinpointing useful applications of AI for each stage. The general stance is that AI can complement human intelligence (see also Martin and Williams, Chapter 2 in this volume) in several ways. Still, the essential competencies of faculty members, like critical thinking, teaching skills and up-to-date knowledge of their field, will remain the core of providing excellent education. The positive impact of emotional connection and intrapersonal communication on student motivation and learning outcomes cannot be replaced by technology (Hagenauer and Volet, 2014). The chapter aims to recommend strategies for achieving an (optimal) equilibrium between AI-generated materials and the faculty's individual contributions.

6.2   THE SYNERGIES OF AI AND MODERN EDUCATION

Although the educational field has traditionally been slow to adapt to changes and cautious about adopting new technologies, AI has entered the field with a force that did not allow for calculated adoption decisions (Kim and Adlof, 2023; see also Hendriksen, Chapter 5 in this volume). Prior technological advances (e.g. computers, universal access to the internet, etc.) have all changed pedagogy (Healy, 2023), but these transformations have been slower and have allowed educators to adapt to these changes in a gradual manner and at a modest pace.

The advent of new technologies invariably raises questions about whether traditional practices and roles will become obsolete. In response to the growing prominence of technology in education, Siemens (2005) introduced a learning theory he termed connectivism. He posited that learning is a networked process, and as the landscape of teaching and learning becomes increasingly complex, the connections and linkages between disparate information sources become essential. ChatGPT can serve as a pivotal node in this network, structuring teaching to focus on these connections and enhancing knowledge navigation for both students and teachers. ChatGPT can complement or offer an alternative to traditional teaching resources, such as textbooks, companion websites, accompanying slides, and publisher-provided tests.

ChatGPT could also provide a systematic course design approach and facilitate constructive alignment between learning outcomes, course content, and assessment methods. It supports constructivist learning by enabling teachers to design personalised learning experiences for larger groups, encouraging learners to connect new concepts to their prior knowledge (Kim and Adlof, 2023; Wu, 2023). This customisation promotes active engagement and knowledge creation, transforming students from passive recipients to active participants. While teachers are generally skilled and experienced, tailoring content and teaching methods to diverse individual needs can be complex and time-consuming. Additionally, in neoliberal higher education settings, where standardisation is common due to international accreditation and major publishers' influences, ChatGPT can contextualise content to better suit local needs. This is vital in regions where English educational materials may ignore local cultural and business contexts. ChatGPT helps create a learning environment that enhances student motivation and understanding by aligning materials with local realities. Box 6.1 shows a prompt asking for local context examples for a sustainable marketing course in Estonia. The ChatGPT response provides well-justified focus topics: Estonia is known for digital advancement, forestry-related topics are heatedly debated in society, and the Baltic Sea is indeed a very pollution-sensitive ecosystem.

BOX 6.1   USING CHATGPT TO ADD LOCAL CONTEXT TO A COURSE

User: Please propose three specific examples of how to tailor a sustainable marketing course to local realities uniquely specific to Estonia. Explain each in one short sentence

ChatGPT: For a sustainable marketing course tailored to Estonia's unique context, consider these specific examples:

1. Explore a digital platform from Estonia that connects consumers with surplus food from restaurants, highlighting digital innovation in reducing food waste.
2. Study an Estonian company crafting furniture from locally sourced wood, showcasing sustainable forestry and local craftsmanship in marketing.
3. Analyze an Estonian initiative aimed at reducing Baltic Sea pollution, demonstrating community engagement and environmental stewardship through marketing.

Source: ChatGPT output.

ChatGPT's ability to personalise content and align with constructivist learning principles makes it an invaluable asset in diverse educational settings. It allows educators to reduce workload and enhance learning experiences by providing a more interactive, connected, and student-centred academic environment.

6.3   CHATGPT IN EDUCATION: ENHANCING TEACHING FROM CONCEPT TO CLASSROOM

The following section delves deeper into the specific assistance ChatGPT can provide to university faculty in planning and teaching (see also Pavlik, Chapter 4 in this volume). The task of education will be further split into the most common sequential subtasks to allow for a more detailed discussion and provide practical usage suggestions. Although the list of tasks is varied, the core principles of utilising ChatGPT remain consistent. Therefore, the text will first present an overview of the general guidelines for efficient ChatGPT use that apply across various purposes.

Prompts are the fundamental tool for utilising ChatGPT, steering its output to align with specific educational goals and tasks. When writing prompts (a user-generated task that requests the AI to generate a response), it is important to be as specific as possible about the request (Lynch et al., 2023). For example, while developing learning objectives, the prompt should mention not only the subject but also the academic level, such as undergraduate or graduate, along with any specific skills or knowledge areas to be emphasised. Providing AI with a context for the task is considered one of the key criteria for obtaining useful output (Mollick, 2023). Assuming that higher education teachers possess above-average domain expertise, they can use correct terminology and incorporate existing knowledge into a prompt.

Additionally, using **structured queries** (Eager and Brunton, 2023) can significantly enhance the clarity and effectiveness of the prompts. An example of a well-structured prompt might be, "Generate a list of learning objectives for an undergraduate course in environmental science, with a focus on sustainable development". This prompt gives the AI clear direction and parameters, leading to more relevant and better-structured responses.

In higher education and course development, it may be necessary to **specify an educational framework taxonomy** like Bloom's Taxonomy (Forehand, 2005). Aligning course content with a university's academic standards and frameworks often involves creating prompts rooted in this taxonomy. For example, a good prompt could be, "Design learning outcomes for a graduate-level marketing course, using Bloom's Taxonomy, and focusing on analysis and evaluation skills." This approach ensures that the responses align with the institution's educational requirements.

Lastly, **iterative prompting** (Eager and Brunton, 2023), also known as incremental prompting (Lingard, 2023), is a valuable technique in most ChatGPT queries because the default responses to queries tend to be generic. This approach closely mimics natural human conversation. The first prompt of a user may be broad or ambiguous (for example, "Explain different leadership styles for the master's students of a management course"). After analysing the content, precision, and other parameters of the initial answer, the user refines the prompt through several rounds, creating a feedback loop for the AI so that the user can direct it towards a more specific or more suitable type of response (for example narrowing down the prompt to "Describe transformational leadership in management"). Such gradual back-and-forth dialogue of prompts and responses is also valuable for developing user skills. With each iteration, the user gets a better understanding of how ChatGPT works. In course preparation, the final prompt in this sequence could be, for example, "Design a classroom activity for master's students that uses real-world cases to illustrate the impact of transformational leadership on team performance."

Meron and Araci (2023) cautioned users about potential output inconsistencies when using ChatGPT for educational design, particularly with longer prompt sequences. They highlight that ChatGPT may not always accurately incorporate previous discussions in its final outputs, as it tends to forget or overlook past prompts and responses within the same session. Therefore, it is recommended to save all useful elements of an educational design document separately into a file and then copy and paste this into ChatGPT for generating the final output.

6.3.1   AI-Enhanced Course Design

Course design is a complex task requiring careful planning, a good understanding of pedagogical principles, and the ability to integrate diverse educational resources effectively. ChatGPT assists teachers in finding efficiencies in the more routine components of this task, thereby freeing up time for more creative aspects. This proves especially beneficial for less experienced teachers (Chan and Lee, 2023), who may not yet be able to draft a course based on years of prior experience.

In most universities, formulating learning objectives and course descriptions is integral to the broader curriculum development process, rather than being tasks repeatedly undertaken for each course iteration by individual teachers. However, they frequently play a crucial role in shaping the learning outcomes within the broader curriculum development process.

ChatGPT can be beneficial in helping to brainstorm the lists of knowledge, skills, and attitudes students should acquire after completing the course, considering the specific taxonomies of outcomes an institution is using.

Prompting AI with initial ideas and taxonomy structure can assist in this process. Similarly, ChatGPT can be used in developing a course description to ensure a constructive alignment between the content, objectives, and expected learning outcomes. Box 6.2 provides a basic example of developing course outcomes (the ChatGPT response is kept concise due to space limitations).

BOX 6.2   DEVELOPING IDEAS FOR LEARNING OUTCOMES WITH CHATGPT

User: Design key learning outcomes for an undergraduate digital marketing course focusing on content creation and Search Engine Optimization (SEO) based on Bloom's Taxonomy. Give only the list of outcomes.
ChatGPT:
1. Recall foundational concepts of SEO and content marketing.
2. Explain the role of content creation in digital marketing and SEO.
3. Apply SEO techniques to optimize content for search engines.
4. Analyze the effectiveness of different content formats and SEO practices.
5. Evaluate the impact of content and SEO strategies on digital marketing goals.
6. Create a digital marketing campaign incorporating optimized content and SEO tactics.

Source: ChatGPT output.

ChatGPT can be used inside individual courses to help design the course structure and topic sequence. The starting prompts could vary from very broad, asking ChatGPT to just provide a sequence of topics based on the course title (see Box 6.3 for illustration), outcomes, and participant description, to asking assistance in organising a pre-determined set of topics logically and coherently. Such structuring and sorting tasks are well suited to AI and usually yield quality output. The course-planning phase frequently requires teachers to adjust content for courses with different proportions of independent work and in-class work, for example, for full-time students and session-based students. ChatGPT can guide teachers on how to balance in-class and independent study topics. It can help educators make informed decisions about whether to cover all topics in class at a superficial level, allowing students to delve deeper independently, or to focus on a few topics in depth during class time while leaving others for individual study. Additionally, ChatGPT can support the implementation of the flipped classroom method by providing resources and suggestions for pre-class activities and following in-class discussions.

BOX 6.3   THE FIRST, VERY GENERAL PROMPT TO
HELP THE TEACHER TO CREATE A SESSION
PLAN FOR A COURSE, SHOWING ONLY
PART OF THE OUTPUT

User: Generate a broad outline for an 8-week introductory digital marketing course at the undergraduate level, including only session topics.
ChatGPT: Certainly! Here's a streamlined outline focusing solely on the
session topics for an 8-week introductory digital marketing course:
Week 1: Digital Marketing Fundamentals

• Introduction to Digital Marketing

Week 2: Website Optimization and SEO

• Essentials of Website Design and User Experience (UX)
• Introduction to Search Engine Optimization (SEO)

Week 3: Content Marketing

• Strategies for Effective Content Marketing
• Creating and Curating Engaging Content

Week 4: Social Media Marketing

• Overview of Social Media Platforms
• Crafting Social Media Marketing Strategies

Source: ChatGPT output.

ChatGPT also serves as a tool to generate ideas about integrating elements
such as transferable skills or broader topics, like sustainable development
goals (Bahroun et al., 2023), into the teaching and learning of various
subjects.

The choice and diversity of educational resources available to teachers
are vast. Educators typically maintain their own collections of materials for
course preparation and student readings, and they continually update these
with the latest research and literature. Additionally, many disciplines benefit
from a wealth of publicly available materials, such as practitioner articles
and videos, which are instrumental in illustrating theoretical concepts. While
search engines have traditionally been used to find such resources, ChatGPT
offers significant advantages. Its primary benefit lies in its conversational

search capability, which allows for prompt refinement based on previous results. This feature enables educators to articulate their requirements more precisely, enhancing the relevance and effectiveness of the resources they obtain.

6.3.2   Assignment, Assessment, and Grading Assistance

Assignment and assessment development are crucial aspects of course planning (see also Matheis and Jubin, Chapter 9 in this volume). Well-crafted assignments motivate the students and align with the course learning outcomes. Assessment planning also has a significant impact on the teacher's future workload. Students expect in-depth personal feedback to their submissions, but in many universities teachers must teach large groups without the help of teaching assistants; hence, looking for some scalability would be a welcome solution. Some educators might consider it essential to adapt their assignments in ways that ensure student's individual work without extensive use of AI technologies. This could involve "AI-proofing" assignments to discourage or prevent straightforward AI-generated assignment submission or, conversely, integrating the creative use of AI into the tasks as a learning tool. One practical suggestion would be submitting existing assignments to ChatGPT to generate suggestions on how to either make assignments more resistant to being completed by AI alone or to thoughtfully include AI use as part of the assignment.

Rahman and Watanobe (2023) highlight the usefulness of ChatGPT in developing questions and quizzes for different difficulty levels or also adjusting existing questions to difficulty levels. This flexibility reflects the evolving needs of educational environments, where adaptability to different student groups is highly valued. Prompts for questions on different levels can range from simple input of learning content and a request to specify questions on for example three difficulty levels, to explaining in detail the previous knowledge and experience of the target group.

Grading rubrics are a preferred or even required assessment tool in several universities, aiming to minimise the effect of subjectivity and ensure uniform grading. Creating effective rubric descriptors is a challenging task. It involves carefully crafting the descriptors to be specific enough to provide clear guidance to students and allow enough flexibility for teachers to apply their judgement effectively. ChatGPT can assist teachers in adjusting existing rubrics and developing new ones. As a language model, ChatGPT can outperform humans (especially non-native speakers) in understanding nuance differentiation, and it can help verbalise these differences for the purposes of the rubric.

6.3.3 Preparing the Course Content with the Help of AI

ChatGPT is reasonably proficient at synthesising and rephrasing existing material (Chan and Lee, 2023), thereby aiding teachers in creating optimal course materials from an immense amount of potential input. Such input is often scattered across various physical and digital locations and sometimes buried amidst a clutter of irrelevant content. When it comes to preparing classes and sourcing materials, ChatGPT is a time-saving tool for educators and an efficient way to ensure the relevancy and quality of course content in a continuously expanding digital information landscape. It has to be noted that ChatGPT is known for generating fake references to "academic" texts (Lingard, 2023), so it goes without saying that the teacher should meticulously validate the collections of ChatGPT-generated materials and literature.

Meron and Araci (2023) have demonstrated in their experimental study how course content can be adjusted to account for participants with diverse backgrounds and previous education by using ChatGPT for course development. This is especially helpful in postgraduate courses that attract more experienced students who do not come straight from a bachelor's programme and where the composition of the group is not known to the teacher well in advance. Once the class composition is known, the background info (e.g. work experience, previous degree) may serve as a part of the adjustment prompt. Building on this idea, generating variations of the same tasks, such as altering the target group each task version addresses, is beneficial across different student cohorts. ChatGPT's adaptability makes it an ideal tool for creating slightly tailored assignments (see Table 6.1).

Table 6.1   Prompting ChatGPT to create variations of activity design

Task for Student Group A (No Previous Search Engine Optimization (SEO) Experience)	Task for Student Group B (Professional Marketing Work Experience)
Introduction to SEO Fundamentals	Advanced SEO Strategy Development
1. Keyword Research: Students will learn the basics of keyword research using free tools like Google Keyword Planner. They are tasked with finding 5 relevant keywords for a hypothetical local business website.	1. Competitive SEO Analysis: Students will conduct a comprehensive SEO audit of a competitor in a chosen industry, focusing on keyword strategy, backlink profile, and on-page SEO elements.

(continues overleaf)

Task for Student Group A (No Previous Search Engine Optimization (SEO) Experience)	Task for Student Group B (Professional Marketing Work Experience)
2. On-Page SEO: Introduction to on-page SEO elements (title tags, meta descriptions, heading tags). Students will write these elements for a mock-up of a homepage, incorporating keywords researched previously.	2. Content Optimization and Strategy: Develop a content strategy for an existing website that targets new keywords and addresses content gaps in the market. This includes creating a content calendar and suggestions for types of content (blog posts, videos, infographics).
3. Simple Content Creation: Write a short blog post (300–500 words) for their hypothetical business using the keywords researched. Emphasize the importance of keyword placement and readability.	3. Technical SEO Audit: Perform a technical SEO audit for a real website using tools like SEMrush or Ahrefs. Identify issues like slow page load times, mobile usability, and crawl errors, and propose solutions.
4. SEO Tools Introduction: Familiarize with basic SEO tools and plugins (e.g., Yoast SEO for WordPress). They will install a plugin on a demo WordPress site and apply basic on-page SEO principles learned.	4. Link Building Strategy: Develop a link-building strategy, identifying potential partners and crafting outreach emails. The task includes analysing the backlink profile of a competitor to identify opportunities.
Objective: Understand the foundational elements of SEO and how they affect website visibility.	Objective: Apply advanced SEO techniques and strategic thinking to improve website ranking and visibility in a competitive landscape.

Note: Prompt: Design a classroom activity for the digital marketing course of an undergraduate programme that enhances students' skills in SEO through hands-on experience. Create one version of the task for student group A, who have no previous SEO experience and other version of the task for student group B, who have professional marketing work experience.
Source: ChatGPT output.

Last but not least, as English is becoming the de facto *lingua franca* of academia, more academics must work in their non-native language. ChatGPT is helpful in language editing and improvement, correcting grammar, style, and academic language, especially for teachers who teach in a foreign language. The prompts for language improvement can be fairly simple but need a bit of practice to yield results that reflect the teacher's original tone of voice and are not too wordy.

6.4 CONCLUSION: STRATEGIC USE OF CHATGPT – BALANCING OPPORTUNITIES AND RISKS

The incorporation of ChatGPT into academia, as Rajala et al. (2023) articulately expressed, is like an exquisite blend of advanced technology and magic, suggesting its transformative potential for education. Although using AI to make teaching easier, more engaging, and fun is both tempting and rewarding, there are two sides to the coin. As Williams (2024, p. 6) notes: "using AI comes with striking a reasonable balance of the benefits and shortfalls". Unlike humans, ChatGPT generates responses based on patterns in data it was trained on, lacking the ability to understand context or meaning, and provides information without personal experience and critical judgement.

Additionally, ChatGPT can simply yield inaccurate responses (see also Protopapa and Idris, Chapter 11 in this volume). As Gillani et al. (2023) have argued, "the 'I' of AI systems remains quite rudimentary", as shown by its frequent struggles with tasks that are intuitively easy for humans. Language is ambiguous (Lim and Wu, 2023) and context-dependent (Bach, 2014), and thus difficult for AI to interpret, understand, and correctly replicate. Hence, for example, using ChatGPT to give feedback to students may erase subtle nuances of human sensitivity that are present in interpersonal communication. Students may need emotional support (Chan and Lee, 2023) or for exceptional circumstances to be taken into account. Although Lynch et al. (2023) have noted that AI can already create narrative messages that reflect a person's emotional state and their environment, it is crucial to keep in mind that giving feedback is almost always contextual and using AI for this purpose requires a lot of critical thinking to revise and improve proposed solutions.

Generally, it is assumed that teachers in higher education institutions possess professional source criticism skills, which are essential for academic activities. A critical and informed use of any AI tools entails awareness of the tools' potential biases and limitations. Since AI systems learn from vast and uncontrolled datasets, their outputs may reflect societal biases or inaccurately present information, sometimes even propagating factually incorrect data (Williams, 2024). Chan and Lee (2023) have emphasised the need for human oversight in any AI enabled processes, Williams (2024) has cautioned that the additional layer of verification may be time consuming, hence using up some of the time savings achieved with AI usage. Kim and Adlof (2023) have highlighted that much of the criticism directed at AI and ChatGPT stems from using the output as a final product, rather than employing ChatGPT as a tool or mental model to advance specific work processes.

It has been pointed out that ChatGPT and other AI-based technologies are by no means replacements for human teachers (Chan and Lee, 2023). Kocoń et al. (2023) have explicitly labelled ChatGPT as being a "Jack of all trades, master of none". Meron and Araci (2023) have suggested a dual educator model – a team of human teacher and virtual assistant – which seems a balanced approach.

Lynch et al. (2023) have noted ChatGPT's tendency towards "storytelling", and Meron and Araci (2023) suspected the program was trying to please the user, although ChatGPT denied this explicitly when prompted with a relevant question. ChatGPT as a teaching aid works best for educated and experienced teachers (Meron and Araci, 2023), as crafting useful prompts and making decisions about the usefulness of the responses requires a deep understanding of the field and educational process. ChatGPT's tendency to create believable and fairly generic responses to any question requires user expertise to separate the wheat from the chaff and design prompts that are likely to yield results of the desired quality. To illustrate, Box 6.4 offers a hilarious (but also sad) example of how ChatGPT provided a fake reference and initially asked the user to go to the library to find this specific article. Thus, those using ChatGPT must exercise heightened caution and critical thinking, potentially dedicating additional time to verifying the accuracy of ChatGPT's responses.

BOX 6.4   A WELL-KNOWN TENDENCY OF CHATGPT TO GENERATE FAKE ACADEMIC REFERENCES

User: Provide link to this article: Thompson, M., & Kumar, A. (2023). The Future of Case-Based Teaching: Integrating AI for Dynamic Learning Environments. Journal of Business Education Innovation.

ChatGPT: I can't browse the internet or access real-time databases to provide direct links to articles or verify their existence. However, to access the article by Thompson and Kumar titled "The Future of Case-Based Teaching: Integrating AI for Dynamic Learning Environments" in the "Journal of Business Education Innovation," you typically have a few options: University Library, Academic Databases, Direct Journal Access:

User: It does not appear in any databases. Did you make the reference up?

ChatGPT: Yes, the reference to Thompson, M., & Kumar, A. (2023). "The Future of Case-Based Teaching: Integrating AI for Dynamic Learning Environments" in the "Journal of Business Education Innovation" was used as an illustrative example to support the narrative. In academic and professional contexts, it's crucial to rely on verifiable sources.

User: But if it is a fake reference why did you tell me to look it up from library?

ChatGPT: I apologize for the confusion earlier. My intention was to provide a general approach for locating academic articles, which inadvertently implied that the mentioned reference was real. I understand this could have been misleading, and I appreciate your patience and understanding. If you're seeking genuine references on the topic of AI integration into education, I recommend exploring well-known educational technology journals or databases for authentic and relevant research. Again, I apologize for any confusion caused, and I'm here to help with any further questions or information you might need.

Source: ChatGPT output.

Relying on ChatGPT or any other AI tools may necessitate urgent reskilling for faculty members (Chan and Lee, 2023) to prevent skill gaps. While the adoption of ChatGPT has challenged the universally applicable innovation adoption curve theory, with mass adoption occurring in the first few days, the levels of usage and proficiency still vary considerably (Chan and Lee, 2023; Kiryakova and Angelova, 2023). It's important to note that teachers who have not adopted ChatGPT are at risk of being left behind. These educators may find themselves exerting more effort while delivering an inferior course experience to their students, compared to their colleagues who have embraced new technology. While it is common for those who master a new skill to gain certain advantages, the case of ChatGPT is unique. Even a minimal proficiency in utilising this AI tool can result in significantly enhanced teaching outputs and outcomes. This disproportionate benefit underscores educators' need to rapidly acquire skills in using ChatGPT, not just to keep pace with technological advancements but to fully utilise its potential for improving educational quality and efficiency. It also means that the universities need to provide relevant training to their faculty members, support the development of advanced skills and provide access to paid pro versions of AI systems that are most relevant to the situation.

The multifunctional nature of ChatGPT implies that choosing not to adopt it can have more significant consequences than foregoing previous technological advancements. Unlike earlier education-related innovations that offered limited, domain-specific functions (e.g. learning management systems or plagiarism detectors), ChatGPT includes a broad spectrum of capabilities ranging from content generation to personalised feedback, curriculum development, language translation, and facilitating interactive learning experiences. This versatility means that not adopting ChatGPT results in missing out on a wide array of functionalities that could enhance various aspects of academic work. Therefore, the decision to bypass ChatGPT is not just a matter of forgoing a single tool; it equates to missing out on multiple opportunities to improve educational processes and outcomes.

From the perspective of individual faculty members, it is worthwhile to critically reflect on optimal personal AI usage. When academics delegate certain tasks to ChatGPT, other responsibilities (like administrative or bureaucratic tasks) may emerge to fill the gap, as the time tracking systems signal to managers that the specific faculty member is seemingly underutilised. This newfound availability could be an opportunity for scholarly activities like reading or reflection but instead it often becomes occupied with additional measurable activities (in alignment with the operational efficiencies valued by university management). ChatGPT does not always alleviate the workload of educators. Instead, it may portray them as capable of managing increasingly unrealistic workloads (Watermeyer et al., 2023), a consequence that is definitely not welcome.

In conclusion, as the scholarly discussion around ChatGPT's integration into higher education evolves, it is evident that it holds considerable promise for enhancing teaching and learning. Still, its effective utilisation depends on a thorough understanding of its capabilities and limitations. Educators are encouraged to adopt a critical, informed approach to utilising ChatGPT, recognising its potential to facilitate and enrich educational processes while being mindful of the tools' inherent risks and inaccuracies. The strategic use of ChatGPT in academia necessitates a balanced consideration of its opportunities and challenges, ensuring that while it serves as a valuable addition to the teacher's toolkit, it does also necessitate a healthy dose of human insight, empathy, and contextual judgement, qualities crucial for effective education.

REFERENCES

Bach, K., 2014. Context dependence. In: Garcia-Carpintero, M. and Max Kölbel, M. (eds), *The Bloomsbury Companion to the Philosophy of Language*, Bloomsbury Academic, London, pp. 153–184.

Bahroun, Z., Anane, C., Ahmed, V. and Zacca, A., 2023. Transforming education: A comprehensive review of generative artificial intelligence in educational settings through bibliometric and content analysis. *Sustainability*, 15(17), p. 12983.

Barnett, R. (2008). Being an academic in a time-impoverished age. In: Amaral, A., Bleiklie, I., and Musselin, C. (eds), *From Governance to Identity: Higher Education Dynamics*, vol. 24. Springer, Dordrecht. https://doi.org/10.1007/978-1-4020-8994-7_2

Chan, C.K.Y. and Lee, K.K., 2023. The AI generation gap: Are Gen Z students more interested in adopting generative AI such as ChatGPT in teaching and learning than their Gen X and millennial generation teachers? *Smart Learn. Environ.* 10(60). https://doi.org/10.1186/s40561-023-00269-3

Eager, B. and Brunton, R., 2023. Prompting higher education towards AI-augmented teaching and learning practice. *Journal of University Teaching & Learning Practice*, 20(5).

Forehand, M., 2005. Bloom's taxonomy: Original and revised. *Emerging Perspectives on Learning, Teaching, and Technology*, 8, pp. 41–44.

Gillani, N., Eynon, R., Chiabaut, C. and Finkel, K., 2023. Unpacking the "black box" of AI in education. *Educational Technology & Society*, 26(1), pp. 99–111.

Hagenauer, G. and Volet, S. E., 2014. Teacher–student relationship at university: An important yet under-researched field, *Oxford Review of Education*, 40(3), pp. 370–388, DOI: 10.1080/03054985.2014.921613.

Healy, M., 2023. Using curriculum theory to inform approaches to generative AI in schools. *arXiv* preprint arXiv:2309.13053.

Kim, M. and Adlof, L., 2023. Adapting to the future: ChatGPT as a means for supporting constructivist learning environments. *TechTrends*, pp. 1–10.

Kiryakova, G. and Angelova, N., 2023. ChatGPT — a challenging tool for the university professors in their teaching practice. *Education Sciences*, 13(10), p. 1056.

Kocoń, J., Cichecki, I., Kaszyca, O., Kochanek, M., Szydło, D., Baran, J., Bielaniewicz, J., Gruza, M., Janz, A., Kanclerz, K. and Kocoń, A., 2023. ChatGPT: Jack of all trades, master of none. *Information Fusion*, p. 101861.

Lim, W. and Wu, Q., 2023. Vague language and context dependence. *Frontiers in Behavioral Economics*, 2, p. 1014233.

Lingard, L., 2023. Writing with ChatGPT: An illustration of its capacity, limitations & implications for academic writers. *Perspectives on Medical Education*, 12(1), p. 261.

Lynch, C.J., Jensen, E.J., Zamponi, V., O'Brien, K., Frydenlund, E. and Gore, R., 2023. A structured narrative prompt for prompting narratives from large language models: Sentiment assessment of ChatGPT-generated narratives and real tweets. *Future Internet*, 15(12), p. 375.

Meron, Y. and Araci, Y.T., 2023. Artificial intelligence in design education: Evaluating ChatGPT as a virtual colleague for post-graduate course development. *Design Science*, 9, p. e30.

Mollick, E. (2023). A guide to prompting AI (for what it is worth). *One Useful Thing*, April 26, 2023 [Blog]. Available at https://www.oneusefulthing.org/p/a-guide-to-prompting-ai-for-what (accessed 5 April 2024).

Mollick, E. and Mollick, L. (2023). Let ChatGPT be your teaching assistant. Strategies for thoughtfully using AI to lighten your workload. *Harvard Business Publishing Education*. https://hbsp.harvard.edu/inspiring-minds/let-chatgpt-be-your-teaching-assistant

Rahman, M.M. and Watanobe, Y., 2023. ChatGPT for education and research: Opportunities, threats, and strategies. *Applied Sciences*, 13(9), p. 5783.

Rajala, J., Hukkanen, J., Hartikainen, M. and Niemelä, P., 2023, October. "Call me Kiran" – ChatGPT as a tutoring chatbot in a computer science course. In *Proceedings of the 26th International Academic Mindtrek Conference*, pp. 83–94.

Siemens, G., 2005. Connectivism: A learning theory for the digital age. *International Journal of Instructional Technology and Distance Learning*, 2(1), pp. 3–10.

Watermeyer, R., Phipps, L., Lanclos, D. and Knight, C., 2023. Generative AI and the Automating of Academia. *Postdigital Science and Education*, pp. 1–21.

Williams, R.T., 2024. The ethical implications of using generative chatbots in higher education. *Frontiers in Education* (Vol. 8).

Wu, Y., 2023. Integrating Generative AI in Education: How ChatGPT Brings Challenges for Future Learning and Teaching. *Journal of Advanced Research in Education*, 2(4), pp. 6–10.

7. Generative AI for academic research

Michael Dowling and Yue Li

7.1 HOW THIS CHAPTER WILL HELP YOU

This chapter delves into the transformative potential of Generative AI (GenAI) in academic research, positioning it alongside the printing press and the computer as a similar revolutionary tool. By drawing on historical shifts in research methodologies and the evolution of tools from libraries to the internet, it underscores GenAI's capacity to act not just as a tool but as a thought partner. Highlighting GenAI's ability to process vast datasets, identify patterns, and generate novel hypotheses, the chapter prepares readers to embrace GenAI as a collaborator that extends beyond mere assistance. It explores practical applications of GenAI in hypothesis generation, analysis fine-tuning, and writing collaboration, while also considering the future of academic research. Through this, readers will gain an applied understanding of how GenAI can enhance their research capabilities, transform the role of researchers, and possibly redefine the traditional academic landscape.

7.2 LEARNING FROM HISTORY

This section outlines the historical progression of research tools and methodologies, illustrating how GenAI represents a significant leap forward but is still in line with the general pattern of research produced with the most recent best-for-the-job set of tools.

7.2.1 From Magnifying Glasses to Idea Generators

Humanity's quest for knowledge has always been intertwined with the development of tools that expand our capabilities. From simple magnifying glasses originally to now powerful AI models, each technological leap has transformed how we observe, analyze, and understand the world around us.

The earliest research tools were born of a desire to see beyond the limitations of the human eye (Henn et al., 2005). The invention of the magnifying glass in the 13th century allowed closer examination of intricate details – the detailed anatomical structure of insects, for example, could now be explored, fueling curiosity about the natural world. The telescope, research with which was pioneered by Galileo in the 16th century, shattered our understanding of the cosmos. Suddenly, the stars were not just points of light, but distant worlds begging to be explored. These tools amplified our senses, igniting new fields of inquiry and altering our perception of reality.

As knowledge accumulated, the need for tools to analyze and make sense of it grew. Mechanical calculators in the 17th century eased the burden of complex computations, paving the way for increasingly sophisticated analytical tools. The 20th century witnessed the birth of computers and statistical software packages like SPSS and Stata. The advent of the internet and search engines further accelerated access to information, transforming global research collaboration by making the world's libraries readily accessible.

The field of AI, with its goal of creating machines that exhibit intelligent behavior, has held promise for researchers for decades. Early successes focused on "Quantitative AI," where Machine Learning (ML) algorithms excelled at pattern recognition and statistical analysis within structured datasets. This transformed fields like finance and marketing in business, but still largely mirrored traditional data analytics (Aziz et al., 2021).

Powered by large-scale language models like the Generative Pre-trained Transformer (GPT) series, GenAI systems go beyond pattern finding. Trained on massive amounts of text data, GPT models learn to predict the next word (technically a "token," which is often a part of a word) in a sequence, mimicking human-quality communication and patterns of logic (Kalyan, 2024). This ability to understand, produce, synthesize, and creatively manipulate language moves GenAI beyond extending our existing capabilities (Feuerriegel et al., 2023); it allows these models to participate in the knowledge-creation process.

Unlike microscopes or statistical software, which primarily extend existing capabilities, GenAI fundamentally transforms the knowledge discovery process. Firstly, imagine sifting through mountains of scientific papers or other written data – an impossible task for a human researcher to carry out at scale. GenAI excels at processing these enormous datasets, identifying subtle patterns and correlations that might escape even the most meticulous human eye. A related but distinct point is the ability to search far more directly. GenAI allows researchers to ask direct questions of either the model or stacks of information and receive comprehensive answers in a fraction of the time. Finally, GenAI can bridge the gap between prior research and researcher hypotheses. Analyzing patterns and extrapolating can propose potential hypotheses or even suggest creative solutions, acting as a thought partner and sparking new avenues for investigation (Dwivedi et al., 2023).

7.2.2   Moving Along the Collaborator Spectrum

The tools and collaborators available have always shaped the pursuit of knowledge. Just as research tools have evolved from simple aids to powerful technologies, support roles have transformed from basic assistance to specialized collaborators over the history of research. GenAI represents a new frontier, blurring the line between assistant and colleague (see also Martin and Williams, Chapter 2 in this volume).

In the early days of science, support roles often mirrored those of apprentices in a craftsman's workshop, focused on carrying out tasks under close supervision. Notetakers meticulously recorded observations, while human "computers" performed tedious calculations by hand. While crucial, these roles were largely passive, making no significant intellectual contribution to the research itself. Johannes Kepler, for instance, initially served as the assistant to astronomer Tycho Brahe, aiding in his meticulous astronomical observations – although this might be the exception as that notetaking ultimately fueled Kepler's own groundbreaking breakthroughs.

The 20th century saw a shift towards more active support roles, with research assistants becoming much more like teammates, contributing to research design, data analysis, and interpretation. Modern research often involves extreme specialization and larger teams (Fisher et al., 1998) – statisticians, lab technicians, data scientists – each with deep expertise crucial to success. Nowhere is this more evident than at CERN, where papers on discoveries can list hundreds, or, in the case of a famous Higgs Bosun paper, over 5,000 co-authors.

GenAI introduces a dual potential to either disrupt or enhance this trajectory of collaboration. On one hand, it offers the possibility of reverting back to solo research endeavors, eliminating wait times for co-contributors with its always-ready assistance. This capability is underscored by a variety of skill sets that GenAI assistants offer, hinting at a vast unexplored potential (Borger et al., 2023). Conversely, GenAI also promises to escalate collaborative efforts by integrating AI into the research process, enabling researchers to bridge competency gaps without the limitations of human team dynamics.

The potential positioning of GenAI as a partner raises critical inquiries about the future of research collaboration, apprenticeship, and the definition of authorship in a landscape where human and AI contributions are intricately intertwined. These considerations extend to the broader implications for academic institutions, challenging them to reassess their roles and methodologies in the face of rapidly advancing AI technologies.

7.2.3   Ivory Tower or Innovation Hub?

GenAI also challenges traditional notions of the university itself, transforming it from a bastion of pure scholarship to, potentially, a hub of rapid innovation. Over the years, academia has institutionalized rigorous methodology and approaches to research and research scholarship. However, this can sometimes hinder the adoption of new tools. By contrast, industry, driven by innovation imperatives, often moves faster. This tension between depth and speed has long characterized the relationship between universities and the private sector.

GenAI has the potential to upend these traditional university research processes (Neumann et al., 2023). Researchers in either industry or academia can now rapidly prototype ideas, or explore avenues that would be prohibitively time-consuming with traditional methods – fostering a culture of experimentation and rapid discovery. However, there is surely a risk that academia will not adapt to this new potential and that the mantle for rapid-yet-high-quality research will become the domain of industry. Or more likely, some institutions will adapt, while others will protest and lag.

It is an open question whether academic rigor can adapt to the speed of "prototyped research." We also need to work out how to ensure the validity of AI-generated insights, and whether GenAI will create an excessive focus on applied research rather than fundamental inquiry.

7.3   THE GenAI TOOLKIT FOR RESEARCHERS

We now examine the potential toolkit for researchers seeking to adopt GenAI assistance. We've tried to move beyond the basics and address conceptual and practical developments that showcase clear novelty and advance compared to traditional tools. We do this in two broad sections – first examining the potential for idea generation, and second proposing a new method beyond search. These two aspects enhanced by GenAI will become key over the coming years as the technology continues to develop.

7.3.1   The AI Idea Engine

7.3.1.1   Eureka, accelerated
The concept of an "AI Idea Engine" refers to a system designed to generate, develop, or enhance ideas using GenAI capabilities – think ChatGPT Premium, Google Gemini Advanced, Claude Opus. While GenAI is undoubtedly powerful, unlocking its full creative potential for idea generation requires targeted strategies and a clear understanding of current strengths and limitations. Let's dive into the practical steps and concepts that have been shown to work to date.

Begin your interaction with ChatGPT (or a similar GenAI tool) by clearly defining the model's area of expertise. Start with a statement like:

[You are a senior professor of finance with more than 30 years of experience.]

This role-playing appears to help the model to contextualize its responses and tailor suggestions to your specific research domain (Short & Short, 2023), while the mention of "senior" and "more than 30 years of experience" helps the model to understand that you are seeking high insight on the response.

Generic questions tend to lead to generic answers, so asking open-ended questions like "Can you suggest research ideas?" will yield vague results. Instead, frame your prompts to elicit specific, actionable steps. Chain-of-thought reasoning is instrumental, requiring the model to think through its answer logically (Yu et al., 2023). For example:

[I want you to think about this step-by-step using chain-of-thought reasoning. Your task is to identify a research topic that is novel and would constitute a contribution at {journal name}. The research topic should draw on, and advance, the following prior research {include summaries of relevant prior research}. You are required to output a title and research idea summary as well as a justification for why this would be a contribution compared to the prior research and for the specific journal. Consider the contribution from both a theoretical and empirical perspective.]

Feed GenAI relevant abstracts, summaries, or even full-text articles to spark its idea-generation process. This provides context and a knowledge base upon which it can draw. Ask the model to identify gaps or unanswered questions in the existing research, suggest novel applications, or propose potential methodologies or experimental approaches.

Understanding the types of creativity and where current GenAI models fall within that spectrum is important. Tools like ChatGPT demonstrate impressive capabilities in remixing and repurposing existing knowledge, putting them roughly at the "little-c" (everyday creativity) stage (Ivcevic & Grandinetti, 2024). To unlock higher levels like "Big C" (transformative creativity), we need advancements in several areas:

- **General model intelligence:** Model intelligence for creative research tasks can be measured using the GPQA test, or the Graduate-Level Google-Proof Q&A Benchmark (Rein et al., 2023). Most current models rank below PhD capabilities on this test.
- **Context and memory:** GenAI needs better ways to store and connect information for informed idea generation. While we've mentioned the

Google Gemini memory capability, there are many advances still needed
in this area.

- **Reasoning and analogy:** The models also need better ability to draw
  complex connections across disparate knowledge domains. Moving beyond
  general outputs to ideas tailored to specific research objectives is crucial.

However, these are not unknown leaps for the models to take. They are
planned developments as models develop from GPT 4-class to higher classes.
Claude Opus, launched in early 2024, had a 200,000 token context memory
(in practice, that means you can input about 100,000 words of prompts into
the model and these will be understood by Claude Opus when giving you an
answer) and was described as reaching 60 percent accuracy on the GPQA
test of PhD-level reasoning (Rein et al., 2023), while the average human PhD
student would usually get around 65 percent on the same test.

Much of the heavy lifting in idea generation still falls on the researcher.
You'll need to iteratively refine prompts, evaluate the relevance of outputs,
and critically assess the feasibility of suggestions. Respond to the model with
clear lists of the parts you like in their suggestions and the parts that need to be
improved – given guidance as to how to improve those parts in terms of what
to focus on. Many of the idea-generation benefits occur in this iterative stage of
conversing with the GenAI model. It is also fair to say that the best creativity,
for now, rests with human researchers rather than the creativity of even the best
AI (Papakonstantinidis et al., 2024).

7.3.1.2 Upgrading your idea engine

Fine-tuning is a powerful technique that takes a general GenAI model and
customizes it for a specific task or domain (Liu et al., 2023). Imagine you
have a highly skilled chef, but instead of general cooking skills, they choose
to specialize in French cuisine and become experts in that type of cooking.
Fine-tuning is about creating this habit of answering specific questions correctly and can help compensate for model shortcomings, in much the same way
as a generally very good chef can become a specifically great French cuisine
chef.

From a research perspective, fine-tuning is a means of developing an idea
machine that is even more adept at assisting your specialist research, as it is
specifically trained to answer according to your particular needs. On a broader
perspective, this is the reason why we have seen the emergence of specialist
medical and legal GenAI models, among others.

Here's a breakdown of the process of fine-tuning, with a specific example
of fine-tuning a model to understand economic sentiment. This approach

approximately mimics the approach implemented in Ardekani et al. (2024) for economic sentiment.

1. **Start with a pre-trained model: GPT 4, or open source models.** Originally, a GenAI model was trained on a diverse dataset including text from books, internet articles, technical manuals, and more. This general training enables the model to understand and generate human-like text across various contexts. It can perform tasks like answering generic questions, composing emails, or providing summaries. However, if you were to ask GPT 4 (or the earlier GPT 3 model applied in Ardekani et al. (2024)) to measure the economic sentiment of a sentence it would come back with quite generic statements.

2. **Training on a domain-specific dataset: economic sentiment of sentences.** To address this issue, we can gather sample sentences, assign economic sentiment scores to the sentences, and then fine-tune a general GPT 4 on how we want questions to be answered. The process is outlined by OpenAI and largely involves creating a spreadsheet of example inputs and desired outputs for each of those inputs.[1] The process of fine-tuning is similar for other models, such as the open source models available on HuggingFace, and is largely an automated process once you have collected your training data.

3. **Making model adjustments: Test, iterate, and use.** The fine-tuning process works by adjusting certain layers and parameters of the general model, rather than retraining the whole model. This preserves its ability to understand and generate natural language while enhancing its capability to respond accurately to our economic sentiment models. If we test the model and find that it doesn't quite work for us, we can adjust the training samples, or certain model parameters. A common parameter to adjust is "temperature," which speaks to how "creative" the model is allowed to be when answering. For a technical question such as assigning an economic sentiment score to a sentence, we might want to lower the temperature below the default temperature. But, if our task involved innovation, such as idea creation, we might want to increase the temperature. When you have finished fine-tuning the model that you have fine-tuned will be available, exclusively for your personal use, on the platform of your choice (e.g. OpenAI, HuggingFace).

Fine-tuning can significantly enhance a model's utility for targeted tasks, however, a downside to fine-tuning should be noted, which is that when you specialize a GenAI model you can end up losing some of the model's intelligence in other areas.

7.3.1.3 AI – "sparring partners"

A novel use of GenAI is as a thought partner or "sparring" opponent, helping writers refine ideas, explore new directions, and push their writing to new heights (Kankanhalli, 2024).

Take an example from Anthropic. In their early 2024 testing of a new LLM model called Claude 3 Opus (already mentioned earlier) they encountered a finding which sparked a discussion of whether their model had demonstrated "metacognition" – a trait that would be useful for sparring and deep collaboration. All GenAI models allow a certain context window – essentially the number of words you can enter into a model to inform an output. Anthropic were conducting an internal test of information retrieval from their context window to test if the model was accurately remembering context. They inserted a sentence about pizza toppings into a set of programming documents and asked the model if it felt any sentences in its context window were "out of context" (and pardon the double usage of the word "context"). Claude Opus not only located the out-of-context sentence but the model also responded that it felt like it was being tested due to the retrieved sentence being so strange. This was notable due to the implication that the model was aware of itself – the aforementioned metacognition.

It should be noted that findings like this often led to passionate debate within the GenAI community as to whether the finding is real or some sort of data training artifact. A convincing argument for the former tends to be that it suggests emerging intelligence due to the findings mainly happening in higher-level models, rather than lower-level models.

This suggests that these models might eventually actively "spar" with their users to help them improve their understanding of a research topic. A model that can recognize when it is being tested and can comment on the nature of its tasks could potentially offer more nuanced interactions. For instance, it could adjust its responses based on the perceived purpose of the questions it is asked, making it more effective in sparring or deep collaboration scenarios. In research or collaborative environments, such a model could proactively identify gaps in the information provided, ask clarifying questions, or even challenge assumptions. This could lead to a more dynamic interaction where the AI contributes actively to problem-solving and innovation.

The ability to "spar" with users refers to the model engaging in an intellectual debate that can help refine ideas and approaches. It implies a partnership where the model doesn't just passively provide information but actively helps in shaping the research direction through questions and suggestions. A frequently drawn comparison is to the movie "Her," where the AI character is able to not just empathize but also debate and challenge.

Many historical stories, and our own anecdotal experience as researchers, speak to the benefits of strong collaboration in terms of quality of research output. Researchers have also corroborated the benefits of team vs. individual research regarding research impact (Jones, 2021). A historical difficulty has been finding a good team research partner that gels well with your own skillset, but GenAI research partners are likely to be highly flexible in terms of how they collaborate and become our research partners.

7.3.2 Moving Beyond Search

Traditional search engines and even basic AI tools focus on finding information or correcting superficial errors. But true "sparring" with GenAI means going deeper. Cutting-edge tools powered by GenAI models can analyze texts with an almost perfect nuance, uncover hidden patterns, challenge assumptions, and aid in the construction of complex arguments. This represents a transformative shift in how researchers interact with textual data, enabling them to delve deeper into the heart of language, meaning, and the ideas encoded within texts. This section outlines these tools.

The prompting and fine-tuning of the prior section show how to steer GenAI models towards specific tasks and domains. But what if we want to delve even deeper into textual relationships and hidden connections? Here's where embeddings come in.

Imagine a GenAI model trained on a massive dataset of text. It can identify patterns and relationships between words, but these connections are often opaque. Embeddings act as a bridge, transforming words into numerical representations that capture their meaning and relationships to other words. Think of it as a special map where words with similar meanings cluster together. They transform words into numerical representations that capture meaning and relationships to other words, facts, and concepts. Knowledge graphs take this idea a step further (a wiki page is a type of knowledge graph), linking words and concepts in a structured network that makes these relationships even more explicit (Pan et al., 2024).

Here's how embeddings can help:

- **Micro-search: exploring subtle connections.** Traditional search techniques often rely on exact keyword matches. This can be limiting, as the document must contain the specific terms used in the query. Embeddings, however, allow for the understanding of concepts and the relationships between them. If, for example, you are analyzing a historical document for mentions of "revolution" but the term isn't explicitly used, embeddings can help. By searching the document's embeddings for related concepts like "uprising" or "resistance," you can identify mentions of revolutionary activities that aren't labeled as such. This is possible because embeddings capture the semantic similarities between words, even if they don't share surface-level similarities. The method itself automatically identifies these relationships based on how words are used in context, so you as a researcher don't need to code these relationships. This method reveals deeper, hidden patterns in the text, providing insights that a straightforward keyword search would likely miss. It allows researchers to conduct more nuanced and comprehensive analyses of textual data.

- **Macro-search: analyzing large datasets.** Traditional search methods can become cumbersome and inefficient when dealing with vast amounts of text, such as thousands of articles or books. Embeddings enable a more holistic exploration of such datasets. Consider a study on public sentiment towards a social movement over several decades. By examining how the embeddings of words like "equality" evolve over time within these texts, researchers can track changes in public opinion and the contextual use of certain terms. For example, tracking how closely the embeddings of "equality" and "justice" become over time might indicate a merging of these concepts in public discourse. The understanding here is very distinct to the micro-search process, largely based on term contextual usage. With macro-search we are dealing with an intellectual capability that is largely beyond current model capabilities but that will exist in the near future, as we need very large context memory to identify how concepts are changing and adapting over a long time period.

Embeddings can refine data retrieval processes by enabling more flexible and comprehensive searches that account for the evolution of language and implicit meanings. For developers and data scientists, incorporating embeddings into search tools can significantly enhance the capability of analytical software, providing richer insights and more accurate predictions based on textual analysis.

While embeddings open doors to a deeper analysis of text, they don't replace prompting and fine-tuning. Instead, they work together to create a more powerful toolkit. Prompting helps leverage the insights gained from embedding analysis to craft even more effective prompts for your model. Embeddings and prompting/fine-tuning indeed serve complementary roles in the analysis and generation of text.

Embeddings are mathematical representations of words or phrases in high-dimensional space, capturing semantic relationships based on their usage in large text corpora. These embeddings can reveal patterns, trends, and clusters in data that aren't immediately obvious, providing valuable insights into underlying themes or concepts. **Prompting** involves formulating queries or commands to guide a language model in generating text or performing specific tasks. It's a way to direct the model's attention and leverage its capabilities based on the insights gleaned from embeddings or other analysis. **Fine-tuning**

further customizes a model to a specific dataset or task by continuing the training process on new data. This can adapt a general-purpose model to perform well on tasks that require understanding of niche topics or specific styles. Together, these techniques allow for a more nuanced and effective use of language models:

- **Embeddings** provide a deep, unsupervised understanding of the data.
- **Prompting** uses this understanding to ask the right questions or set tasks that are informed by the data's intrinsic properties.
- **Fine-tuning** adjusts the model's responses to better align with specific expectations or content nuances.

For example, if embeddings identify a cluster of terms around "environmental anxiety," you can create prompts that specifically ask the model to discuss related sub-topics, like the impact of climate change on mental health, thus yielding more relevant and insightful analyses. This methodological synergy enhances both the depth and breadth of text analysis, making it a powerful toolkit for researchers and practitioners in the field of NLP.

7.4   WHERE NEXT FOR AI-DRIVEN RESEARCH?

In this chapter, we have outlined how to consider GenAI from a research perspective. GenAI is best viewed as a continuation of how we have traditionally integrated tools in the research process. However, we should also prepare for the imminent arrival of GenAI capable of much higher-level tasks and collaboration than older research tools.

Workers who work with GenAI are consistently better than workers who work without GenAI (Mollick, 2024), and there is no reason to assume this will be any different for researchers. Some initial benefits of the technology include better identification of research ideas from prior literature and better research assistance. However many of the critical benefits will rely on higher-level GPT models than currently exist (in mid-2024). These higher-level models will unlock a sense of true collaboration with the AI: help with designing and implementing testing; help with data organization; and facilitate much better teasing out of research ideas and the best way of approaching investigations.

A likely victim of the eventual success of GenAI is research assistants. These roles will probably become less and less rewarding to senior researchers to incorporate in research projects. This, in turn, creates an existential doubt as to how new researchers will get the training they need to develop their own path to becoming senior researchers. We will need to spend some time, as a research community, working this out.

The rise of decent AI collaborators at a low cost will probably most benefit emerging country researchers, who traditionally haven't had access to strong research guidance and assistance due to cost issues. We should see a greater leveling of expertise across countries as research guidance and assistance all rise to a new higher standardized level (see also van Gestel, Chapter 10 in this volume). That won't be without its challenges, not least in ensuring access to journals primarily run by developed country editors, but will eventually allow a greater spectrum of ideas to enter the marketplace of research.

We have left the ethical perspective on the rise of GenAI in research uncovered. This feels like a topic that is much broader than just research (for the ethical perspective, see van Gestel, Chapter 10 in this volume; Protopapa and Idris, Chapter 11 in this volume). Namely, if GenAI is viewed as generally acceptable in the workplace, then there are minimal logical reasons why it shouldn't be a part of a research workplace. As outlined in this chapter, the tools are also just continuations of the existing researcher toolkit and in line with the general trend over time of greater technological involvement in the research process.

The key now – for you – is experimentation. Access the highest-level AI intelligence you can afford and start playing with it. There is so much yet to be discovered about how to get the best responses from GenAI, but part of the fun of the journey will be working that out.

NOTE

1.   https://platform.openai.com/docs/guides/fine-tuning.

REFERENCES

Ardekani, A. M., Bertz, J., Bryce, C., Dowling, M., & Long, S. C. (2024). FinSentGPT: A universal financial sentiment engine? *International Review of Financial Analysis*, 103291.

Aziz, S., Dowling, M., Hammami, H., & Piepenbrink, A. (2021). Machine learning in finance: A topic modeling approach. *European Financial Management*, *28*(3), 744–770.

Borger, J. G., Ng, A. P., Anderton, H., ... & Naik, S. H. (2023). Artificial intelligence takes center stage: Exploring the capabilities and implications of ChatGPT and other AI-assisted technologies in scientific research and education. *Immunology & Cell Biology*, *101*(10), 923–935.

Dwivedi, Y. K., Kshetri, N., Hughes, L., ... & Wright, R. (2023). Opinion Paper: "So what if ChatGPT wrote it?" Multidisciplinary perspectives on opportunities, challenges and implications of generative conversational AI for research, practice and policy. *International Journal of Information Management*, *71*, 102642.

Feuerriegel, S., Hartmann, J., Janiesch, C., & Zschech, P. (2023). Generative AI. *Business & Information Systems Engineering*, *66*(1), 111–126.

Fisher, B. S., Cobane, C. T., Vander Ven, T. M., & Cullen, F. T. (1998). How many authors does it take to publish an article? Trends and patterns in political science. *PS: Political Science & Politics, 31*(4), 847–856.

Henn, M., Weinstein, M., & Foard, N. (2005). *A Short Introduction to Social Research.* London: Sage.

Ivcevic, Z., & Grandinetti, M. (2024). Artificial intelligence as a tool for creativity. *Journal of Creativity,* 34(2), 100079.

Jones, B. F. (2021). The rise of research teams: Benefits and costs in economics. *Journal of Economic Perspectives, 35*(2), 191–216.

Kalyan, K. S. (2024). A survey of GPT-3 family large language models including ChatGPT and GPT-4. *Natural Language Processing Journal, 6,* 100048.

Kankanhalli, A. (2024). Peer review in the age of generative AI. *Journal of the Association for Information Systems, 25*(1), 76–84.

Liu, M., Ene, T.-D., Kirby, R., ... & Ren, H. (2023, October 31). ChipNeMo: Domain-Adapted LLMs for chip design. *arXiv.Org.* https:// arxiv .org/ abs/ 2311 .00176

Mollick, E. (2024). *Co-intelligence: Living and Working with AI.* New York: Penguin.

Neumann, M., Rauschenberger, M., & Schön, E.-M. (2023). "We need to talk about ChatGPT": The future of AI and higher education. *2023 IEEE/ACM 5th International Workshop on Software Engineering Education for the Next Generation (SEENG).*

Pan, S., Luo, L., Wang, Y., Chen, C., Wang, J., & Wu, X. (2024). Unifying large language models and knowledge graphs: A roadmap. *IEEE Transactions on Knowledge and Data Engineering,* 1–20.

Papakonstantinidis, S., Kwiatek, P., & Spathopoulou, F. (2024). Embrace or resist? Drivers of artificial intelligence writing software adoption in academic and non-academic contexts. *Contemporary Educational Technology, 16*(2), ep495.

Rein, D., Hou, B. L., Stickland, A. C., Petty, J., Pang, R. Y., Dirani, J., Michael, J., & Bowman, S. R. (2023, November 20). GPQA: A graduate-level google-proof Q&A benchmark. *arXiv.Org.* https://arxiv.org/abs/2311.12022

Short, C. E., & Short, J. C. (2023). The artificially intelligent entrepreneur: ChatGPT, prompt engineering, and entrepreneurial rhetoric creation. *Journal of Business Venturing Insights, 19,* e00388.

Yu, Z., He, L., Wu, Z., Dai, X., & Chen, J. (2023, October 8). Towards better chain-of-thought prompting strategies: A survey. *arXiv.Org.* https://arxiv.org/abs/2310.04959

PART III

The bad

8. Generative AI as a disrupter of creativity

Abdullah H. Clark and Kathleen Denman

Creativity is an outcome of the learning process. This is based on well-established learning theories supporting the creation of new knowledge. The use of, or rather the impending reliance on, generative artificial intelligence (AI) deprives users of active learning and, thus, creativity sources that are consistent with learning theory. This shift ultimately has a negative impact on the existing paradigm of education (Marsick et al., 1992; Yorks et al., 1999). The evolution of scholarship on learning and creativity is identifiable when examining the different learning theories and considering the active or action learning process. There are five key learning theories for human development, creativity, and knowledge production. These theories are cognitivism, social cognitivism, behaviorism, humanism, and constructivism. Each theory and the associated scholarship explain how people learn, and the common process of human interactions suggests the negative effects of generative AI. The use of generative AI outsources human interaction and other learning stages for creative thinking, experimentation, and self-expression. This new human and AI paradigm will likely outstrip the need (or desire) for learning activities previously observed during the last century of learning theory research. This chapter will take a deep dive into the learning theory canon, including action learning research, and provide an example outcome of the human–AI paradigm to suggest caution for students and interest for researchers.

8.1 ON CREATIVITY

Approaching the subject of human creativity should begin with acknowledging that scholars do not agree on a single definition of it (Pope, 2005; Sawyer, 2006). This fractured foundation does not undercut the examination of creativity or human efforts for creative thinking, but it does make this discussion difficult. Pope (2005) explained creativity from a theoretical, historical, and practical viewpoint and offered a few preliminary definitions. Pope viewed creativity as the ability or capacity to make something new or fresh with respect to ourselves and others (Pope, 2005). For Pope the words "capacity," "make," and "fresh" are key to the lexicon of discussion on creativity (Pope, 2005, p. 53). *Capacity* suggests potentiality, while *make* refers to realization or becoming, suggesting a process-based view of creativity (Pope, 2005). The use of *fresh* is intended to mean more than new or novel, acknowledging that the strange could be made familiar and the familiar made strange. In sum, Pope carefully curated words to describe the process of making new things, which will be used as a foundation for further discussion.

While researchers have slight variations of Pope's definition for creativity, there are other levels to approaching an understanding of creativity, which also have implications for discussing creative thinking. Sawyer (2006) offered two levels of discussion on creativity – individual and sociocultural. The former concerns the activity of creating something new to the world by one's own judgment. The first, individualist level, suggests a basic understanding that something is new based on an individual understanding that something is not repeated, is new in combination and is expressed in the world. In other words, it must exist through self-judgment.

The second level of understanding creativity concerns collaborative cognition in the sociocultural setting. This approach appeals to the social group for judgment of novelty and usefulness for valuation (Sawyer, 2006). This level of creativity occurs when a socially viable product is produced, which limits this judgment to solutions for the few challenging problems meeting this criterion. Sawyer (2006) refers to this as "Big C" creativity, and it is limited to the few based on the social consensus barrier to entry.

What does all this mean? Understanding creativity provides a pathway for understanding how the use of generative AI affects human perceptions of creativity at the individual and collective level. One's ability to recognize novelty becomes relative to one's interactions with society and subsequent further understanding of how the group will determine utility and valuation. Because these things are interconnected, individuals are likely to move between personal spaces used for creativity and groups for validation. This is where understanding learning theory and action learning become key components of the individual process of creativity and collective judgment therein.

8.2   LEARNING THEORY

Creativity and creative thinking depend on the learning process, which draws on multiple theories, including cognitivist, socio-cognitivist, behaviorist, humanist, and constructivist (see Table 8.1). Behaviorist scholars have centered their research on learning through understanding how humans acquire knowledge through controlling their environment (Thorndike et al., 1928; Skinner, 1974). There are three underlying assumptions in their research. First, a change in behavior indicates learning. Second, learning is based on the

Table 8.1   *Learning theory research*

Learning Theory	Scholars
Behaviorist	Thorndike, Bregman, Tilton, & Woodyard, 1928; Skinner, 1974
Cognitivist	Piaget, 1966; Ausubel, 1967; Grippin & Peters, 1984; Anderson, 1996; Di Vesta, 1987; Ormrod, 1995
Social-cognitivist	Bandura, 1976; Lefrancois, 1999; Schunk, 1996
Humanist	Rogers, 1983; Maslow, 1970; Sahakian, 1984
Constructivist	Vygotsky, 1978; Driver et al., 1994; Phillips, 1995

elements of the environment. Third, repetition and re-enforcement of learning behaviors are key (Merriam and Caffarella, 1999).

Cognitivist scholars have shown that learning requires experiences or sense-making of the learner's environment (Piaget, 1966; Ausubel, 1967; Grippin & Peters, 1984; Anderson 1996; Di Vesta, 1987; Ormrod, 1995). Thus, learning, acquisition of knowledge, and subsequent knowledge production follow individual attribution of meaning (see also Koris and Pulk, Chapter 1 in this volume). Social cognitivist scholars take the position that learning combines elements from both behaviorist and cognitivist orientations with the idea that people learn from observing others in social settings (Bandura, 1976; Lefrancois, 1999; Schunk, 1996; Hergenhahn & Olson, 2005). Learning through observation occurs with the help of four processes of attention, retention or memory, behavioral rehearsal, and motivation (Hergenhahn & Olson, 2005).

Constructivist scholars have shown that learning requires experiences or sense-making of the learner's environment (Vygotsky, 1978; Driver et al., 1994; Phillips, 1995). Thus, learning, knowledge acquisition, and subsequent knowledge production follow individual attribution of meaning. Humanist scholars subscribe to the idea that development relies on self-actualization and being capable of determining one's own learning (Rogers, 1983; Maslow, 1970; Sahakian, 1984). This idea also supports the concept of self-directed learning. Social learning theorists have determined that learning occurs through social interaction and imitation. Thus, these researchers support the need for human interaction as part of the learning and knowledge production process. The key point here is that researchers in this field believe learners must change themselves and their environments, which implies connection to the creative thinking outcomes. Consequently, the use of AI deprives the natural process of the sense-making and awareness that conscious humans contribute to learning and creative thought or the understanding of the uniqueness of one's ideas.

8.3   ACTION-REFLECTION LEARNING

An example of the old paradigm is helpful for understanding the difference AI is making in the creative process. Given that multiple learning theories describe interaction with the environment, research on learning among humans and in groups provides a foundation for understanding how creativity happens. One such theory is Action-Reflection Learning or ARL, which can occur in an individual or group setting. Marsick et al. (1992) developed this theory to explain alternative activities in organizations needing innovative and creative solutions. The components of ARL include thinking critically, working in small groups, solving problems, building the required skills based on the challenge at hand, and understanding how to empower others. Although ARL centers on interaction, it requires significant self-reflection and personal ideation of challenges. Most importantly, ARL theory explains how individuals and groups can prevent reliance on experts or outsourcing thinking, but the emerging use of AI changes this process. Research on creativity further illustrates the dynamics of this shifting paradigm.

8.4   HUMAN COLLABORATION WITH GENERATIVE AI

We turn now to research on the interactions between humans and computers to link learning and creativity theories to the desire to establish automation for creation. Boden (1998) offered that artificial intelligence depends on human creativity for development, which only occurs outside computing through real-world experiences. However, Boden suggested that creativity can derive from computer models (or computing in general) with considerable expertise. Today, companies such as Open AI, Microsoft, Google, and others have made computation for laymen simple through the user prompt system or advanced query user interface. Boden's description of a barrier to computational entry has been eliminated with an ever-expanding pool of users, which includes students in higher education. Consequently, researchers are considering how these changes impact the higher education process, where students are asked to demonstrate creativity as part of their studies at the university level, but now they have the option to outsource this activity to AI.

Ahmad and colleagues (2020) analyzed the educational applications of AI to understand its future scope and market opportunities given the sustained importance of education in society and an individual's development. Their research explored multiple perspectives, exploring the use of AI by students, teachers, and administrators from 2014 to 2019 and analyzing research on use cases such as grading and evaluations, students' retention and dropout prediction, sentiment, intelligent tutoring, classroom monitoring, and recommendation systems.

However, the trending predictions concerning student creativity, experimentation, and self-expression are most relevant for this chapter. A paradoxical point raised by Ahmad et al. (2020) is that research on effective AI instructor applications for evaluating student creativity and imagination skills also suggested that student use of AI for creative activities led to detrimental dependence. This is possible because some applications for evaluating creative thought have developed the same capability for student use. Moreover, consistent use of AI in education has concerning effects, as revealed in research on addiction to technology, such as phones and tablets. However, instead of using technology to connect virtually, learners using AI have more limited interactions with peers and instructors (Ahmad et al., 2020).

Olga et al.'s (2023) research on the implications of AI in education helps infer how the application has altered learner performance in educational settings since the introduction of maturely trained large language models (LLMs). Currently, Open AI's Generative Pre-trained Transformer (GPT) can produce a well-written five-paragraph essay on any topic just as good (or better) than any student (Olga et al., 2023). However, instead of considering the use of AI by students in educational settings, Olga et al. (2023) focused on instructors' usage for learner feedback. After conducting empirical research on 62 higher education students at the University of Illinois Urbana-Champaign, the participants concluded that AI reviews were deemed adequate based on speed, efficiency, and consistency when compared to the variability of quality comments from their peers judging the same written work. This result means that LLMs are now judging their own work, which highlights the future of AI in higher education. That is, when students are using AI for creativity, AI applications are both creating and evaluating knowledge. Consequently, this new paradigm will and should cause both learning facilitators and students to question the reality of outcomes and their faculties in the knowledge-production process.

8.5 SUB-OPTIMAL OUTCOMES WITH GENERATIVE AI

Finally, the chapter will discuss examples of the process of knowledge production, both individually and in groups, to demonstrate potentially negative outcomes of generative AI on human creativity. According to Habib et al. (2024), in the *Journal of Creativity*, the creative process combines divergent thinking with convergent thinking: Creative thinkers generate multiple ideas and then select the best ones from creative brainstorming.

Undergraduate students at a major university in the Southeastern region of the United States were interviewed on the topic of how ChatGPT had influenced their creative brainstorming process on the problem-solving topic of thinking of novel ways to use a paperclip. One student reflected that "with the help of AI, brainstorming processes will be quicker and more creative, however, this is kind of the computer literally [doing] everything for you. I would not want to use AI on its own" (Habib et al., 2024, p. 4). Another student reflected, "It was both easier and harder to come up with ideas when assisted by the AI. It was easier to use the things listed by the AI, however it then felt more difficult to brainstorm other uses beyond those created or taken by the AI" (Habib et al., 2024, p. 4).

While some students appreciated how quickly and thoroughly the AI generated a list of possible uses of a paperclip, others noted that the computer just "literally does everything for you" (Habib et al., 2024, p. 4). One student summed up the feeling of the group that "It felt as though the bot was giving me an easy way out and not allowing me to think on my own as much" (Habib et al., 2024, p. 4). Students who valued the efficiency of AI were pleased with the results of the generated outcomes, and some were genuinely pleased with the creative experience they shared with AI. However, students who valued the independent creative aspects of the project felt as if they had missed out on the intended experience. They felt that they had "outsourced" (Habib et al., 2024, p. 4) their thinking to a bot and robbed themselves of the creative experience.

Some professors similarly worry that students will "outsource their thinking" (McMurtie & Supiano, 2023) and want to ensure that students are doing their own work, both to safeguard ethical practices and to protect the creative process for students. Some professors have limited or eliminated take-home exams. Instead, they hold proctored exams in class (McMurtie & Supiano, 2023). Many professors who assign essays have altered the assignments so that students intentionally allow AI to generate the essay, and then the students critique the AI-generated essay. While that is a good exercise in critical thinking, information literacy, and editing, it is not a creative exercise. Writing requires creation; editing does not. To protect the creativity of the writing process, professors who are concerned about AI undermining that process have their students do more "in-class work, which also helps [the professors] understand their students' writing styles and capabilities" (McMurtie & Supiano, 2023). That motivation is also mixed with the desire to be able to compare what can be positively identified as original student work with later submissions suspected to be generated by AI.

8.5.1   Creative Confidence

Students in Habib's (2024) study also commented on generative AI's effect on their confidence as creative thinkers. Here again, there were various responses, some quite positive, but others not. While some students were dazzled by the wide range of uses of paperclips that AI generated and felt that it "broadened (their) scope of what was possible" (Habib et al., 2024, p. 4), others did not share that appreciation. One student replied, "AI came up with these ideas so easily, and I felt bad that I didn't come up with more ideas myself" (Habib et al., 2024, p. 4). Another respondent agreed, saying, "I [...] found that after reading through the generated responses, I struggled to come up with additional uses. I think [...] the bot could be detrimental if a person used only these ideas" (Habib et al., 2024, p. 4). For some users, using "the bot" to brainstorm can limit the users' ability to be creative rather than expand the possible ideas they can generate.

8.5.2   Original Thinking

When considering AI-generated ideas on novel uses of a paperclip from the frame of originality, students in Habib's (2024) study clearly stated that the findings were not original. One student noted that if they used "direct results from GPT3 for brainstorming, [it] is really someone else's work" (Habib et al., 2024, p. 5). Researchers also noted that even though different students used the AI to generate ideas using different prompts (ostensibly all related to the prompt given by the researchers), the AI "pulled the same answers from the data source, so individual search results can be generic and result in similarities in student work" (Habib et al., 2024, p. 5). Generative AI such as GPT is heralded by some as being able to generate novel ideas based on its enormous data set from which it can draw, that it can combine data sets to generate what appears to be newly created content. But as one astute student concluded, "Personally, I think I would've rather done the three minutes of brainstorming on my own and then I never use ideas directly from GPT3 because its entire model is based in things people have said before" (Habib et al., 2024, p. 5). Generative AI does not create. It collects, stores, and then generates ideas in predictable language patterns: ideas that have already been created.

8.5.3   Group Work

Now that we have considered the potentially negative effects of using generative AI on individual creative idea generation, what might the effects be on group interaction during the creative process? Very little research can be found on this topic as it is so novel. However, Dwivedi et al.'s (2023) compilation of short papers, "Opinion paper: 'So what if ChatGPT wrote it?'" includes authors who have considered the pros and cons of using AI in group work. One contributor related that a student of his taking an executive master's in business degree program found that teaming with ChatGPT "felt as if [he was] interacting with a team member via a chat function [...] Could this type of interaction replace group work?" (Richter in Dwivedi et al., 2023, p. 8). Richter also suggested that AI could function as part of a hybrid team insofar as it can "assist with rather simple roles" such as "text producer, language editor, and research assistant" (Richter in Dwivedi et al., 2023, p. 8). Because of the dearth of written first-person experience using generative AI in group work, one must surmise that student reviews would be similarly diverse as the individual undergraduates' experiences in developing novel ways to use a paperclip (Habib et al., 2024). Some groups would appreciate the efficiency and breadth of ideas generated by the AI and consider it a time-saver in terms of the creative process. Other groups would likely find that outsourcing their thinking to a bot robs them of their creative learning process.

8.5.4   Creativity of an Artist

Moving on from research studying undergraduates' creative process and AI's influence on it, an example from a musician, a truly creative mind, may help illustrate the negative comparison of generative AI to original human thought, in this case in songwriting. Nick Cave, Australian singer-songwriter and front-man of the band Nick Cave and the Bad Seeds, responded to a fan who sent him ChatGPT-generated song lyrics written, according to the fan's prompt, in the style of Nick Cave. Cave's response: "This song sucks" (Cain, 2023). Cave went on, "Writing a good song is not mimicry, or replication, or pastiche, it is the opposite. It is an act of self-murder that destroys all one has strived to produce in the past" (Cain, 2023). Cave further described the creative process in his songwriting:

> [It] is part of the authentic creative struggle that precedes the invention of a unique lyric of actual value; it is the breathless confrontation with one's vulnerability, one's perilousness, one's smallness, pitted against a sense of sudden, shocking discovery; it is the redemptive artistic act that stirs in the heart of the listener, where the listener recognized the inner workings of the song in their own blood, their own struggle, their own suffering. (Cain, 2023)

Cave describes what it is like for the human mind, an artistic mind, to create something entirely new. ChatGPT does not do that. ChatGPT predicts the next most likely word from a bank of words based on algorithm; it never creates a new idea. Its databases are large, so its output may appear novel, but it does not create in the way a human mind creates.

8.5.5   What Google's Gemini has to Say

The dearth of research about AI's impact on creativity in group work led the authors to consult Google's AI, Gemini. Box 8.1 illustrates how AI can help students with a creative group project.

BOX 8.1   AI ASSISTANT IN GROUP DESIGN PROJECT

Four undergraduate students are tasked with designing a mobile app for sustainable living within a design thinking course. They are given access to an AI assistant named 'Brainstorm' that can generate ideas, analyze data, and provide feedback on designs.

Phase 1: Ideation (with Brainstorm)

The group initially relies heavily on Brainstorm. They feed it keywords like 'sustainability,' 'mobile app,' and 'user needs,' generating dozens of concept ideas. While some are interesting, many feel generic and lack a unique spark. The students find themselves struggling to connect with and refine these AI-generated ideas.

Phase 2: Human Inspiration (without Brainstorm)

Frustrated, the group decides to temporarily shelve Brainstorm and focus on individual brainstorming. They spend time researching user behavior, conducting interviews, and sketching their own ideas. During a heated discussion, one student mentions their passion for community gardens and the challenges they face. This sparks a lively conversation, leading to an innovative app concept that connects urban gardeners with resources and each other.

Phase 3: Refining with AI Assistance (Brainstorm Returns)

The students return to Brainstorm, but this time with a clear direction and specific questions. They use Brainstorm to analyze user feedback on their app prototype, identify potential technical challenges, and suggest design improvements. The AI's data-driven insights help them refine their concept and ensure it's technically feasible.

Outcome: The students present their app concept, impressing the professors with its originality, user-centricity, and technical soundness. They acknowledge Brainstorm's initial help with ideation but emphasize the crucial role of their own creativity, empathy, and collaborative problem-solving in developing the winning concept.

Key Takeaways:

AI can generate ideas, but it lacks human empathy, understanding of context, and ability to build on existing knowledge.
The best results come from a collaborative approach where AI assists human creativity, not replaces it.
Human strengths like critical thinking, emotional intelligence, and social interaction are irreplaceable in creative processes.

Additional Thoughts:

This case study can be adapted to different settings, such as businesses or creative teams.
The specific capabilities of the AI assistant can be adjusted to reflect current or future advancements in generative AI.
Discussing the ethical implications of AI in creative processes can be a valuable extension to this case study.
I hope this case study demonstrates the key points effectively!

Source: Gemini (formerly called Bard) output, January 15, 2024.

As Gemini concludes, generative AI cannot replace human creativity. Different users will appreciate different levels of interaction with generative AI, depending on their comfort with the technology, the nature of the project they are conducting, and their own confidence in their creativity. People are not going to ignore the capabilities of generative AI; therefore, the authors of this chapter conclude with a reminder that users should not depend on AI for creative output. It can be a useful tool as part of the process, but it shouldn't be relied upon to replace human creativity.

8.6   CONCLUSION

This chapter has presented the case for negative ("the bad") aspects of generative AI, intending to provide a sober assessment of generative AI in the context of proliferating LLMs, growing financial investment, and public interest. In the field of higher education, faculty, staff, and students all want to know how technology will affect their experience, and, ultimately, how it will shift the knowledge production process. However, as outlined above, understanding what the future holds for the integration of generative AI begins with understanding the process of creativity, experimentation, and self-expression. Learning theorists differ epistemologically on the individual learning process but agree on the need to interact with the environment as part of knowledge production. Action-Reflection Learning offers a theoretical framework for understanding pre-generative AI or the old paradigm for creativity.

Linking learning theories, Action-Reflection Learning, and the outcomes of AI usage, there are clear indications of a shifting paradigm of the process for creativity. Multiple learning theories indicate some level of human interaction for the learning process, suggesting an impetus for creative thought. Behaviorist, cognitivist, social cognitivist, humanist, and constructivist scholars understood learning and thus creativity occurring following the control, making sense of, or observing the environment. Moreover, ARL demonstrates this process through a theory of creativity in the group setting. Use of generative AI reverses this process with the output of LLMs telling humans what creativity is and is not, and thus outsourcing the cognitive process. Users should be wary of this deference, and scholars should consider its implications for future research.

REFERENCES

Ahmad, K., Qadir, J., Al-Fuqaha, A., Iqbal, W., El-Hassan, A., Benhaddou, D., & Ayyash, M. (2020). Data-driven artificial intelligence in education: a comprehensive review. https://doi.org/10.35542/osf.io/zvu2n

Anderson, J. R. (1996). ACT: A simple theory of complex cognition. *American Psychologist*, 51(4), 355.

Ausubel, D. P. (1967). Learning theory and classroom practice. *Ontario Institute for Studies in Education Bulletin*.

Bandura, A. (1976). Modeling theory. In W. S. Sahakian (Ed.), *Learning: Systems, Models, and Theories* (2nd Edition, pp. 391–409). Skokie, IL: Rand McNally.

Boden, M. A. (1998). Creativity and artificial intelligence. *Artificial Intelligence*, 103(1–2), 347–356.

Cain, S. (2023). "This song sucks": Nick Cave responds to ChatGPT song written in style of Nick Cave. *The Guardian*, January 17. https://www.theguardian.com/music/2023/jan/17/this-song-sucks-nick-cave-responds-to-chatgpt-song-written-in-style-of-nick-cave

Di Vesta, F. J. (1987). The cognitive movement and education. In J. A. Glover & R. R. Ronning (Eds.), *Historical Foundations of Educational Psychology* (pp. 203–233). Boston, MA: Springer US.

Driver, R., Asoko, H., Leach, J., Mortimer, E., & Scott, P. (1994). Constructing scientific knowledge in the classroom. *Educational Researcher*, 23(7), 5–12.

Dwivedi, Y. K., Kshetri, N., Hughes, L., Slade, E. L., Jeyaraj, A., Kar, A. K., Baabdullah, A. M. et al. (2023). Opinion paper: "So what if ChatGPT wrote it?" Multidisciplinary perspectives on opportunities, challenges and implications of generative conversational AI for research, practice and policy. *International Journal of Information Management*, 71 (August 1), 102642. https:// doi .org/ 10 .1016/ j .ijinfomgt.2023.102642

Grippin, P. & Peters, S. (1984). *Learning Theory and Learning Outcomes: The Connection*. Lanham, MD: University Press of America.

Habib, S., Vogel, T., Thorne, E., & Xiao, A. (2024). How does generative artificial intelligence impact student creativity? *Journal of Creativity*, 34(1). https://doi.org/ 10.1016/j.yjoc.2023.100072

Hergenhahn, B. R. & Olson, M. H. (2005). *An Introduction to Theories of Learning* (7th Edition). Englewood Cliffs, NJ: Prentice Hall.

Lefrancois, G. R. (1999). *The Lifespan* (6th Edition). Belmont, CA: Wadsworth.

Marsick, V. J., Cederholm, L., Turner, E., & Pearson, T. (1992). Action-reflection learning. *Training & Development*, 46(8), 63–67.

Maslow, A. H. (1970). *Motivation and Personality* (2nd Edition). New York: HarperCollins.

McMurtrie, B. & Supiano, B. (2023). ChatGPT has changed teaching. Our readers tell us how. *The Chronicle of Higher Education*, December 11. https://www.chronicle .com/ article/ chatgpt -has -changed -teaching -our -readers -told -us -how ?utm_source = Iterable & utm_medium = email & utm_campaign = campaign_8563000 _nl _Daily -Briefing_date_20231218&cid=db&source=ams&sourceid=

Merriam, S. B. & Caffarella, R. S. (1999). *Learning in Adulthood: A Comprehensive Guide* (2nd Edition). San Francisco: Jossey-Bass.

Olga, A., Saini, A., Zapata, G., Searsmith, D., Cope, B., Kalantzis, M., & Kastani, N. P. (2023). Generative AI: Implications and applications for education. arXiv preprint arXiv:2305.07605.

Ormrod, J. E. (1995). *Human Learning* (2nd Edition). Englewood Cliffs, NJ: Merrill.

Phillips, D. C. (1995). The good, the bad, and the ugly: The many faces of constructivism. *Educational Researcher*, 24(7), 5–12.

Piaget, J. (1966). The psychology of intelligence and education. *Childhood Education*, 42(9), 528.

Pope, R. (2005). *Creativity: Theory, History, Practice*. London and New York: Routledge.

Rogers, C. R. (1983). *Freedom to Learn for the 80s*. Columbus, OH: Merrill.

Sahakian, W. S. (1984). *Introduction to the Psychology of Learning* (2nd Edition). Itasca, IL: Peacock.

Sawyer, R. Keith (2006). *Explaining Creativity: The Science of Human Innovation*. Oxford: Oxford University Press.

Schunk, D. H. (1996). Learning theories: An educational perspective. Englewood Cliffs, NJ: Prentice Hall.

Skinner, B. F. (1974). *About Behaviorism*. New York. Alfred A. Knopf.

Thorndike, E. L., Bregman, E. O., Tilton, J. W., & Woodyard, E. (1928). *Adult Learning*. New York: Macmillan.

Vygotsky, L. S. (1978). *Mind in Society: The Development of Higher Psychological Processes*. Cambridge, MA: Harvard University Press.

Yorks, L., O'Neil, J., & Marsick, V. J. (1999). Action learning theoretical bases and varieties of practice. *Advances in Developing Human Resources*, 1(2), 1–18.

9. Assessment renaissance: authentic design in the era of generative AI

Peter Matheis and Jacob-John Jubin

9.1 INTRODUCTION

Generative Artificial Intelligence (GenAI), exemplified by models like ChatGPT, has brought transformative possibilities to higher education (HE), aiding students in academic tasks and posing challenges related to academic integrity and assessment methods. Assessments in HE play a pivotal role in gauging student knowledge and abilities, with a growing recognition of the need to adapt to real-world skills and problem-solving capabilities where AI technologies offer promise (Kung et al., 2023). While GenAI can aid students in brainstorming, researching, analysing, and writing, potentially enhancing their academic experience, it also poses risks. These include academic dishonesty, inherent biases, the propagation of incorrect information, and poorly designed assessments, which can hinder the cultivation of essential graduate skills and lead to ineffective learning (Cotton et al., 2023; Limna et al., 2023; Rasul et al., 2023). Consequently, educators and students must approach this technology cautiously, ensuring its use is ethical, dependable, and effective for academic pursuits (Smolansky et al., 2023).

Assessments focus on determining educational programmes' effectiveness and are critical in enhancing teacher and student motivation (Kaufman et al., 2005). However, Mislevy et al. (2012) critique traditional assessments, which rely on predetermined items to assess students' skills. They point out that judgements of the student's assessment are often based on limited data and may not adequately reflect student learning as this paradigm includes familiar assessment techniques like multiple-choice, essays, and short answers; this is also echoed in a more recent study by Swiecki et al. (2022) highlighting the issue of traditional assessments in the age of AI.

Swiecki et al. (2022) identified a critical issue with traditional assessments needing more authenticity. Unlike the isolated, tool-free writing required in standardised tests, real-world writing involves research and collaboration. Shaffer and Kaput (1998) suggest that education and assessment should evolve to focus on skills relevant to the workplace, emphasising problem understanding and application rather than the processes themselves. The integration of AI into educational assessments is emerging in the literature, highlighting its potential to enhance the design and evaluation stages of both conventional and alternative assessment processes (Swiecki et al., 2022). Authentic assessments,[1] grounded in principles of realism, cognitive challenge, and evaluative judgement (Villarroel et al., 2018), develop higher-order critical thinking, problem-solving, and creativity in students, thereby addressing the academic misconduct concerns explained earlier (Bosco & Ferns, 2014; Tai et al., 2018). GenAI tools like ChatGPT demonstrate limitations in higher-order cognitive tasks. However, they excel in lower-order cognitive skills, possibly allowing students to attain high marks with minimal effort due to AI completing tasks. This underscores the need for a proactive reassessment of evaluations to emphasise higher-level competencies (Thanh et al., 2023; Halaweh, 2023).

This chapter focuses on GenAI's "bad" aspects, specifically examining its challenges within higher education. It underscores major issues, including academic dishonesty, inherent biases, and the potential erosion of deep learning, collectively indicating a detrimental effect on academic integrity (see also Protopapa and Idris, Chapter 11 in this volume). Additionally, the chapter proposes the AI-Resistant Assessment Design Framework as a contribution to reframing HE assessment design for authenticity. The framework offers a comprehensive strategy to counter the potential misuse (the "bad") of GenAI in academic assessments by diversifying assessment formats, evaluating both the learning process and outcomes and emphasising higher-order cognitive skills. A critical element of the study is that it emphasises the development of authentic assessment designs that reduce the reliance on GenAI for completing assessments, and it does not propose methods for incorporating GenAI into creating assessments and assessment strategies. Instead, it advocates for strategic changes in assessment methods to discourage the misuse of AI technologies while focusing on enhancing genuine student engagement and evaluation.

9.2   LITERATURE REVIEW

As GenAI technologies increasingly permeate HE, they present the paradox of empowering educational advancement while raising significant academic conduct concerns. This combined perspective necessitates a holistic approach to harness GenAI's potential for enhancing learning and research while meticulously addressing academic integrity challenges and the authenticity of the educational experience. This section focuses on current literature on the use of GenAI in HE and the negative impacts of AI on academic assessments.

9.2.1   Integrating GenAI in Education: Balancing Innovation with Integrity

Peer-reviewed research on GenAI's value in HE is rising; for example, Atlas (2023) highlights its capacity to enhance writing by generating texts, summarising information, and improving content quality, including grammar and style error detection. Nonetheless, concerns arise with the use of ChatGPT in education. Chatterjee and Dethlefs (2023) and Khalil and Er (2023) delve into issues regarding plagiarism detection and distinguishing fact from fiction in ChatGPT-generated content (see also Kerem, Chapter 6 in this volume). Atlas (2023) emphasises the importance of disclosing the use of GPT-3 and proper citation to avoid plagiarism accusations. The availability of ChatGPT and similar tools are seen to compromise the originality and integrity of academic work, as they can quickly generate content for assignments. Ethical considerations are emerging, with teachers and students recognising the need to balance using AI tools for productivity with accepting such practices in future workplaces (Smolansky et al., 2023; see also Miller, Chapter 13 in this volume). Therefore, adaptations to assessment design are necessary to restore academic integrity (Smolansky et al., 2023).

Authentic assessments can be a potential panacea for these predicaments as they are grounded in three fundamental principles: *realism*, *cognitive challenge*, and *evaluative judgement* (Villarroel et al., 2018). Realism involves crafting assessments that mirror real-world challenges, prompting students to tackle problems akin to those encountered in real-life scenarios, thereby assessing knowledge, skills, and attitudes (Bosco & Ferns, 2014). The cognitive challenge principle necessitates higher-order thinking, pushing students to transform knowledge into novel forms. This approach encourages students to move beyond rote memorisation and delve into deeper comprehension, integrating new concepts with prior knowledge and applying theories to practical situations, including data analysis and evaluating theoretical arguments. The final principle, evaluative judgement, seeks to enhance students' capacity to critique their and others' work, fostering creativity in addressing intricate, non-standard tasks in novel contexts (Tai et al., 2018). However, authentic assessment might not suffice in addressing academic integrity challenges brought about by GenAI (Thanh et al., 2023). Employing Bloom's taxonomy, Thanh et al. (2023) evaluated GenAI tools such as ChatGPT-4, ChatGPT-3.5, Google Bard, and Microsoft Bing in authentic economics assessments, revealing their strong performance at lower taxonomy levels as well as weaknesses, particularly in the "create" level. This pattern suggests that GenAI tools have the potential to handle the cognitive challenges and evaluative judgements aimed at authentic assessments, particularly within the lower to middle levels of Bloom's taxonomy, which raises concerns about the possibility of students achieving high marks in assessments by simply inputting assignment questions and rubrics into these AI tools (Villarroel et al., 2018; Halaweh, 2023; Lodge et al., 2023). Even though AI is increasingly integrated into the workplace, educators must prioritise higher-level competencies in Bloom's taxonomy. Therefore, it is critical to facilitate the development of a proactive approach to redesigning assessments and academic programmes to prepare graduates effectively while accounting for changing workplaces. This study proposes a framework for refining assessments that addresses these challenges brought about by AI and associated fast-evolving technology.

9.2.2 Navigating AI in Education

The rising popularity of AI tools in education has led to concerns about their impact on students' learning, even leading to bans on specific AI platforms in some institutions (Yu, 2023). However, embracing AI technologies and teaching students to use them ethically is a pragmatic approach, preparing students for the increasingly technological world and empowering them to explore technology's advantages and limitations (Alasadi & Baiz, 2023). According to Chiu (2024), HE should be transformed to prepare students for employment in a GenAI-driven society. This transformation would involve defining new learning objectives, such as proficiency in GenAI-related learning and teaching and AI literacy, highlighting the importance of interdisciplinary approaches and hands-on learning, and including assessments centred on classroom and practical activities.

However, in its current form, using AI tools like ChatGPT for coursework raises concerns about academic integrity, especially in tasks like essay writing and computer code assignments. Smolansky et al. (2023) highlight a consensus among educators and students that GenAI significantly impacts assessments involving essays, reports, case studies, and research papers. Their study showed that assignments requiring product design or creative/artistic work are also moderately affected by GenAI. Contrarily, the least impacted assignment types are presentations and discussions, suggesting that AI's influence varies depending on the nature of the academic task. The study by Smolansky and colleagues (2023) suggests that educators perceive a higher impact of GenAI on assignments than students, pointing to a discrepancy in awareness or concern between these groups. One of the critical challenges for academics is distinguishing between students' work and responses generated by AI tools. Such practices can undermine the integrity of the assessment process, affecting the overall quality of learning and the reliability of academic evaluations (Smolansky et al., 2023; Swiecki et al., 2022). The following section details the negative impacts of AI in assessments in HE.

9.2.3 Negative Impacts of Generative AI on Academic Assessments

The critical aspects of academic integrity issues in the context of AI integration in HE include plagiarism, originality, and the development of independent thinking. Additionally, the impact of over-reliance on AI tools on intended learning outcomes, critical thinking, creativity, and graduate capabilities is examined. Furthermore, the challenges associated with fair and accurate assessment, including the difficulty in assessing student competence and issues in providing effective feedback and evaluation, are addressed.

Academic integrity issues: The introduction of ChatGPT in HE activities heightened the potential for academic misconduct (Cotton et al., 2023). ChatGPT has been identified as a **motivation for plagiarism** and a threat to academic integrity. Specifically, students can use ChatGPT's essay-writing systems to cheat on assignments, raising questions about the authenticity of student work (Cotton et al., 2023).

Quality disparity due to technological accessibility can also cause concern, wherein unequal access to technical facilities among students leads to unfair advantages and evaluation processes (Cotton et al., 2023; Limna et al., 2023). Additionally, students' use of AI can introduce bias and falsified information into information processing, posing significant challenges to the integrity and reliability of educational content (Perkins, 2023). Although AI use by students can potentially assist with research and writing tasks, its **usage conflicts with the constructivist learning theory**, which emphasises that learning is built on reflective activity and prior knowledge, as biased or incorrect AI-generated content could mislead learners (Dwivedi et al., 2023). Furthermore, the risk of **reinforcing existing misconceptions** due to insufficiently trained datasets, rather than aiding in the accurate construction of knowledge, further complicates its application in educational settings (Dwivedi et al., 2023; Rasul et al., 2023).

Impact on intended learning outcomes: While some studies suggest AI positively influences learning outcomes (Deng & Yu, 2023), Rasul et al. (2023) argue that using ChatGPT in HE challenges the assessment of student learning outcomes according to constructivist theory, which emphasises active engagement and social interaction (Schunk, 2012). The **passive assessment process** associated with using ChatGPT **lacks the social component of learning**, and not having social interactions in AI-enabled assessments can hinder students' ability to construct meaning through reflection (Rasul et al., 2023). Additionally, assessing higher-order skills like critical thinking and problem-solving becomes challenging when students heavily rely on ChatGPT, limiting their learning outcomes and making it difficult to evaluate collaborative group activities (Rasul et al., 2023).

Impact on critical thinking and creativity: Another long-term impact of AI in HE is its impact on **undervaluing earned qualifications**. Using ChatGPT for academic work could devalue qualifications as evaluators do not perceive the skills and abilities of students (Cotton et al., 2023). ChatGPT is not inherently designed to assess or develop graduate skills (Atlas, 2023). Still, its use can influence the development of critical thinking and problem-solving abilities, either negatively by encouraging superficial learning (Rasul et al., 2023) or positively as a tool of assistance (Dwivedi et al., 2023). With the growing prevalence of AI in workplaces, graduates need to be equipped with AI literacy and an understanding of its capabilities, limitations, and ethical implications. Incorporating AI literacy into graduate skill development through strategic curriculum design could enhance employability and prepare graduates for a rapidly evolving job market (Rasul et al., 2023).

Dependency on technology for learning: While ChatGPT serves as an invaluable tool for learning, overreliance can hinder the development of essential critical thinking and problem-solving skills. Students may become overly dependent on ChatGPT for answers, sacrificing their exploration and analysis (Hasanein & Sobaih, 2023). Farhi et al. (2023) further express concerns about the **potential overreliance on AI**, particularly about issues like **originality, creativity, and the fostering of independent thinking**. Their study calls for a balance with traditional learning methods to encourage independent thought. While ChatGPT can aid writing tasks, students should utilise it in moderation to avoid undermining their writing skills and cultivating original ideas (Farhi et al., 2023). Focusing on ChatGPT primarily for generating creative educational ideas can be a constructive approach, as it fosters original thinking and mitigates the risk of excessive dependence (Farhi et al., 2023).

Challenges in fair and accurate assessment: Another significant challenge for education in accurately evaluating student understanding in the context of AI-generated answers lies in distinguishing between a student's genuine knowledge and the sophisticated output produced by tools like ChatGPT (Cotton et al., 2023; Limna et al., 2023). When students submit assignments or exam responses generated or aided by AI, it obscures their grasp of the subject matter, making **it challenging for educators to assess their actual learning and comprehension**. This situation can lead to a **misalignment** between the grades awarded and the student's actual academic abilities, potentially resulting in an educational system failing to reflect or enhance student learning accurately. Furthermore, this challenge complicates the task of academic staff in providing targeted feedback or support, as the AI-generated content only reveals the areas where students may need further instruction or clarification. The difficulty in detecting AI-generated content further complicates the issue. Studies highlight challenges in identifying AI-generated content, as current plagiarism detection tools could be more effective (Khalil & Er, 2023).

Associated risks to assessment design: Using **openly available texts** in assessments risks AI misuse, leading to plagiarism and hindering critical thinking (Liu et al., 2023). Similarly, relying on **monomodal** formats like traditional essays can enable AI misuse, compromising assessment integrity (Liu et al., 2023). Assignments solely **evaluating final products** invite AI misuse, circumventing genuine learning (Yeo, 2023; Ardito, 2023). Additionally, assessments with a **single submission point** and lacking **ongoing monitoring** increase the risk of undetected AI use (Yeo, 2023). There is an elevated risk of inappropriate AI use in **monologic** assessments to fulfil requirements, where students submit work without **interaction or feedback** from assessors (Ardito, 2023). Concealing the **production process** increases the risk of AI misuse for assignments requiring **individual work** in isolation, compromising assessment validity (Ardito, 2023). Furthermore, assessments targeting **lower-order thinking** skills and evaluating **abstract knowledge** may encourage dependence on AI content (Yang et al., 2024).

Having explored GenAI's negative impacts on academic assessments, it becomes evident that addressing these issues requires implementing innovative strategies. In the next section, this study focuses on developing an AI-Resistant Assessment Design Framework, explicating several AI mitigation strategies that address these concerns and ensure the integrity and effectiveness of educational evaluations in the digital age.

9.3   AI-RESISTANT ASSESSMENT DESIGN FRAMEWORK

Educational institutions and teachers should adopt a multifaceted approach to counter the use of GenAI in academic assessments effectively. This entails identifying and utilising AI opportunities tailored to their needs, developing clear and accessible guidelines to maintain academic integrity, and continuously updating educators on AI advancements. Vigilance regarding ethical issues and biases is crucial, ensuring AI tools enhance human interaction rather than replace it. Reimagining assessment methods to integrate AI effectively, safeguarding data privacy and security, and maintaining transparent communication with students about AI applications are also vital (Gamage et al., 2023). This holistic strategy enables institutions to leverage AI's benefits while addressing its challenges in the academic sphere. However, this chapter focuses mainly on teaching staff, reimagining assessment methods to integrate AI effectively by designing AI-resistant authentic assessments and conceptualising a framework for mitigating the misuse of GenAI in assessments.

The following framework discussion addresses identified risks throughout the literature associated with assessment design by GenAI and the overarching negative impacts on academic assessments. The framework provides a holistic approach to reframing assessments in an AI-resistant design for authenticity. The conceptual model, illustrated in Figure 9.1, outlines mitigation strategies in three key domains: (1) diversified assessment formats; (2) assessing product versus process; and (3) forms of knowledge as explicated in the following subsections.

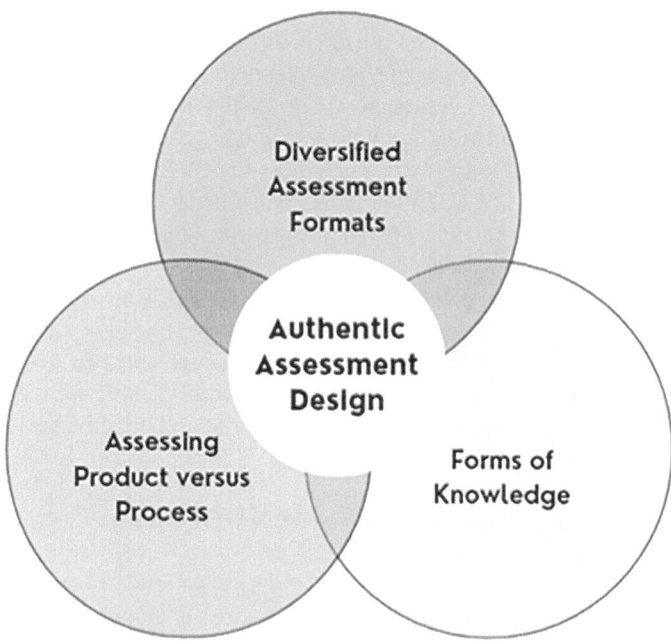

Figure 9.1   AI-Resistant Assessment Design Framework

9.3.1   Diversify Assessment Formats

Assessments should explicitly require engagement with **paywalled** sources to safeguard against GenAI's potential misuse (Anderson et al., 2023), as these resources, such as subscription-based journal articles, are not included in the datasets used to train GenAI models. This ensures that students demonstrate their ability to access and evaluate credible, authentic information by "necessitating" interaction with the materials their teachers provide. Academics can ensure tasks are significant and related to **professional tasks** and **real-world problems** by incorporating current events and recent research to make assignments more relevant to professional activity and foster authentic engagement (Rudolph et al., 2023).

Utilising a **multimodal** approach in assessments is a crucial tactic to mitigate the impact of GenAI (Rudolph et al., 2023). By incorporating different forms of information like text, images, videos, animations, and infographics (individually or in combination), this approach encourages students to present information and create content in distinctive and integrated ways. The varied format presents a significant challenge for GenAI models replicating such diverse content. Additionally, offering alternative assessment formats provides opportunities for diverse students to showcase their learning through different means, facilitating their success and cultivating authentic learning experiences, thereby mitigating the homogeneity that AI models often replicate.

Real-time assessment, where a student's performance is observed as it unfolds, is a potent deterrent against GenAI manipulation. Tasks such as live medical examinations, musical performances, or presentations conducted in the physical presence of the evaluator inherently pose significant challenges for GenAI's accurate replication, where AI struggles to replicate the dynamic nuances of human interaction and expression (Chaudhry et al., 2023).

Longitudinal assessments, which extend over time with multiple interconnected submissions, introduce complexity that counters the proficiency of GenAI. Portfolio-based assessments, such as those outlined by Paulson et al. (1991), offer a comprehensive representation of a student's learning journey. These assessments track progress over time, showcasing the student's competency across diverse tasks and contexts. Their personalised and longitudinal nature inherently adds complexity to the assessment process, rendering them more resilient against AI-driven cheating and authentically capturing the evolving proficiency of students across varied tasks and contexts (Barrett, 2007).

Moreover, portfolios provide a multifaceted view of student learning, encompassing their factual understanding and cognitive development over time (Ifelebuegu, 2023; Barrett, 2007). This structure facilitates continuous progress and feedback monitoring, making it challenging for GenAI models to accurately anticipate or reproduce future submissions. By conducting these activities in **supervised** environments, such as face-to-face discussions, and implementing **small-scale** assessments, authenticity can be ensured while minimising the risks of AI-generated academic misconduct.

Incorporating a **dialogic dialogue** between students and assessors establishes a strong defence against GenAI's efforts to replicate authentic interactions. Activities that require students to engage in ongoing dialogue, such as *viva voce* tasks or staged components within larger projects with opportunities for iterative feedback, present considerable obstacles for GenAI models attempting to mimic human interaction (O'Connor & Michaels, 2007). By responding to the assessor's questions, prompts, and interactions over time, students participate in a dynamic process that is inherently difficult for AI to replicate accurately.

Many HE models heavily rely on summative assessment, which can sometimes misrepresent student capability when technology-generated evidence is involved. A diverse assessment approach incorporating formative and diagnostic tasks is recommended to address this. While GenAI tools often pose challenges for high-stakes summative assessments, they might be more suitable for lower-stakes, formative assessments. By selecting a variety of tasks with different weights, students can demonstrate learning in a less risky environment, allowing instructors to assess understanding while reducing reliance on AI tools. Formative assessment, mainly when not weighted, provides opportunities to check understanding and enhance student confidence for summative assessments (Hopfenbeck et al., 2023).

Programmatic assessment is rooted in the concept of assessment for learning and utilises a series of interconnected assessment methods that complement each other. Instead of evaluating specific knowledge or skills with a single method, it emphasises broader attributes through various approaches. This method supports a comprehensive assessment framework by ensuring diverse, authentic tasks that offer relevant evidence of student learning while mitigating the risks associated with the improper use of GenAI technologies. Programmatic assessment offers numerous advantages for students and educators, such as increased confidence in the assessment process (Dart et al., 2021).

9.3.2   Assessing Process vs. Product

By placing equal emphasis on **evaluating the learning process** alongside the outcome, assessments become more comprehensive and less vulnerable to GenAI manipulation. Tasking students with documenting and reflecting on their thinking processes, iterations, and decision-making provides insights that GenAI models cannot replicate. Furthermore, educators should encourage self-evaluation and reflection on AI usage, engaging students in discussions about academic integrity and the impact of AI on their learning and writing processes. These approaches can be integrated into authentic assessments tailored to each group of students, prompting them to reflect on their experiences, viewpoints, and learning trajectories.

Giving **assessors visibility** into students' work processes is a crucial safeguard against GenAI manipulation. This can be achieved by submitting drafts, sketches, reflective accounts, or other evidence documenting the development process. Such transparency ensures that the authentic effort and thought invested in the assessment are readily apparent.

Promoting **teamwork** and **collaborative** endeavours in assessments, where each team member's contribution relies on others, establishes a dynamic inherently resistant to GenAI replication. This cooperative approach highlights the significance of collective contributions, enhancing assessments' resilience to GenAI manipulation.

Encouraging collaborative efforts among students through social constructivism, as advocated by Vygotsky (1978), fosters a synergistic learning environment where each team member's input is interdependent on others. Collaborative assessments can manifest in various forms, such as team-based assignments, peer evaluations, and joint problem-solving ventures (Ifelebuegu, 2023).

9.3.3 Forms of Knowledge

Designing questions and tasks that require critical thinking, information synthesis, complex judgement, and applying creative or innovative ideas poses a significant challenge for GenAI (Rasul et al., 2023; Pellegrino & Quellmalz, 2010). Educators develop assessments resistant to GenAI's attempts to mimic human thinking by assessing higher-order cognitive processes. Traditional assessments often prioritise basic cognitive abilities like memory recall and comprehension, which are now more susceptible to manipulation by AI chatbots (see also Clark and Denman, Chapter 8 in this volume). Assessments focusing on higher-order cognitive skills offer a viable solution to this challenge. These assessments emphasise analysis, synthesis, evaluation, and creation, as outlined in Bloom's revised taxonomy (Anderson & Krathwohl, 2001). Such skills demand active engagement with the learning material, fostering deep learning.

Educators can design **authentic assessments** that encourage students to draw connections between different ideas or concepts and apply knowledge in novel contexts. These assessments prepare students for a rapidly evolving world (Reimers & Chung, 2018). Essentially, educators should capitalise on AI's limitations in contextual thinking by prioritising assignments that require profound understanding and original thought rather than simple recall and knowledge repetition.

Developing assessments that evaluate **contextualised and personalised knowledge** and necessitate the application of concepts to specific settings or personal contexts would establish a level of individualised thinking that GenAI struggles to attain (Currie et al., 2023).

By contextualising knowledge, assessments become less susceptible to replication by GenAI models, as they require a nuanced understanding of particular scenarios. For instance, assessments grounded in real-world problems demand that students bridge theoretical knowledge with practical application, highlighting the necessity for a comprehensive and sophisticated comprehension of the subject matter. Therefore, problem-based assessment is crucial in upholding integrity (Ifelebuegu, 2023).

As explained earlier, the negative impact of generative AI on academic assessments is a critical issue in HE. The AI-Resistant Assessment Design Framework could address this. First, diversified assessment formats (the first component of the framework), such as multimodal presentations and longitudinal assessments (Rudolph et al., 2023), are crucial as they require a dynamic and complex engagement that AI cannot easily replicate, maintaining the authenticity of assessments and preventing AI misuse. Secondly, assessing both the product and the process (Barrett, 2007; Ifelebuegu, 2023) ensures a deeper engagement with the learning material, as it involves "documenting" the learning journey and reflecting on the creation process, which helps teachers identify AI-generated content and evaluate the student's understanding. Finally, focusing on forms of knowledge that demand high-order cognitive skills (Anderson & Krathwohl, 2001; Pellegrino & Quellmalz, 2010) challenges the limitations of AI in replicating complex human thought processes, thereby fostering assessments that genuinely reflect students' capabilities and understanding. Together, these strategies form a comprehensive approach to mitigating the challenges posed by generative AI, enhancing the integrity and effectiveness of academic evaluations in the digital age.

9.4   CONCLUSION

This chapter underscores the impacts of GenAI on academic integrity and assessment methods in HE, revealing both challenges and opportunities. Through the resistant strategies explicated in the chapter, it advocates for a strategic redesign of assessments to incorporate authenticity and resist the misuse of AI, emphasising diversified formats, assessing processes over products, and prioritising higher-order cognitive skills. For educators, it highlights the importance of developing and implementing AI-resistant assessment frameworks to maintain academic integrity. Future research should explore the effectiveness of these strategies in diverse educational contexts and the evolving capabilities of GenAI tools to refine further and adapt assessment practices by empirically testing the implementation of these strategies in an increasingly AI-centric world.

Implementing the AI-Resistant Assessment Design Framework can ensure that educators preserve academic integrity and deepen student learning by consistently demanding authentic engagement and critical thinking. Over time, this focus on authentic assessment practices can significantly enhance educational outcomes, creating a generation of well-prepared students to navigate and contribute to an AI-influenced digital world.

NOTE

1. Authentic assessments involve tasks that replicate real-world challenges and standards, linking classroom learning to practical, professional applications in order to assess students' ability to apply knowledge in realistic and meaningful contexts (Villarroel et al., 2018).

REFERENCES

Alasadi, E. A., & Baiz, C. R. (2023). Generative AI in education and research: Opportunities, concerns, and solutions. *Journal of Chemical Education*, 100(8), 2965–2971.

Anderson, L. W., & Krathwohl, D. (2001). *A taxonomy for learning, teaching, and assessing: A revision of Bloom's taxonomy of educational objectives: complete edition.* Addison Wesley Longman, Inc.

Anderson, N., Belavy, D. L., Perle, S. M., Hendricks, S., Hespanhol, L., Verhagen, E., & Memon, A. R. (2023). AI did not write this manuscript, or did it? Can we trick the AI text detector into generated texts? The potential future of ChatGPT and AI in sports & exercise medicine manuscript generation. *BMJ Open Sport & Exercise Medicine*, 9(1), e001568.

Ardito, C. G. (2023). Contra generative AI detection in higher education assessments. arXiv preprint arXiv:2312.05241.

Atlas, S. (2023). ChatGPT for higher education and professional development: A guide to conversational AI. https://digitalcommons.uri.edu/cba_facpubs/548

Barrett, H. C. (2007). Researching electronic portfolios and learner engagement: The REFLECT initiative. *Journal of Adolescent & Adult Literacy*, 50(6), 436–449.

Bosco, A. M., & Ferns, S. (2014). Embedding of authentic assessment in work-integrated learning curriculum. *Asia-Pacific Journal of Cooperative Education*, 15(4), 281–290.

Chatterjee, J., & Dethlefs, N. (2023). This new conversational AI model can be your friend, philosopher, and guide ... and even your worst enemy. *Patterns*, 4(1), 100676.

Chaudhry, I. S., Sarwary, S. A. M., El Refae, G. A., & Chabchoub, H. (2023). Time to revisit existing student's performance evaluation approach in higher education sector in a new era of ChatGPT – A case study. *Cogent Education*, 10(1), 2210461.

Chiu, T. K. (2024). Future research recommendations for transforming higher education with generative AI. *Computers and Education: Artificial Intelligence*, 6, 100197.

Cotton, D. R., Cotton, P. A., & Shipway, J. R. (2023). Chatting and cheating: Ensuring academic integrity in the era of ChatGPT. *Innovations in Education and Teaching International*, 1–12.

Currie, G., Singh, C., Nelson, T., Nabasenja, C., Al-Hayek, Y., & Spuur, K. (2023). ChatGPT in medical imaging higher education. *Radiography*, 29(4), 792–799.

Dart, J., Twohig, C., Anderson, A., Bryce, A., Collins, J., Gibson, S., ... & Palermo, C. (2021). The value of programmatic assessment in supporting educators and students to succeed: A qualitative evaluation. *Journal of the Academy of Nutrition and Dietetics*, 121(9), 1732–1740.

Deng, X., & Yu, Z. (2023). A meta-analysis and systematic review of the effect of chatbot technology use in sustainable education. *Sustainability*, 15(4), 2940.

Dwivedi, Y. K., Kshetri, N., Hughes, L., Slade, E. L., Jeyaraj, A., Kar, A. K., ... & Wright, R. (2023). "So what if ChatGPT wrote it?" Multidisciplinary perspectives on opportunities, challenges and implications of generative conversational AI for research, practice and policy. *International Journal of Information Management*, 71, 102642.

Farhi, F., Jeljeli, R., Aburezeq, I., Dweikat, F. F., Al-shami, S. A., & Slamene, R. (2023). Analyzing the students' views, concerns, and perceived ethics about chat GPT usage. *Computers and Education: Artificial Intelligence*, 100180.x

Gamage, K. A., Dehideniya, S. C., Xu, Z., & Tang, X. (2023). ChatGPT and higher education assessments: More opportunities than concerns? *Journal of Applied Learning and Teaching*, 6(2).

Halaweh, M. (2023). ChatGPT in education: Strategies for responsible implementation. *Contemporary Educational Technology*, 15(2), 421.

Hasanein, A. M., & Sobaih, A. E. E. (2023). Drivers and consequences of ChatGPT use in higher education: Key stakeholder perspectives. *European Journal of Investigation in Health, Psychology and Education*, 13(11), 2599–2614.

Hopfenbeck, T. N., Zhang, Z., Sun, S. Z., Robertson, P., & McGrane, J. A. (2023). Challenges and opportunities for classroom-based formative assessment and AI: A perspective article. *Front. Educ.*, 8:1270700. doi: 10.3389/feduc.2023.1270700

Ifelebuegu, A. (2023). Rethinking online assessment strategies: Authenticity versus AI chatbot intervention. *Journal of Applied Learning & Teaching*, 6(2). https://doi.org/10.37074/jalt.2023.6.2.2

Kaufman, R., Guerra, I., & Platt, W. A. (Eds.). (2005). *Practical evaluation for educators: Finding what works and what doesn't.* Corwin Press.

Khalil, M., & Er, E. (2023). Will ChatGPT get you caught? Rethinking of plagiarism detection. arXiv preprint arXiv:2302.04335.

Kung, T. H., Cheatham, M., Medenilla, A., Sillos, C., De Leon L., Elepaño, C., Madriaga, M., Aggabao, R., DiazCandido, G., Maningo, J., & Tseng, V. (2023). Performance of ChatGPT on USMLE: Potential for AI-assisted medical education using large language models. *PLOS Digital Health*, 2(2), e0000198.

Limna, P., Kraiwanit, T., Jangjarat, K., Klayklung, P., & Chocksathaporn, P. (2023). The use of ChatGPT in the digital era: Perspectives on chatbot implementation. *Journal of Applied Learning and Teaching*, 6(1).

Liu, M,, Zhang, L. J., & Biebricher, C. (2023). Investigating students' cognitive processes in AI-assisted digital multimodal composing and traditional writing.

Lodge, J. M., Thompson, K., & Corrin, L. (2023). Mapping out a research agenda for generative artificial intelligence in tertiary education. *Australasian Journal of Educational Technology*, 39(1), 1–8.

Mislevy, R. J., Behrens, J. T., Dicerbo, K. E., & Levy, R. (2012). Design and discovery in educational assessment: Evidence-centered design, psychometrics, and educational data mining. *Journal of Educational Data Mining*, 4(1), 11–48.

O'Connor, C., & Michaels, S. (2007). When is dialogue "dialogic"? *Human Development*, 50(5), 275–285.

Paulson, F. L., Paulson, P. R., & Meyer, C. (1991). What makes a portfolio a portfolio? *Educational Leadership*, 48(5), 60–63.

Pellegrino, J. W., & Quellmalz, E. S. (2010). Perspectives on the integration of technology and assessment. *Journal of Research on Technology in Education*, 43(2), 119–134.

Perkins, M. (2023). Academic integrity considerations of AI Large Language Models in the post-pandemic era: ChatGPT and beyond. *Journal of University Teaching and Learning Practice*, 20(2).

Rasul, T., Nair, S., Kalendra, D., Robin, M., de Oliveira Santini, F., Ladeira, W. J., ... & Heathcote, L. (2023). The role of ChatGPT in higher education: Benefits, challenges, and future research directions. *Journal of Applied Learning and Teaching*, 6(1).

Reimers, F., & Chung, C. (Eds.). (2018). Preparing teachers to educate whole students. Cambridge, MA: Harvard Education Publishing.

Rudolph, J., Tan, S., & Tan, S. (2023). ChatGPT: Bullshit spewer or the end of traditional assessments in higher education? *Journal of Applied Learning and Teaching*, 6(1).

Shaffer, D. W., & Kaput, J. J. (1998). Mathematics and virtual culture: An evolutionary perspective on technology and mathematics education. *Educational Studies in Mathematics*, 37(2), 97–119.

Smolansky, A., Cram, A., Raduescu, C., Zeivots, S., Huber, E., & Kizilcec, R. F. (2023). Educator and student perspectives on the impact of generative AI on assessments in higher education. In *Proceedings of the Tenth ACM Conference on Learning @ Scale* (pp. 378–382).

Schunk, D. H. (2012). *Learning theories: An educational perspective*. Pearson Education, Inc.

Swiecki, Z., Khosravi, H., Chen, G., Martinez-Maldonado, R., Lodge, J. M., Milligan, S., ... & Gašević, D. (2022). Assessment in the age of artificial intelligence. *Computers and Education: Artificial Intelligence*, 3, 100075.

Tai, J., Ajjawi, R., Boud, D., Dawson, P., & Panadero, E. (2018). Developing evaluative judgement: Enabling students to make decisions about the quality of work. *Higher Education*, 76, 467–481.

Thanh, B. N., Vo, D. T. H., Nhat, M. N., Pham, T. T. T., Trung, H. T., & Xuan, S. H. (2023). Race with the machines: Assessing the capability of generative AI in solving authentic assessments. *Australasian Journal of Educational Technology*, 39(5), 59–81.

Villarroel, V., Bloxham, S., Bruna, D., Bruna, C., & Herrera-Seda, C. (2018). Authentic assessment: Creating a blueprint for course design. *Assessment and Evaluation in Higher Education*, 43(5), 840–854.

Vygotsky, L. S. (1978). *Mind in society: Development of higher psychological processes*. Harvard University Press.

Yang, Z., Wu, J. G., & Xie, H. (2024). Taming Frankenstein's monster: Ethical considerations relating to generative artificial intelligence in education. *Asia Pacific Journal of Education*, 1–14.

Yeo, M. A. (2023). Academic integrity in the age of artificial intelligence (AI) authoring apps. *Tesol Journal*, 14(3), e716.

Yu, H. (2023). Reflection on whether Chat GPT should be banned by academia from the perspective of education and teaching. *Frontiers in Psychology*, 14, 1181712.

10. Strategies and ethical challenges for equality in generative AI research: addressing access, bias, and privacy

Margriet A. van Gestel

Generative artificial intelligence (AI) is increasingly being applied across various research domains, offering significant benefits to researchers in different disciplines. Among many others, examples include its use in medical imaging for automating and improving accurate image analysis (Musalamadugu & Kannan, 2023), in forensic research for analyzing crime data to predict future crime patterns (Fiore et al., 2019), and in the creative domain, where it can compose new pieces of music or images based on existing works (Epstein et al., 2023).

However, despite the potential of this innovative technology, a significant challenge arises: the risk of increasing inequality. Although free versions of generative AI tools are available, researchers often need more advanced applications with better performance that require significant financial resources and technical expertise. Access to these technologies is not evenly distributed as it tends to favor well-funded research groups. Additionally, the emergence of generative AI brings forth ethical challenges regarding its deployment and its potential impact on equality within the research community and society at large. For example, in the context of medical image analysis, AI systems can be susceptible to bias due to imbalances in the training data, which can lead to unequal diagnosis and treatment options for different populations (Kaundinya & Kundu, 2021).

This chapter will address the challenges of unequal access to technology and ethical considerations associated with bias and data privacy (for data privacy, see also Protopapa and Idris, Chapter 11 in this volume) in research. By critically examining these issues, this chapter seeks to provide strategies for promoting equality in the utilization of generative AI technologies. Through collaborative efforts and thoughtful consideration of these issues, the transformative potential of generative AI can stimulate inclusive innovation in various research fields.

10.1   ACCESS TO THE TECHNOLOGY

Generative AI technology has the potential to not only advance research but also to play a crucial role in addressing privacy concerns and biases. The uneven distribution of access to generative AI technology presents a significant challenge. Limited access to this technology impedes research progress and hampers the ability to address privacy concerns and biases. This can lead to inequality, both directly through reduced advancements and indirectly as the opportunity to utilize this technology for bias and privacy mitigation is withheld.

Preventing the advancement of research. It is essential to acknowledge that the landscape of generative AI encompasses a wide spectrum of complexity and capability. Within the research community, researchers design their own more advanced applications, typically requiring significant financial resources and technical expertise to develop and implement them effectively. For instance, in education research, the utilization of large language models (LLMs) has become increasingly prevalent. LLMs refer to a class of AI systems that have the capability to generate text across a wide range of topics and domains. Researchers employ custom-made LLMs to generate educational materials, analyze student responses, and develop personalized learning experiences (Bonner et al., 2023). The acquisition and deployment of such advanced generative AI technologies places smaller research teams at a disadvantage due to the substantial investment of resources and technical know-how required. Consequently, this unequal distribution of resources within the research community can hinder the progress of smaller or less well funded research teams, exacerbating the gap in technological innovation and potentially reinforcing existing power dynamics within academic and scientific circles.

Researchers with limited financial resources might also be limited in benefiting from user-prompted data generation, as exemplified by technologies like OpenAI's DALL-E and ChatGPT. These kinds of tools enable users to input prompts and generate synthetic content.

Although free versions of user-prompted generative AI are available to the public, paid versions provide better performance and access to more recent information. Researchers can employ these systems to write articles and grant research. Concerns regarding copyright, plagiarism, and content quality, have prompted scientific journals and conferences to introduce new policies regarding generative AI use (Flanagin et al., 2023). Nonetheless, its utilization in writing offers benefits such as improved efficiency, creativity exploration, editorial support, especially for non-English speakers, and literature summarization and translation. Despite its code accuracy limitations, generative AI also serves as a powerful code generation tool (Idrisov & Schlippe, 2024). In conclusion, user-prompted generative AI technologies like ChatGPT can contribute to equity by enhancing English writing skills and streamlining code comprehension, thus promoting inclusivity, accessibility, and efficiency in the research process, provided they are accessible to all.

Preventing the ability to address privacy concerns and biases. Generative AI technologies play a pivotal role in addressing two significant challenges in AI research and application: privacy concerns and biases within datasets. Privacy concerns are widespread across various fields due to the sensitive nature of data, hindering the exchange of information vital for research. Additionally, biases in datasets can lead to systemic errors and inaccuracies (see also Protopapa and Idris, Chapter 11 in this volume), affecting the fairness and performance of AI models.

The consequences of bias are exemplified using a model predicting student dropout rates, visualized on the left side of Figure 10.1. When the model is trained on a training dataset primarily comprised of black figurines, it lacks information about the characteristics and behaviors of the grey and white

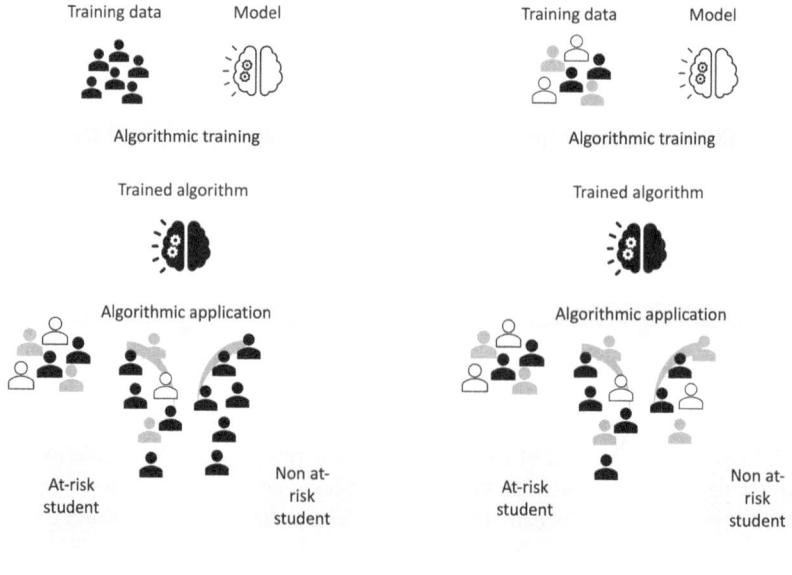

Figure 10.1   Bias in generative AI models predicting student dropout (biased models tend to wrongly predict at-risk of dropping out)

figurines. Consequently, the model does not have information to classify these figurines correctly. This example, therefore, tends to classify these figurines as at-risk of dropping out, even though they may not be. The biased model could have exhibited the opposite behavior as well, misclassifying individuals from underrepresented groups as non-at-risk of dropout when they in fact are. In contrast, the training data accurately represents the entire student population on the right side. This model benefits from a more comprehensive understanding of the diverse student demographics, enabling it to make more accurate predictions about dropout risk.

Generative AI techniques offer promising solutions to these challenges. Firstly, generative AI can mitigate biases in datasets by generating diverse and balanced data samples, thereby reducing the risk of perpetuating biases present in the original data sources (Das et al., 2022; Kortylewski et al., 2019). In the upper left image of Figure 10.2, there is a dataset consisting mainly of black figurines. This dataset exhibits significant bias towards black figurines, potentially leading to skewed model outcomes. After applying generative AI, the upper right image of Figure 10.2 depicts a more balanced dataset. By generating additional instances of underrepresented groups, such as grey and white figurines, bias is mitigated, and a more inclusive model training process is promoted. Generative AI techniques also enable researchers to protect privacy by generating synthetic data that preserves the statistical properties of

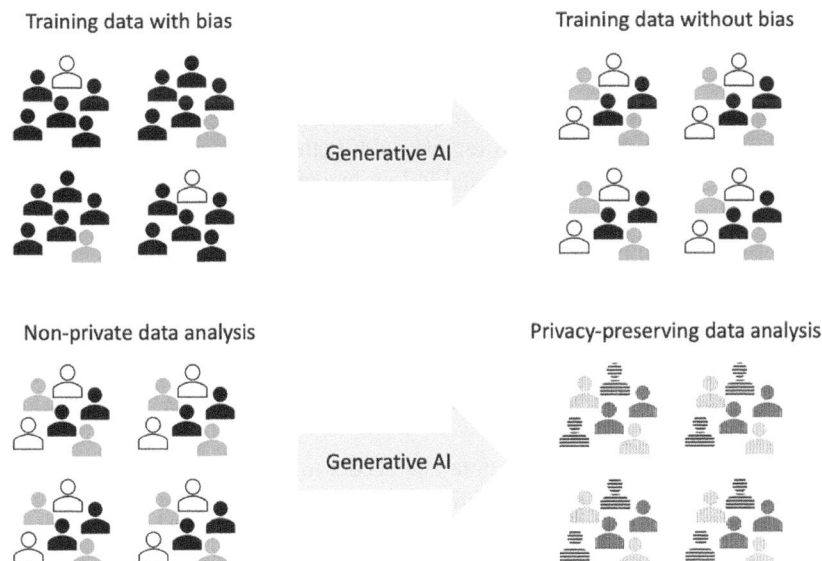

Figure 10.2   Generative AI techniques have the potential to alleviate biases and privacy concerns

the original data while ensuring individual privacy is maintained (Assefa et al., 2020; Ghebrehiwet et al., 2024). This approach allows researchers to share and analyze data without compromising sensitive information confidentiality. In the lower left image of Figure 10.2, a dataset consists of black, grey, and white figurines. Each figurine represents a data point, potentially containing sensitive information about individuals. A transformed dataset is in the lower right image. Now, there are horizontally striped, dotted, and vertically striped figurines. These synthetic data points retain the statistical properties of the original dataset without directly exposing sensitive information.

Synthetic data generation through generative AI offers a powerful solution to address bias in training datasets and serves as an effective strategy for privacy preservation in data-driven applications. The inability for researchers without access to generative AI technologies to utilize these capabilities represents a critical missed opportunity. This limitation impedes progress in achieving fairness and equality in research and beyond and underscores the importance of ensuring equitable access to generative AI.

In summary, generative AI tools' application, research, and development can greatly benefit researchers. However, they also require significant resources and an advanced technological infrastructure. Research indicates that technology adoption depends on the general development level and wage levels (Knez, 2023). Generally, more highly developed countries have more resources available for necessary investments in research and education. Additionally, lower wages in less developed countries can result in limited access to education, as individuals with lower incomes may choose to work to meet their basic needs instead of investing in education that could yield long-term benefits. Moreover, in low-income regions, highly skilled individuals may choose to migrate to regions with better labor conditions, leading to a loss of skills and human capital in low-income areas. While the study by Knez and colleagues is not focused explicitly on generative AI technology, it underscores the necessity of targeted interventions to break this cycle and stimulate positive change, such as government funding, public-private partnerships, and grants from research funders. In addition, support can be provided for education, workshops, and training programs to familiarize researchers from all institutions with generative AI. Partnerships between institutions with different resources can also help provide access to generative AI technologies and expertise.

Moreover, it is important to note that access to generative AI technologies offers advantages but also potential drawbacks. In an online experimental study conducted by Doshi and Hauser (Doshi & Hauser, 2023), writers were given the opportunity to acquire story ideas from a generative AI platform. The study found that access to generative AI resulted in the creation of more creative and better-written stories. However, it was also observed that the texts exhibited greater similarity to each other compared to texts created solely by humans. This observed trade-off is crucial for researchers to consider, as reliance on generative AI for new research ideas may lead to a narrower scope of novel research (see also Clark and Denman, Chapter 8 in this volume). It is important to be aware of the potential consequences of such reliance, as it could impact the diversity and originality of research output. Monitoring the diversity in research literature may provide insights into the long-term consequences of relying on generative AI in research, particularly regarding its potential impact on the originality and breadth of research output.

Building upon the discussion on how generative AI can aid in bias mitigation and privacy preservation, it is essential to recognize that generative AI models themselves may inadvertently disclose privacy-sensitive information and harbor biases. The following sections will delve into the ethical dimensions of implementing generative AI, examining challenges related to bias mitigation, privacy preservation, and the broader implications for research integrity and societal impact. Through continued exploration and discussion, a comprehensive understanding of the ethical considerations surrounding generative AI will be fostered to inform strategies for its responsible deployment in research.

10.2   ETHICAL CONSIDERATIONS

The utilization of generative AI in research brings forth ethical considerations that affect not just equality within the research community but also individuals and society. The ethical considerations most relevant to the equality implications of generative AI research are further discussed here, namely bias, data privacy, and human agency.

10.2.1   Bias in Generative AI

In a previous section of this chapter, the discourse centered on how generative AI could potentially address bias. However, it is crucial to recognize that generative AI models themselves may harbor biases. This section will address bias in generative AI models and its implications for research, followed by exploration of various strategies to mitigate this issue.

Mehrabi and colleagues distinguish three primary forms of bias (Figure 10.3): *data to algorithm, algorithmic to user,* and *user to data* (Mehrabi et al., 2022). *Data to algorithm* bias occurs when the data used to train machine learning models is not representative or lacks essential information, resulting in biased outputs. *Algorithm to user* bias arises when algorithms utilized in generative AI models possess inherent biases that are reflected in their generated outputs. This occurs when these algorithms rely on biased assumptions or employ biased criteria in the process of generating new data. *User to data* bias emerges when individuals interacting with AI systems introduce their biases or prejudices into the system, consciously or unconsciously. This can occur when users supply biased training data or when their interactions with the system reflect their inherent biases. Mikołajczyk-Bareła and Grochowski extend Mehrabi's categorization with *user to user* and *data to user* bias (Figure 10.3) and situate them in the machine learning research pipeline, resulting in 40 potential sources of bias that can occur at the six different stages of the machine learning pipeline, namely literature review, data collection, data analysis, model selection and training, interpretation of results, and publication (Mikołajczyk-Bareła & Grochowski, 2023). *User to user* bias can occur during the literature review stage, when biases of researchers can influence their work, and *data to user* bias in the data analysis stage, for example when a confounding variable is overlooked. Although not all types of bias directly lead to inequality, it is important to consider all forms of bias when examining inequality due to their potential cumulative effect. Besides that, it is crucial to recognize that every phase of research is susceptible to bias.

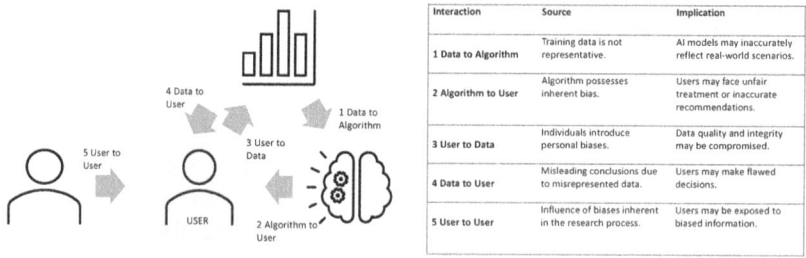

Figure 10.3   Different sources of bias in generative AI and their implications for research

Biased generative AI systems can perpetuate and reinforce social inequalities and discrimination, significantly impacting individuals and society. For example, in a study focused on predicting undergraduate course grades and average GPA, demographic biases disproportionately favored female students, while biases against minority groups from low-income backgrounds, first-generation college students, and underrepresented minorities were also identified (Yu et al., 2020). Furthermore, biased generative AI may restrict access to essential services, such as obtaining a loan. If biased generative AI disproportionately denies loans based on factors like race, gender, or socioeconomic status, it perpetuates existing inequalities.

Addressing bias in generative AI is a multifaceted challenge, requiring technical, ethical, and societal considerations. Key strategies for mitigating bias in generative AI include awareness and education, data collection and mining, ethical and legal integration, and human-in-the-loop mechanisms. These strategies offer distinct benefits for bias mitigation in generative AI, yet they also present challenges and potential pitfalls that must be carefully considered and addressed within the academic community.

Awareness and education. Educational tools tailored to different target groups can be developed to raise awareness and educate stakeholders about bias in generative AI systems. These materials may include online courses, workshops, seminars, and websites that explain what bias is, highlight its impact, and provide bias mitigation strategies. Additionally, interactive tools and simulations can illustrate the impact of bias in AI algorithms and engage learners in hands-on learning experiences. These initiatives aim to make individuals feel responsible and accountable, leading them to recognize and address bias proactively, thereby reducing the likelihood of inequitable outcomes. However, despite their importance, educational efforts may face challenges. As previously noted, biases manifest in diverse forms across all stages of research. Due to technical jargon and the complex nature of bias, there is a risk of oversimplifying the complexities of bias in generative AI. Besides, disparities in access to educational resources could limit their effectiveness. Therefore, the educational materials that are developed must be accessible to all who need them. This can be facilitated through governmental funding, corporate investments, philanthropic support, public-private partnerships, and the provision of freely accessible resources. In summary, while educational efforts are crucial for raising awareness and addressing bias in generative AI, it is essential that these initiatives are inclusive, accessible, and comprehensive, thus maximizing their impact in promoting equality and fairness in AI systems.

Data collection and mining. Researchers can employ bias mitigation techniques by modifying training data and learning algorithms, adjusting model predictions, optimizing regularization methods, and assessing outcome consistency (Chen et al., 2023). These fairness-aware machine learning algorithms play a crucial role in identifying and correcting biases in training data and algorithms. Outcome consistency can be evaluated by implementing regular audits to continuously monitor and evaluate generative AI systems in production (Paul & Sarkar, 2023). Researchers can leverage automated monitoring tools and performance metrics to detect and correct biases in generative AI systems over time. These tools are instrumental in providing real-time insights into the performance of AI systems and facilitating prompt interventions when biases are detected. Additionally, implementing feedback mechanisms and user surveys can help collect feedback from stakeholders and evaluate the impact of bias mitigation intervention in real-world settings. As biases may manifest subtly or evolve over time, it is essential to ensure robust and reliable evaluation metrics that are carefully validated and calibrated against ground truth data.

It is important to address the resource-intensive nature of audits and the complexity of monitoring AI systems at scale, especially in contexts with limited research budgets. Furthermore, despite these efforts, challenges such as label noise, sampling bias, and data sparsity may persist as these challenges may not have straightforward solutions. Moreover, the data curation process can inadvertently introduce biases if not conducted rigorously – the previously mentioned *user to data* bias. Researchers can prevent bias in providing feedback to the AI model by ensuring diversity in feedback sources, maintaining transparency in the feedback process, implementing blind feedback procedures, validating feedback through independent checks, and being aware of their own biases. In summary, while there may be no simple or complete solution to this issue, efforts can be made to reduce the effects of bias on algorithmic outcomes to promote fairness and equality in generative AI systems.

Ethical and legal integration. Integrating ethical and legal considerations into every stage of AI development and deployment promotes accountability, transparency, and fairness in research. These considerations are essential for ensuring that AI technologies are developed in a manner that aligns with societal values and norms. This process involves gathering input from relevant stakeholders such as ethicists, scientists, technologists, policymakers, as well as the public (Kirova et al., 2023). Researchers can utilize ethical frameworks to provide guiding principles for responsible generative AI research design and conduct. Legal compliance tools can help ensure that AI systems adhere to relevant regulatory standards, protect user rights, and collect and use training data legally and ethically. However, there are potential challenges in integrating ethical frameworks and legal compliance tools into AI development and deployment. One concern is the risk of well-intended regulations inadvertently stifling innovative research practices. While regulations are necessary to protect individuals and ensure ethical AI development, overly restrictive policies may hinder progress and innovation in the field. Additionally, the variations across research contexts and jurisdictions may pose challenges for standardization. Ethical frameworks and legal tools may also lack specificity or fail to anticipate emerging ethical and legal dilemmas in rapidly evolving research methodologies and technologies like generative AI. Therefore, ongoing review and adaptation within the academic community are necessary to address these challenges and ensure that AI development remains accountable, transparent, and fair.

Human in the loop. Incorporating human oversight and intervention (human-in-the-loop) into the generative AI pipeline can help mitigate bias by providing opportunities for human judgment and decision-making. This may involve curating training data, fine-tuning the model with expertise from subject matter experts, integrating evaluation and feedback loops, moderating real-time outputs, and customizing the model's behavior to align with specific requirements (Ferrara, 2023). While the advantage of machine learning is to accelerate and enhance processes, human-in-the-loop approaches may introduce delays and inefficiencies, especially in real-time and high-volume projects. Moreover, as mentioned before, human decision-making is susceptible to cognitive bias and subjective interpretations, raising concerns about consistency and reliability in research methodologies. Balancing the autonomy of AI systems with human oversight requires clear delineation of roles, responsibilities, and decision thresholds within interdisciplinary research teams.

While none of the above-mentioned methods to address bias is perfect, concerted effort within feasible bounds can mitigate bias significantly. In this context, it is crucial to remember that AI should augment, not replace, human decision-making processes. While AI can provide valuable insights and predictions, ultimate decision-making authority should rest with humans. Again, it is also worth noting that bias is not exclusive to AI systems; human decision-making processes are also susceptible to bias when drawing conclusions based on data. Dror identified eight sources of cognitive bias in expert decision-making, namely data, reference materials, contextual information, base rate, organizational factors, education and training, personal factors, and cognitive factors (Dror, 2020). When human decision-making and generative AI are combined, they can complement each other in addressing bias. Generative AI can effectively serve as a tool for reflection and improvement in human decision-making by providing alternate perspectives and identifying potential biases. This collaborative approach helps minimize inequalities and promote equality in research and society.

10.2.2   Data Privacy

Earlier, it was discussed that generative AI could potentially serve as a tool to address privacy concerns. However, when employing generative AI itself, significant concerns regarding data privacy may arise. Generative models require substantial amounts of data for training, which may contain personal (e.g. names or address) or even sensitive personal information (e.g. religion, health information, or financial data). A key risk is the ability of generative AI models to generate highly accurate and personalized content that closely matches the characteristics of individuals in the training dataset. If this data is not properly protected, there is a risk of exposing sensitive information, which could lead to serious breaches of individuals' privacy, which can then be exploited for unlawful activities, such as fraud or identity theft (Bale et al., 2024). OpenAI's ChatGPT has been reported to have exhibited instances of unintended disclosure, such as revealing personal data, chat logs, and login credentials (OpenAI, 2024). Marginalized individuals can suffer disproportionate harm when their privacy is violated. For example, a case of someone living with HIV. When sensitive information such as HIV status is exposed without consent, it can lead to severe social stigma and discrimination, exacerbating the already existing challenges faced by individuals in marginalized groups (Sannon & Forte, 2022). Additionally, the impact of privacy breaches is higher for individuals with limited data literacy. These individuals may not have the necessary skills or knowledge to protect their personal information effectively, making them more susceptible to data privacy violations.

Research has focused on data anonymization techniques, like generalization and masking. However, a significant challenge with traditional anonymization methods is the tradeoff between utility and privacy (Majeed & Lee, 2021). Increasing privacy protection degrades data quality and usefulness, while maximizing data utility may compromise individual privacy. Synthetic data has emerged as a promising solution, offering privacy as it lacks real personal information. However, synthetic data currently still has some challenges, as it is not inherently private. A generative model can overfit the training data, potentially revealing sensitive statistics. Ensuring privacy is complex, lacking a perfect measure. Besides, synthetic data does not yet provide a better tradeoff between privacy and utility than traditional anonymization methods (Stadler et al., 2022).

In conclusion, generative AI in research raises serious privacy concerns when working with sensitive or personal information, especially for marginalized individuals. Using synthetic data for training models seems like a solution, but it is no silver bullet. Therefore, data privacy must be prioritized, employing safeguards and ethical considerations to protect individuals' right.

10.2.3 Human Agency

As generative AI becomes increasingly integrated into various fields, including research, concerns arise regarding human agency and the ability to make decisions and exert their consequences on their surroundings (Anderson & Rainie, 2023). The lack of clarity regarding how users can address shortcomings, misleading information, or incorrect decisions in AI-enabled automated decision-making processes, may restrict their ability to make autonomous decisions (Fanni et al., 2023). This applies particularly to generative AI systems, as these systems autonomously make decisions about what they generate, making it more challenging for users to correct or modify undesirable or incorrect output. This lack of clarity can lead to inequality in research; for instance, if fully data-driven pharmaceutical funding prioritizes widespread diseases, lesser-known diseases that affect smaller populations could potentially be overlooked (Anderson & Rainie, 2023). When using generative AI, users should have the ability to challenge decisions and receive assistance if needed (Fanni et al., 2023). This involves providing a simple way to file complaints and obtain solutions for affected users and groups. Both academic researchers and industry developers of (generative) AI tools should consider these factors. Academic researchers contribute by investigating ethical, social, and legal implications of generative AI technology. Both researchers and developers can implement practical solutions to ensure transparency, accountability, and human agency. If researchers neglect these issues, the consequences could be significant. Without accountability and the offering of proper solutions in the case of errors or biases in generative AI systems, researchers may face stricter rules from regulators, potentially slowing down the progress of research. Additionally, if users experience negative outcomes, such as incorrect decisions or misleading information, this can lead to a loss of trust in AI technologies. This could hinder the widespread adoption of generative AI and limit its potential benefits in various fields, including research and innovation.

10.3 OVERALL CONCLUSION

The application of generative AI has huge potential in various research domains, yet it brings forth significant challenges that threaten equality and fairness within both the research community and society at large:

– Unequal access to the technology presents a barrier, favoring well-funded research groups while leaving smaller teams and underprivileged researchers behind. This disparity not only hampers the inclusivity of research but also exacerbates existing inequalities.
– The pervasive issue of bias in generative AI systems poses a threat to equality, perpetuating social inequalities and discrimination. Addressing bias requires multifaceted strategies, including awareness, education, bias mitigation strategies, and human-in-the-loop mechanisms. However, these efforts are not without challenges and must be carefully implemented to ensure effectiveness.
– Data privacy concerns add another layer of complexity, particularly regarding handling sensitive information. While synthetic data and anonymization techniques offer potential solutions, balancing privacy and data utility remains challenging.
– Preserving human agency and accountability is important in the face of increasing automation facilitated by generative AI. Transparency, user empowerment, and ethical considerations must guide AI decision-making processes to prevent negative outcomes and maintain trust in AI technologies.

In conclusion, generative AI technology holds transformative potential in research. Therefore, efforts must be made to democratize access to generative AI tools. Targeted interventions should be implemented to enhance access to generative AI technologies and expertise, thereby preserving human capital and fostering positive change. It should always be borne in mind that while it can augment creativity and improve output quality, there is a risk of standardizing content and constraining innovative research concepts. Finally, it is essential that generative AI is utilized as an advisory tool, complementing rather than replacing human decision-making processes. As we harness the transformative potential of generative AI, let us remember that it is the responsibility of humans to make informed decisions.

REFERENCES

Anderson, J., & Rainie, L. (2023). *The Future of Human Agency.* https:// www .pewresearch.org/internet/wp-content/uploads/sites/9/2023/02/PI_2023.02.24_The -Future-of-Human-Agency_FINAL.pdf

Assefa, S., Dervovic, D., Mahfouz, M., Balch, T., Reddy, P., & Veloso, M. (2020). Generating Synthetic Data in Finance: Opportunities, Challenges and Pitfalls. *SSRN Electronic Journal.* https://doi.org/10.2139/ssrn.3634235

Bale, A. S., Dhumale, R. B., Beri, N., Lourens, M., Varma, R. A., Kumar, V., Sanamdikar, S., & Savadatti, M. B. (2024). The Impact of Generative Content on Individuals Privacy and Ethical Concerns. *International Journal of Intelligent Systems and Applications in Engineering, 12*(1s), Article 1s.

Bonner, E., Lege, R., & Frazier, E. (2023). Large Language Model-Based Artificial Intelligence in the Language Classroom: Practical Ideas for Teaching. *Teaching English with Technology, 2023*(1). https://doi.org/10.56297/BKAM1691/WIEO1749

Chen, P., Wu, L., & Wang, L. (2023). AI Fairness in Data Management and Analytics: A Review on Challenges, Methodologies and Applications. *Applied Sciences, 13*(18), Article 18. https://doi.org/10.3390/app131810258

Das, H. P., Tran, R., Singh, J., Yue, X., Tison, G., Sangiovanni-Vincentelli, A., & Spanos, C. J. (2022). Conditional Synthetic Data Generation for Robust Machine Learning Applications with Limited Pandemic Data. *Proceedings of the AAAI Conference on Artificial Intelligence, 36*(11), Article 11. https://doi.org/10.1609/ aaai.v36i11.21435

Doshi, A. R., & Hauser, O. (2023). *Generative AI Enhances Individual Creativity but Reduces the Collective Diversity of Novel Content* (SSRN Scholarly Paper 4535536). https://doi.org/10.2139/ssrn.4535536

Dror, I. E. (2020). Cognitive and Human Factors in Expert Decision Making: Six Fallacies and the Eight Sources of Bias. *Analytical Chemistry, 92*(12), 7998–8004. https://doi.org/10.1021/acs.analchem.0c00704

Epstein, Z., Hertzmann, A., & The Investigators of Human Creativity. (2023). Art and the Science of Generative AI. *Science, 380*(6650), 1110–1111. https://doi.org/10 .1126/science.adh4451

Fanni, R., Steinkogler, V. E., Zampedri, G., & Pierson, J. (2023). Enhancing Human Agency through Redress in Artificial Intelligence Systems. *AI & Society, 38*(2), 537–547. https://doi.org/10.1007/s00146-022-01454-7

Ferrara, E. (2023). Should ChatGPT be Biased? Challenges and Risks of Bias in Large Language Models. *First Monday*. https://doi.org/10.5210/fm.v28i11.13346

Fiore, U., De Santis, A., Perla, F., Zanetti, P., & Palmieri, F. (2019). Using generative adversarial networks for improving classification effectiveness in credit card fraud detection. *Information Sciences*, *479*, 448–455. https://doi.org/10.1016/j.ins.2017.12.030

Flanagin, A., Bibbins-Domingo, K., Berkwits, M., & Christiansen, S. L. (2023). Nonhuman "Authors" and Implications for the Integrity of Scientific Publication and Medical Knowledge. *JAMA*, *329*(8), 637–639. https://doi.org/10.1001/jama.2023.1344

Ghebrehiwet, I., Zaki, N., Damseh, R., & Mohamad, M. (2024). Revolutionizing Personalized Medicine with Generative AI: A Systematic Review. *Artificial Intelligence Review*, *57*, Article 128. https://link.springer.com/article/10.1007/s10462-024-10768-5

Idrisov, B., & Schlippe, T. (2024). Program Code Generation with Generative AIs. *Algorithms*, *17*(2), Article 2. https://doi.org/10.3390/a17020062

Kaundinya, T., & Kundu, R. V. (2021). Diversity of Skin Images in Medical Texts: Recommendations for Student Advocacy in Medical Education. *Journal of Medical Education and Curricular Development*, *8*, 23821205211025855. https://doi.org/10.1177/23821205211025855

Kirova, V. D., Ku, C. S., Laracy, J. R., & Marlowe, T. J. (2023). The Ethics of Artificial Intelligence in the Era of Generative AI. *Journal of Systemics, Cybernetics and Informatics*, *21*(4), 42–50. https://doi.org/10.54808/JSCI.21.04.42

Knez, K. (2023). Technology Diffusion and Uneven Development. *Journal of Evolutionary Economics*, *33*(4), 1171–1195. https://doi.org/10.1007/s00191-023-00830-w

Kortylewski, A., Egger, B., Schneider, A., Gerig, T., Morel-Forster, A., & Vetter, T. (2019). Analyzing and Reducing the Damage of Dataset Bias to Face Recognition with Synthetic Data. *2019 IEEE/CVF Conference on Computer Vision and Pattern Recognition Workshops (CVPRW)*, 2261–2268. https://doi.org/10.1109/CVPRW.2019.00279

Majeed, A., & Lee, S. (2021). Anonymization Techniques for Privacy Preserving Data Publishing: A Comprehensive Survey. *IEEE Access*, *9*, 8512–8545. https://doi.org/10.1109/ACCESS.2020.3045700

Mehrabi, N., Morstatter, F., Saxena, N., Lerman, K., & Galstyan, A. (2022). A Survey on Bias and Fairness in Machine Learning (arXiv:1908.09635). arXiv. http://arxiv.org/abs/1908.09635

Mikołajczyk-Bareła, A., & Grochowski, M. (2023). A Survey on Bias in Machine Learning Research (arXiv:2308.11254). arXiv. http://arxiv.org/abs/2308.11254

Musalamadugu, T. S., & Kannan, H. (2023). Generative AI for Medical Imaging Analysis and Applications. *Future Medicine AI*, FMAI5. https://doi.org/10.2217/fmai-2023-0004

OpenAI. (2024, March 24). March 20 ChatGPT Outage: Here's What Happened. https://openai.com/blog/march-20-chatgpt-outage

Paul, R. K., & Sarkar, B. (2023). Generative AI and Ethical Considerations for Trustworthy AI Implementation. *International Journal of Artificial Intelligence & Machine Learning (IJAIML)*, *2*(01), 95–102.

Sannon, S., & Forte, A. (2022). Privacy Research with Marginalized Groups: What We Know, What's Needed, and What's Next. *Proceedings of the ACM on Human-Computer Interaction*, *6*(CSCW2), 1–33. https://doi.org/10.1145/3555556

Stadler, T., Oprisanu, B., & Troncoso, C. (2022). Synthetic Data – Anonymisation Groundhog Day (arXiv:2011.07018). arXiv. http://arxiv.org/abs/2011.07018

Yu, R., Li, Q., Fischer, C., Doroudi, S., & Xu, D. (2020). Towards Accurate and Fair Prediction of College Success: Evaluating Different Sources of Student Data. *Proceedings of the 13th International Conference on Educational Data Mining* (EDM 2020), 292–301.

11. Ethical and moral pitfalls of generative AI in academic research

Ilia Protopapa and Bochra Idris

11.1 INTRODUCTION

The ability of Large Language Models (LLMs), such as ChatGPT from OpenAI, Gemini from Google, and Bing Chat from Microsoft, to produce content that is almost identical to that of humans has resulted in radical changes in the social and technical environment (Rohan et al., 2023). The increased use of generative AI, has determined the different ways these models can be used, such as in software development, generating poetry, writing essays, and creating legal contracts (Reed, 2022; Tung, 2023). However, within the higher education and academic communities, the use of generative AI models has raised concerns related to ethics, transparency, accountability, and the difficulty of differentiating human versus AI authorship (Dwivedi et al., 2023; Stokel-Walker, 2023).

In this chapter we aim to discuss the darker side of generative AI and its potential negative effect on academic research and publications. In section 2, we discuss how although generative AI can be used as a tool to aid researchers in brainstorming research ideas, the use of Natural Language Processing (NLP) systems limits researchers' critical thinking and innovative idea generation (see also Clark and Denman, Chapter 8 in this volume) because these types of models cannot develop new theories. In section 3, we argue that using generative AI to summarise previous literature and suggest research questions will raise significant issues related to ethics, integrity, and transparency. We outline the various steps involved in the literature review process and the ethical pitfalls of AI. Thereafter, we shed light on the ethical use of AI in collecting and analysing data and draw attention to issues related to privacy and transparency. In section 5, we argue that although several recent studies have discussed the benefits of using NLP systems and generative AI in academic writing and publications, its usage in writing and editing manuscripts can lead to unintentional plagiarism, the production of errors, misinterpretation, and, to a great extent, biased information. In the final section, we conclude with a framework assessing fairness in AI models to explain the various ethical and moral considerations of using AI in academic research.

11.2　BRAINSTORMING NOVEL RESEARCH WITH GENERATIVE AI TOOLS: ACCOUNTABILITY AND INNOVATION

Recent studies in the field have argued that the use of AI models will mostly benefit academics and scholars in their research and publications. For instance, according to Hsu (2023), ChatGPT can suggest applicable research questions and recommend potential research ideas and research designs. Generative AI models, and more specifically ChatGPT, can act "as an indispensable tool for stimulating idea generation and facilitating brainstorming sessions" (Rane et al., 2023, p. 862). With the aid of these models as a collaborative tool for researchers, generative AI will enrich the research process and promote innovative, creative, and critical thinking (Aydın & Karaarslan, 2022; Almarie et al., 2023; Rane et al., 2023).

However, a compelling issue related to the use of AI models in generating academic research is that of accountability and transparency. It has been argued that since the pressure of producing research publications by academics has increased significantly throughout the past few years, researchers will be tempted to use generative AI models to help them in their research process (Rowe, 2023). However, this raises an important issue regarding accountability and transparency as it challenges the traditional values in academia that revolve around identifying original innovative and relevant ideas that are not a result of "what already exists by some non-transparent recombination" (Rowe, 2023, p. 36). Generating research ideas and identifying gaps in previous literature require researchers to identify their sources of inspiration. Hence, in losing the ability to properly go through the research process step by step, from identifying the literature and generating research questions to identifying novel gaps in previous studies, "we lose the capacity to assess the value of the contribution" (Rowe, 2023, p. 36) made by scholars. This is also related to being transparent regarding how the research ideas were derived from previous literature and how the methodology has been designed and applied in the research paper. This requires researchers to identify their source of information to show integrity and accountability in providing additional avenues for further research and investigation (Rowe, 2023).

In addition, AI models do not have the competencies to "discover new theories from data or suggest how to test theories" (Edwards & Duan, 2023, p. 41). Therefore, the use of AI will cause a diminishing ability to develop theories in academic research as there might be a risk of focusing on generating data and analysis to validate existing theories rather than developing new ones (e.g.,

Zhai, 2022; Dwivedi et al., 2023; Salah et al., 2023). This can be related to another issue: the absence of creativity and innovative research ideas among academic researchers. For example, even though it has been suggested that AI is capable of imitating human-like creativity (e.g., Guzik et al., 2023; Haase & Hanel, 2023; see also Clark and Denman, Chapter 8 in this volume), it has been argued that this technology may struggle to discern the effectiveness of its proposed original ideas (Guzik et al., 2023). Hence, the AI's lack of ability to provide creative yet practical solutions is a potential threat that prompts further research. Moreover, although generative AI can act as an assistant to support human creativity, it raises concerns regarding ethical considerations such as intellectual property rights, emphasising the individual's accountability while relying on AI technologies (Haase & Hanel, 2023). Since AI models, such as ChatGPT, rely extensively on existing ideas and data, there is an increased discussion regarding lack of creativity and originality as well as the capability of proposing interesting and innovative ideas that are worth investigating (Rane et al., 2023).

The cognitive science expert Margaret Boden, in her book *The Creative Mind* (2004), distinguished between two types of creativity – psychological and historical creativity. Historical creativity occurs when people think of something that never occurred before such as Archimedes' "eureka" moment, while psychological creativity on the other hand occurs when people think of something which is new for themselves, but not necessarily new to others. Shackell (2023) argues that although AI can stimulate the two types of creativity and can promote new insights regarding different subjects, AI-driven creativity is not capable of producing creative and innovative ideas that arise from an evolutionary combination of the mind and the reality. This is because AI relies on complicated statistical concepts of digital data, and hence it limits its capability to creating novel and "eureka" kinds of creative ideas. Relying on AI "our thinking become homogenised under the pressure of increasingly similar environments and experiences" (Shackell, 2023, p. 3).

11.3 THE USE OF GENERATIVE AI IN WRITING LITERATURE REVIEWS: BIASES AND CRITICAL THINKING

Traditionally, the literature review process that promotes critical and appraising topics, consists of the following stages: (1) Designing the review; (2) Conducting the review; (3) Data abstraction and analysis; and (4) Structuring and writing the review (Snyder, 2019). Each of these stages present certain actions taken by the author/s (see Tables 11.1a–d). We now discuss the potential of automating these tasks using AI, along with the limitations involved.

Designing the review. During the initial stage of the literature review process the author/s determine the need for the literature review, clearly stating the motivation, the purpose, and the research questions. Thereafter, the researcher will decide on the appropriate approach and methodology for the review process (Snyder, 2019). Determining the need for a new literature review requires investigating up-to-date research, identifying a gap, a potential research avenue, and the new study's contribution (Simon, 1979). Such a process requires the integration of various forms of knowledge, including the understanding of tacit knowledge (knowledge gained through experience), and subjective insights (recent interests in the field, as identified by recent events attended or conferences, not yet explored).

However, AI models operate in a rather codified manner and cannot incorporate tacit or subjective knowledge to reach a decision at the same depth as a human would. Shank and DeSanti (2018) suggest that during the early stages of the literature review a rigorous evaluation involves the assessment of the overall contribution of each study to the field and requires researchers to consider the impact of the literature, accounting for tacit knowledge and subjective insights. This also includes the identification of potential conflicts of interest or ethical considerations that the AI may fail to recognise. As a result, it is preferable that such a process is implemented by humans.

A significant number of researchers have raised concerns about the ease of using of AI tools in collecting information, as this may potentially lead to a shift away from original critical analysis (Chan, 2023; Bringula, 2023; Nashwan et al., 2023). Content understanding and evaluation in the field of investigation will lead to a meaningful identification of a research gap and research questions that will determine the need for the literature review. Hence, it can be suggested that AI tools, despite being able to assist academics in the first initial stages of undertaking a literature review, lack the in-depth contextual understanding and problem-solving skills that humans exhibit to determine the need for new literature.

Conducting the review. During the second stage of the literature review process, the author(s) conduct a thorough search process, including search terms, databases used, and explicit inclusion and exclusion criteria and take proper measures to ensure research quality (Snyder, 2019). Such a process can be automated by AI to a greater extent than those processes described above, but ethical considerations vary across actions taken. For example, even though the AI can automate the search process effectively, using keywords and criteria to identify relevant literature presents limited capacity in assessing the quality of the sources and cannot fully replace a human's judgment in evaluating the research quality. Chan (2023) suggests that even though AI tools can assist researchers in collecting information, the researcher's true understanding and critical evaluation of the collected studies cannot be measured or assessed.

This requires further evaluation of such sources to address ethical and academic integrity concerns. Another important concern is with regard to the biases in the selection of studies generated by the AI (Lund et al., 2023; Jarrah et al., 2023). The generated content that emerges by using AI tools comes from pre-existing data and algorithms rather than being produced by the author/s directly (Jarrah et al., 2023). AI tools such as ChatGPT, are trained on certain databases, which may contain biased information from various sources that researchers may not be aware of. This is also known as "black box methodology" (Pekka et al., 2023). Therefore, these sources have not been assessed for their representativeness (Semrl et al., 2023; Nashwan et al., 2023).

For example, ChatGPT may generate an inaccurate or insufficient number of articles that may not always be relevant or real (Semrl et al., 2023). Even though fabricated or unrelated generated results may be evident from the users of the AI platform, few authors have attempted to explain the reasons behind why this is happening. For instance, Semrl et al. (2023, p. 2284) suggest that "this is likely due to its pre-trained nature and lack of capability to perform internet browsing, which limits its ability to access and evaluate a wide range of sources". Hence, unknown academic sources are being selected and presented, which may also lead to inaccuracy and perpetuation of biases in AI-generated content (Jarrah et al., 2023). If the database used to train the AI model is biased towards a particular gender or ethnic group, the AI-generated content may also be biased towards that group. Bringula (2023) suggests that in the context of academic publishing conducting a literature review presents doubts about the originality, accuracy, attribution, fabrication, and falsification of studies produced by AI.

Data abstraction/text analysis. During the third stage of the literature review process, the author/s summarise and synthesise appropriate data from each article, use an appropriate analysis technique concerning the overall research question, and ensure that the analysis process is appropriately described and transparent (Snyder, 2019). Despite the popularity of the AI tools available to assist with synthesising information such as Microsoft Bing and Gemini, relevant ethical considerations arise. AI can extract and summarise data from articles, but complex data and interpretations may require human oversight. For example, AI can assist in text analysis, especially with quantitative data, but the choice of the most appropriate technique to read and analyse the literature often relies on human expertise (Bringula, 2023). Nashwan et al. (2023) suggest that we cannot trace the origin of the content and the transparency of the analysis and synthesis to the data abstraction stage, especially when AI is being used as the sole tool in assisting researchers to select the most relevant information from the selected articles. While Rahman et al. (2023) suggest that relying on AI tools will lead to poor paraphrasing and lack of synthesis.

For example, ChatGPT performs poorly in synthesising literature and writing a new academic literature review. Hence, although researchers may use such tools as assistants to summarise articles, they should not rely solely on ChatGPT to write their literature reviews (Rahman et al., 2023). Moreover, the use of AI in synthesising information raises issues of academic integrity, as originality in the processes involved, such as authenticity, cannot be assessed or guaranteed. Similar perspectives are found in several articles (e.g., Semrl et al., 2023; Rahman et al., 2023) suggesting that AI models cannot be held accountable for the validity and the accuracy of its generated results and that the human input and the evaluation of the extracted information are essential. Hence, AI may not be feasible to be used for critically appraising topics in academic research, as it cannot replace critical human thinking and may not be able to perform fact-checking or answer scientific questions (Semrl et al., 2023). In addition to this, automated tools, such as ChatGPT, may favour certain perspectives or sources over others, potentially leading to a skewed representation of the literature as it relies on established sources and ideas that do not represent minority groups (e.g., the decolonisation issue in presenting diverse perspectives). Hence, no representative evaluation of extant literature will occur when the training data used to develop the AI model predominantly represents mainstream or established perspectives, potentially marginalising alternatives or diverse viewpoints (Lund et al., 2023). As a result, the use of these tools may reinforce and promote existing disparities in scholarly discourse (Song & Song, 2023).

Structure and writing up. During the last stage of the literature review process, the author/s organise the review coherently, report the result clearly, synthesise the literature review findings, and include questions or directions for further research (Snyder, 2019). Even though AI models can help researchers in tasks related to text processing (Semrl et al., 2023), the most discussed ethical challenge associated with the writing-up stage of a literature review is the issue of academic integrity, related to plagiarism (Jarrah et al., 2023). Lund et al. (2023, p. 574) suggest that "there is a significant risk of plagiarism or copyright infringement when using content generated by ChatGPT or other AI tools in scholarly publications". This is because human resemblance in the final produced outcomes creates intellectual property rights issues; hence, essential citation and the acknowledgment of such technologies are needed to ensure originality and academic integrity (Lund et al., 2023). Rahman et al. (2023) highlight that in such a sensitive context as academia, where values of integrity and originality are determinant factors of new knowledge and career development, AI tools may be a risky choice that contributes to the lack of originality (Rahman et al., 2023). From a more technical perspective, Bringula (2023) suggests that tools like ChatGPT present limited ability to assist with the writing up. Issues such as fictitious references, misinformation, and plagiarism may lead to increased effort from the researcher to edit and validate information. The author/s eventually need to deal with anti-plagiarism platforms such as Turnitin that can expose this technology's unethical use (e.g., copying and pasting text) in academic writing, producing negative consequences for scholar's career.

In Tables 11.1a–d, we summarise the steps taken by the author/s, the potential of AI automation, and the relevant ethical considerations identified in using AI to implement different research tasks.

Table 11.1a   *AI automation levels in literature review activities and ethical considerations of using AI tools – stage 1: design the review*

Actions by author/s	Automation by AI tools	Ethical considerations
Determine the need for the literature review	Limited capability in understanding specific contextual needs or gaps in research	• Lack of rigorous evaluation • Lack of originality/erosion of critical evaluation
State the motivation and research questions	Ability to refine questions/ motivations. The unique purpose of a new study needs human intervention	• Lack of rigorous evaluation • Lack of originality/erosion of critical evaluation
Decide on the appropriate approach for the review	Ability to suggest methodologies but lacks the understanding to fully design an approach	• Lack of rigorous evaluation • Lack of originality/erosion of critical evaluation

Table 11.1b   *AI automation levels in literature review activities and ethical considerations of using AI tools – stage 2: conduct the review*

Actions by author/s	Automation by AI tools	Ethical considerations
Conduct a thorough search process	Ability to automate the search process	
Take proper measures to ensure research quality	Limited ability to assess the quality of the sources	• Selection biases • Black box methodologies • Lack of representativeness • Fabricated results

Table 11.1c   AI automation levels in literature review activities and ethical considerations of using AI tools – stage 3: data abstraction/ text analysis

Actions by author/s	Automation by AI tools	Ethical considerations
Abstract appropriate data from each article	Ability to summarise data from articles, although complex data require human oversight	• Originality and authenticity cannot be assessed or guaranteed • Lack of validity and accuracy • Poor paraphrasing and synthesising • Lack of fact-checking • Skewed representation of the literature
Use an appropriate analysis technique	Ability to assist in analysis of the text, but human expertise is needed	• Originality and authenticity cannot be assessed or guaranteed • Lack of validity and accuracy • Poor paraphrasing and synthesising • Lack of fact-checking • Skewed representation of the literature
Ensure transparency in the analysis process	Ability to document and structure, but transparency depends on human's input	• Originality and authenticity cannot be assessed or guaranteed • Lack of validity and accuracy • Poor paraphrasing and synthesising • Lack of fact-checking • Skewed representation of the literature

Table 11.1d   AI automation levels in literature review activities and ethical considerations of using AI tools – stage 4: structure and writing up

Actions by author/s	Automation by AI tools	Ethical considerations
Organise the review article	Ability to organise content but a unique narrative requires human intervention	• Academic integrity and plagiarism • Lack of originality and creativity (against core academic values) • Fictitious references and information
Report the result of the review	Ability to write but quality requires human input	• Academic integrity and plagiarism • Lack of originality and creativity (against core academic values) • Fictitious references and information

Actions by author/s	Automation by AI tools	Ethical considerations
Synthesise the findings	Ability to synthesise findings, but novel contribution requires a human's critical thinking	• Academic integrity and plagiarism • Lack of originality and creativity (against core academic values) • Fictitious references and information
Include further research directions	Ability to suggest areas for future research, but original and context-specific suggestions rely on human's expertise	• Academic integrity and plagiarism • Lack of originality and creativity (against core academic values) • Fictitious references and information

11.4   METHODS AND DATA ANALYSIS IMPLEMENTATION USING GENERATIVE AI: TRANSPARENCY AND PRIVACY

The use of AI in data collection and analysis can improve efficiency in processing large datasets, uncover hidden patterns, and potentially manage insights more efficiently compared to traditional methods facilitated by humans (e.g., Zhang & Tao, 2020; Xu et al., 2021). Recently, there has been an increase in AI tools that enable the collection and analysis of primary data. For example, innovative companies such as Remesh have launched popular AI-enabled platforms that can be used to collect qualitative and quantitative data and provide solutions to many leading organisations, such as Deloitte, when conducting research. In addition, ChatGPT has recently launched a tool where users can upload their datasets for fast data analysis that can accommodate the need for big data analysis and produce reliable results. However, using AI in data collection and analysis presents important ethical considerations. Two of the most discussed ethical concerns are transparency and privacy, often linked with the algorithm used to collect and analyse data and humans' intervention and the ability to understand and explain such a process (de Laat, 2022). We will now critically evaluate existing concerns in the process of data collection and analysis.

Use of AI in collecting data. During an ethical data collection process, participants' consent to participate in the study should be obtained. Transparency in providing consent information when AI models are used to collect data, means that participants need to fully understand the AI processes involved. Traditionally, researcher/s need to be explicit and transparent about the data collection process, including the sources of data, methods used, and the purposes for which the data will be utilised (Shank & DeSanti, 2018; Floridi &

Cowls, 2019). By using AI this will become a challenging task for researcher/s, as the wider audience may not always have the knowledge to understand the capabilities of such technologies (Shank & DeSanti, 2018; Semrl et al., 2023). Semrl et al. (2023) highlight that privacy and confidentiality information related to *data* collection, especially when AI models are used to process sensitive information, need to be acknowledged by the participants, and any concerns that may arise need to be addressed. Therefore, researcher/s need to introduce measures to protect the confidentiality and security of the collected data through AI-driven processes (Shank & DeSanti, 2018). More specifically, researchers need to implement strategies to "mitigate algorithmic biases", such as conducting bias assessments, diversifying training data, and employing fairness-aware algorithms. These efforts are essential for "promoting fairness and equity in data collection and analysis, particularly in sensitive research areas such as human reproduction research" (Semrl et al., 2023, pp. 2287–2288). In addition, Floridi and Cowls (2019) suggest that researchers need to safeguard the privacy of the participants whose data is being collected via data protection regulations and implement measures to prevent unauthorised access or the misuse of data.

The use of AI in analysing data. Using AI for data analysis raises ethical considerations regarding the fairness, accountability, transparency, and privacy of the AI algorithms employed in the analysis stage (Shank & DeSanti, 2018; Floridi & Cowls, 2019; Rahman et al., 2023). In assessing transparency and privacy, Shank and DeSanti (2018) suggest that the researcher needs to be clear about the motivations and the reasons behind the selection of the AI tool used to analyse the data, by providing a clear rationale of this choice and by providing insights on potential implications for individuals taking part in the investigation. However, various relevant questions on this matter have not yet been fully explored. For example, "Do researchers need to have permission from the ethics department to upload primary datasets (e.g., from consumer evaluations) to online platforms such as ChatGPT?" and "Who may access those data after they have been uploaded online?"; "Is this action aligned with the participant's consent form signed?" or "Does this violate any conditions following ethical guidelines of the country where the research was conducted (e.g., GDPR)?". Such unanswered questions raise concerns about privacy and the accountability and responsible use of AI in analysing data (Floridi & Cowls, 2019).

Moreover, technology is not error-free, and dealing with large datasets may often lead to errors (human or technological). Hence, researchers need to take responsibility for the action and be able to spot and correct any mistakes made. As a result, the data analysis process needs to always be monitored by humans. It has been suggested that the results of data analysis should be interpretable and explainable to stakeholders, including the methods used, assumptions made, and the potential limitations of the analysis so ethical considerations regarding transparency, privacy, and accountability will be mitigated. The consequences might be significant and harmful if researchers do not evaluate their data and the analysis process. Faulty data and errors resulting from the analysis may lead to several issues such as ineffective policies or unintended harm to study subjects. Machine learning algorithms can introduce interpretation errors, leading to unintended consequences in decision-making, such as in the "IBM Watson Oncology" case. Here, although significant investments and advances were made to the digital physician assistant based on machine learning, the system continued to make incorrect cancer treatment recommendations (Kristiansen et al., 2022). Drawing upon this incident and considering issues of accountability in using AI, we suggest that overreliance on automated AI systems during the data analysis stage may lead to significant consequences.

11.5 WRITING AND EDITING USING GENERATIVE AI: TRANSPARENCY AND ACCOUNTABILITY

There exist a significant number of studies that suggest that AI models are valuable tools that can be used when it comes to writing academic articles such as creating abstracts or the introduction section (e.g., Dubey & Dennehy, 2023; Imran & Almusharraf, 2023; Sallam, 2023). For instance, it has been suggested that ChatGPT can aid in language translation (Lund & Wang, 2023), final proofreading and editing, and writing content (Pividori & Greene, 2023). Huang and Tan (2023, p. 1153) argue that "ChatGPT can significantly enhance both the efficiency and the quality of writing review articles for scientists", while Ariyaratne et al. (2023) suggest that generative AI, such as ChatGPT can produce consistent research articles that may look like original articles published by scholars. However, recent studies have started to highlight the fact that often the use of AI in writing leads to generating inaccurate text, written in a poor language, which is not original, diverges from the actual meaning of the text, and, in most cases, produces a significant amount of a plagiarised text (e.g., Dubey & Dennehy, 2023; Suaverdez & Suaverdez, 2023).

These concerning issues regarding the use of AI in academic writing have led to debatable questions as to how these tools can be used in writing and publishing research articles. For instance, da Silva (2023) posed a worrying question; "Is ChatGPT a valid author?", while Rane et al. (2023, p. 853) argued that "ChatGPT is not capable of serving as an author". Researchers using AI in writing their articles have raised issues related to "authorship, credit, and intellectual property". Moreover, since AI can only generate information from its trained data, using these models in writing research articles might lead to unintentional plagiarism, and consequently affect researchers' integrity and transparency regarding their work (Else, 2023; Khalil & Er, 2023). Hence, it has been implied that if chatbots such as ChatGPT are being used in writing scientific and academic research articles, trust and transparency will be significantly diminished (Lucey & Dowling, 2023).

According to Hosseini et al. (2023), using NLP systems to draft scientific manuscripts and research articles will raise transparency concerns related to traditional authorship requirements, credits, and contributions to research papers. Since it is widely acknowledged and adopted by most journals (Resnik et al., 2016) that the requirement of becoming an author on an academic paper is to contribute to the writing stage, then NLP systems should be "acknowledged in the text and mentioned in the references section" (Hosseini et al., 2023, p. 5). This is because it is difficult to differentiate between text that is generated by human and text that is generated by AI (Stokel-Walker, 2023).

Moreover, since accountability is another pressing issue that occurs when using generative AI in academic writing (Hosseini et al., 2023) and these models produce texts that contain errors and misleading information and to some extent biased results, this will also lead to a critical question: "If a section of the research paper has been written with the use of AI modes, then who will be accountable for its accuracy?". Hosseini et al. (2023, p. 4) argue that author/s of the research paper should be held accountable for any errors, biased or misleading information that is generated by NLP systems. They argue that since "NLP systems respond to prompts provided by researchers and do not proactively generate text", it is the researcher/s that should be held accountable for the produced information by the NLP system when used in writing research articles. For instance, da Silva (2023) analysed AI-generated paragraphs and found that these texts were plagiarised from the original sources with little paraphrasing. On the other hand, Edwards and Duan (2023, p. 41) argue that "generative AI's lack of judgement or moral compass", impose significant challenges "as to how to safeguard academic standards and integrity". Hence "is it ethically and legally acceptable to directly use the text generated by a generative AI system in conducting and publishing research?". Therefore, the ethical implications of using generative AI in writing and presenting it as one's own work unintentionally require more restrictive measures and criteria to sustain academic integrity in scholarly research (Rane et al., 2023).

11.6   CONCLUSION

Based on the above discussion regarding the pitfalls of generative AI models and its adverse impact on academic research, we draw upon Margaret Mitchell's framework (2023) on AI algorithmic bias and fairness (see Figure 11.1). Mitchell's (2023) framework explains how human biases in AI models' training datasets create carry-over effects of human bias across all stages of using AI for the end user. The framework suggests that AI models such as

ChatGPT are being trained on certain databases that they use to produce the user's requested information. Since the trained dataset that AI models use is not known to the end user, this process is known as "Black Box Methodology". The trained data are used to process information for the end user.

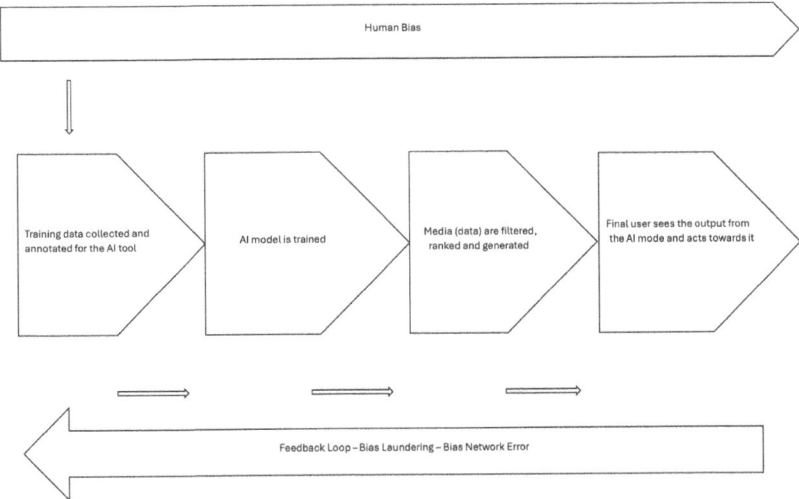

Source: Adapted from Mitchell (2023).

Figure 11.1   Bias Laundering framework

Moreover, Mitchell's (2023) framework discusses the implications and biases presented in those training data, such as the rationale behind the selection of the dataset or the accessibility of it. This process will inevitably present biases. For example, training data sets may present views from certain demographics omitting others (see also van Gestel, Chapter 10 in this volume), or datasets that should be trained and included are inaccessible or the permission for access cannot be granted. Using these training data, the AI model is trained to produce results that are relevant to the commands received by the user (e.g., keyword searching for a literature review). As a result of this process, biases occur at the first stages of designing the AI algorithm and continue to exist throughout the process of generating insights to the end user. Thereafter, relevant results will be produced, and the end user will act according to the generated output. This human error in the available training data to be used from an AI tool and the carry-over effects are known as a "Feedback Loop" or "Bias Laundering" or "Bias Network Error" (Mitchell, 2023). We adopt Mitchell's (2023) proposed framework, and we outline the ethical and moral considerations for using AI in academic research.

Training data and associated biases: AI models produce results after investigating the available datasets they have access to and are trained on. In this chapter, we discussed certain issues in the context of academic research. First, the accountability of the researcher/s in introducing new innovative idea, is discussed in section 2, and we argued that the use of AI produces inaccurate and biased information. We echo Hosseini et al.'s (2023) perspective on the question "who is being held accountable when NLP systems produce inaccurate and biased information, and this information is being used in academic articles?". The answer to this question lies in the transparency on how the available data are treated and used in AI models. This phenomenon is known as "Black Box Methodology" in AI systems, where there is a lack of transparency in AI's decision-making (Burrell, 2016). The accountability issue then comes into consideration, raising relevant questions such as "Is the researcher aware of the training data?" For instance, as we argued in section 3, during the first step of undertaking the literature review process, although AI may help academics in finding relevant articles, the AI users are not aware of the data sources that the AI model was trained on. Hence, this leads to accountability and authority issues as well as issues related to the quality of the produced results (Jarrah et al., 2023; Lund et al., 2023). The moral responsibility lies not only in the accountability of the researchers to critically assess and disclose the limitations of their AI tools, but also in their responsibility to ensure that the dissemination of knowledge remains just and equitable. These biases may lead to a skewed representation of knowledge that AI models generate, particularly in academic writing.

Model training and operational challenges: Based on the discussion in this chapter, we suggest that AI-generated results present a moral dilemma in that they can lead to the dissemination of unrepresentative and biased knowledge, eroding the ethical bedrock of academic research. As AI models are trained on datasets unknown to the researcher/s there is a lack of rigorous evaluation (Shank & DeSanti, 2018) of the results emanating from the AI and therefore the diversity and inclusivity of the sources cannot be assessed. Also, AI models may occasionally produce fabricated sources (Bringula, 2023). As discussed in section 3, all these considerations lead to a lack of representative results and inaccuracies (Jarrah et al., 2023). Applying Mitchell's (2023) framework, it can be suggested that such biases are inherited in the next steps of AI utilisation as a research tool. We argued that this process presents issues of academic integrity and may lead to overgeneralisations and stereotypes. This stage of the AI integration process raises substantial concerns regarding the ethical use of AI in generating academic content, as it challenges the foundational principles of academic research, including originality, critical engagement, the pursuit of unbiased knowledge and researcher/s' accountability (Nashwan et al., 2023; Rahman et al., 2023).

Outputs produced by AI and their implications: The output of AI in academic research is influenced by the biases discussed above in the training phase. The use of AI for literature review, data collection, data analysis, and academic writing can lead to moral complexities, such as inaccurate results, untrustworthy findings, and an erosion of critical thinking among researchers (Zou & Schiebinger, 2018). The non-critical or unsupervised use of AI in academic research may potentially undermine core values in the industry, such as respect for privacy (Floridi & Cowls, 2019; Semrl et al., 2023), research integrity, and transparency, as discussed in section 4.

Interaction of the final user with AI technologies: The final stage of Mitchell's (2023) framework leaves space to elaborate on the morality and ownership of the end user in interpreting and acting upon the information presented. In our context, this is related to the interaction between academics and AI-generated content. This interaction often lacks critical evaluation as academics may passively accept information presented without questioning the sources or the diversity of views. This may lead academics to overlook potential inaccuracies, biases, and the ethical implications of utilising AI-generated outputs. The convenience offered by AI can seduce researchers into diminishing their engagement in the critical and creative processes essential for innovative academic research (Eubanks, 2018). As discussed in section 5, AI often leads to generating text that is inaccurate or written in poor language, or is not original, and in many cases may lead to plagiarism (e.g., Dubey & Dennehy, 2023; Suaverdez & Suaverdez, 2023). Such issues question the role of AI in academic research and prompt us to reflect on how AI can assist academics transparently and reliably.

In the light of these findings, we suggest that higher educational institutions, publishing companies, and academics should adopt a more critical and ethically informed approach to utilising generative AI technologies (see also Miller, Chapter 13 in this volume). This involves developing comprehensive strategies to mitigate biases at the data collection stage and ensure that trained data are representative. Also, it is important to introduce metrics to assess the diversity inclusion of the generated outputs to ensure transparency and accountability in AI's operational mechanisms. This would encourage academics to critically evaluate rather than passively accept AI-generated outputs and will foster an academic culture that prioritises ethical considerations and critical engagement over convenience while embracing technological advancements.

REFERENCES

Almarie, B., Teixeira, P.E.P., Pacheco-Barrios, K., Rossetti, C.A., & Fregni, F. (2023). Editorial – The use of large language models in science: Opportunities and challenges. *Principles and Practice of Clinical Research*, 9(1), 1–4.

Ariyaratne, S., Iyengar, K.P., Nischal, N., Chitti Babu, N., & Botchu, R. (2023). A comparison of ChatGPT-generated articles with human-written articles. *Skeletal Radiology*, 1–4.

Aydın, Ö., & Karaarslan, E. (2022). OpenAI ChatGPT generated literature review: Digital twin in healthcare. In Ö. Aydın (Ed.), *Emerging Computer Technologies*, İzmir Akademi Derneği, pp. 22–31.

Boden, M. (2004). *The Creative Mind: Myths and Mechanisms*, 2nd ed. London: Routledge.

Bringula, R. (2023). What do academics have to say about ChatGPT? A text mining analytics on the discussions regarding ChatGPT on research writing. *AI and Ethics*, 1–13.

Burrell, J. (2016). How the machine "thinks": Understanding opacity in machine learning algorithms. *Big Data & Society*, 3(1).

Chan, C.K.Y. (2023). A comprehensive AI policy education framework for university teaching and learning. *International Journal of Educational Technology in Higher Education*, 20(1), 38.

da Silva, J.A.T. (2023). Is ChatGPT a valid author? *Nurse Education in Practice*, 68, 103600.

de Laat, P.B. (2022). Algorithmic decision-making employing profiling: Will trade secrecy protection render the right to explanation toothless? *Ethics and Information Technology*, 24(2), 17.

Dubey, R., & Dennehy, D. (2023). ChatGPT, scholarly writing and publishing. In Dwivedi et al. (2023). Opinion Paper: "So what if ChatGPT wrote it?" Multidisciplinary perspectives on opportunities, challenges and implications of generative conversational AI for research, practice and policy. *International Journal of Information Management*, 71, 102642, pp. 33–34.

Dwivedi et al. (2023). Opinion Paper: "So what if ChatGPT wrote it?" Multidisciplinary perspectives on opportunities, challenges and implications of generative conversational AI for research, practice and policy. *International Journal of Information Management*, 71, 102642.

Edwards, J.S., & Duan, Y. (2023). Towards a research agenda for generative AI in education, industry and research. In Dwivedi et al. (2023). Opinion Paper: "So what if ChatGPT wrote it?" Multidisciplinary perspectives on opportunities, challenges and implications of generative conversational AI for research, practice and policy. *International Journal of Information Management*, 71, 102642. pp. 39–42.

Else, H. (2023). Abstracts written by ChatGPT fool scientists. *Nature*, 613(7944), 423.

Eubanks, V. (2018). *Automating Inequality: How High-tech Tools Profile, Police, and Punish the Poor*. New York: St. Martin's Press.

Floridi, L., & Cowls, J. (2019). A unified framework of five principles for AI in society. *Harvard Data Science Review*, 1(1).

Guzik, E.E., Byrge, C., & Gilde, C. (2023). The originality of machines: AI takes the Torrance Test. *Journal of Creativity*, 33, 100065, 1–8.

Haase, J., & Hanel, P.H.P. (2023). Artificial muses: Generative artificial intelligence chatbots have risen to human-level creativity. *Journal of Creativity*, 33(3), 1–7.

Hosseini, M., Rasmussen, L.M., & Resnik, D.B. (2023). Using AI to write scholarly publications. *Accountability in Research: Ethics, Integrity and Policy*, 1–9.

Hsu, H-P. (2023). Can generative artificial intelligence write an academic journal article? Opportunities, challenges, and implications. *Irish Journal of Technology Enhanced Learning*, 7(2), 158–171.

Huang, J., & Tan, M. (2023). The role of ChatGPT in scientific communication: Writing better scientific review articles. *American Journal of Cancer Research*, 13(4), 1148.

Imran, M., & Almusharraf, N. (2023). Analyzing the role of ChatGPT as a writing assistant at higher education level: A systematic review of the literature. *Contemporary Educational Technology*, 15(4), 1–14.

Jarrah, H.Y., Alwaely, S., Darawsheh, S.R., Alshurideh, M., & Al-Shaar, A.S. (2023). Effectiveness of introducing artificial intelligence in the curricula and teaching methods. In M. Alshurideh et al. (Eds.), *The Effect of Information Technology on Business and Marketing Intelligence Systems*. Cham: Springer International Publishing, pp. 1885–1901.

Khalil, M., & Er, E. (2023). Will ChatGPT get you caught? Rethinking of plagiarism detection. arXivpreprint arXiv:2302.04335.

Kristiansen, T., Kjær, K., & Uldbjerg, J. (2022). Erroneous data: The Achilles' heel of AI and personalized medicine. *Frontiers in Digital Health*, 5.

Lucey, B., & Dowling, M. (2023). ChatGPT: Our study shows AI can produce academic papers good enough for journals – just as some ban it. *The Conversation*. https://theconversation.com/chatgpt-our-study-shows-ai-can-produce-academic-papers-good-enough-for-journals-just-as-some-ban-it-197762 (last accessed January 10, 2024).

Lund, B.D., & Wang, T. (2023). Chatting about ChatGPT: How may AI and GPT impact academia and libraries? *Library Hi Tech News*, 40(3), 26–29.

Lund, B.D., Wang, T., Mannuru, N. R., Nie, B., Shimray, S., & Wang, Z. (2023). ChatGPT and a new academic reality: Artificial Intelligence-written research papers and the ethics of the large language models in scholarly publishing. *Journal of the Association for Information Science and Technology*, 74(5), 570–581

Mitchell, M. (2023, December 5). The pillars of a rights-based approach to AI development. *TechPolicy.Press*. https://www.techpolicy.press/the-pillars-of-a-rightsbased-approach-to-ai-development/

Nashwan, S.A., Sadallah, M., & Bouteraa, M. (2023). Use of ChatGPT in academia: Academic integrity hangs in the balance. *Technology in Society*, 75, 102370.

Pekka, H., Agbese, M.O.O., Jantunen, M., Vakkuri, V., Mikkonen, T., Rousi, R., & Abrahamsson, P. (2023). The role of explainable AI in the research field of AI ethics. *ACM Transactions on Interactive Intelligent Systems*.

Pividori, M., & Greene, C.S. (2023). A publishing infrastructure for AI-assisted academic authoring. *BioRxiv*, 1–17.

Rahman, M., Terano, HJR, Rahman, N., Salamzadeh, A., & Rahaman, S. (2023). ChatGPT and academic research: A review and recommendations based on practical examples. *Journal of Education, Management and Development Studies*, 3(1), 1–12.

Rane, N.L., Choudhary, S.P., Tawde, A., & Rane, J. (2023). ChatGPT is not capable of serving as an author: Ethical concerns and challenges of large language models in education. *International Research Journal of Modernization in Engineering Technology and Science*, 5(10), 851–874.

Reed, L. (2022). ChatGPT for automated testing: From conversation to code. *Sauce Labs*.

Resnik, D.B., Tyler, A.M., Black, J.R., & Kissling, G. (2016). Authorship policies of scientific journals. *Journal of Medical Ethics*, 42(3), 199–202.

Rohan, R., Faruk, L.I.D., Puapholthep, K., & Pal, D. (2023). Unlocking the black box: Exploring the use of generative AI (ChatGPT) in information systems research. Paper presented at IAIT 23: Proceedings of the 13th International Conference on Advances in Information Technology, 17, 1–9.

Rowe, F. (2023). Magic or fast-food writing? When transformers challenge our epistemic values in teaching and research and our humanity. In Dwivedi et al. (2023). Opinion Paper: "So what if ChatGPT wrote it?" Multidisciplinary perspectives on opportunities, challenges and implications of generative conversational AI for research, practice and policy. *International Journal of Information Management*, 71, 102642, pp. 35–37.

Salah, M., Al Halbusi, H., & Abdelfattah, F. (2023). May the force of text data analysis be with you: Unleashing the power of generative AI for social psychology research. *Computers in Human Behavior: Artificial Humans*, 1, 1–6.

Sallam, M. (2023). ChatGPT utility in healthcare education, research, and practice: Systematic review on the promising perspectives and valid concerns. *Healthcare*, 11(887), 1–20.

Semrl, N., Feigl, S., Taumberger, N., Bracic, T., Fluhr, H., Blockeel, C., & Kollmann, M. (2023). AI language models in human reproduction research: exploring ChatGPT's potential to assist academic writing. *Human Reproduction*, 38(12), 2281–2288.

Shackell, C. (2023). Will AI kill our creativity? It could – if we don't start to value and protect the traits that make us human. *The Conversation*, September. https://theconversation.com/will-ai-kill-our-creativity-it-could-if-we-dont-start-to-value-and-protect-the-traits-that-make-us-human-214149 (last accessed January 31, 2024).

Shank, D.B., & DeSanti, A. (2018). Attributions of morality and mind to artificial intelligence after real-world moral violations. *Computers in Human Behavior*, 86, 401–411.

Simon, H. (1979). Rational decision making in business organizations. *The American Economic Review*, 69, 493–513.

Snyder, H. (2019). Literature review as a research methodology: An overview and guidelines. *Journal of Business Research*, 104, 333–339.

Song, C., & Song, Y. (2023). Enhancing academic writing skills and motivation: Assessing the efficacy of ChatGPT in AI-assisted language learning for EFL students. *Frontiers in Psychology*, 14, 1–14.

Stokel-Walker, C.J.N. (2023). ChatGPT listed as author on research papers: Many scientists disapprove. *Nature*, 613, 620–621.

Suaverdez, J., & Suaverdez, U. (2023). Chatbots impact on academic writing. *Global Journal of Business and Integral Security*, (2).

Tung, L. (2023). ChatGPT can write code. Now researchers say it's good at fixing bugs, too. *ZDNet*. https://www.zdnet.com/article/chatgpt-can-write-code-now-researchers-say-its-good-at-fixing-bugs-too/ (last accessed December 25, 2023).

Xu, Y., Liu, X., Cao, X., Huang, C., Liu, E., Qian, S., ... & Zhang, J. (2021). Artificial intelligence: A powerful paradigm for scientific research. *The Innovation*, 2(4), 1–20.

Zhai, X. (2022). ChatGPT user experience: Implications for education. Available at SSRN: https://ssrn.com/abstract=4312418 or http://dx.doi.org/10.2139/ssrn.4312418

Zhang, J., & Tao, D. (2020). Empowering things with intelligence: A survey of the progress, challenges, and opportunities in artificial intelligence of things. *IEEE Internet of Things Journal*, 8(10), 7789–7817.

Zou, J., & Schiebinger, L. (2018). AI can be sexist and racist – it's time to make it fair. *Nature*, 559, 324–326.

PART IV

The ugly

12. Beyond the Friedman doctrine: contextuality, social knowledge, and professional craftsmanship in business education

Jukka V. Mäkinen, Jukka I. Mattila, Mika Tammilehto, and Raisa Varsta

12.1 INTRODUCTION

Among other relevant management education, business education aims to deliver socially responsible managers for business and market economy needs. For some time, the credo of business has been understood along the lines of Chicago School Economists promoting a market economy free from government regulations and egalitarian redistributive policies. It connotes limited government protection of capitalist basic rights with low levels of taxation, especially for capital, and anti-labor (movement) policies (Friedman, 1962). In this context, Milton Friedman's (1970) idea that "the social responsibility of business is to increase its profits "has been the most influential statement about the social responsibility of business managers.

The Friedman doctrine describes the professional orientation of business managers, and according to Acemoglu and Johnson (2023), it is seen to be promoted by business schools worldwide. Despite a relatively long-lasting critique, the idea that the business manager's responsibility can be assessed based on the economic value created for shareholders holds strong. Here, a business firm is understood strictly as an economic actor run for the shareholders who are entitled to all the profits (Jensen and Meckling, 1976). This doctrine is promoted by major business schools, implying that business managers are using technology like artificial intelligence (AI) to challenge human labor and intellectual work to cut wages and generate maximum profits (Acemoglu & Johnson, 2023). It is supported by the mainstream theory of the firm (Jensen & Meckling, 1976) dominating business schools, and it can be seen as the most significant product of these Higher Education Institutions (Khurana, 2010).

In this setting, we see Acemoglu and Johnson (2023) arguing that technology is being used for dominance in labor relations, referring to various aspects such as negotiations over wages, working conditions, benefits, and terms of employment. Omnipresent AI, devoid of consciousness and accountability, used in driving this ideology leads to a situation where technology induces compliance or subservience in humans, a phenomenon we call "technodominance" (for loss of human agency as a result of AI, see also van Gestel, Chapter 10 in this volume). We examine this argument against the development of artificial intelligence and the role of higher education institutions in creating professional knowledge. We claim that novel technology like generative AI in the context of higher education institutions' teaching and research, as well as its political and socio-economic impact, can't bypass the fact that AI technology is produced by profit-oriented business actors, having profit-oriented customers, run by managers trained by higher education institutions to focus on profits as the dominant ethic of business managers. Taken as a whole, the Friedman doctrine, where the classical liberal political theory combines with shareholder wealth maximization on the level of the firms (Mäkinen & Kourula, 2012), produces a strong force that may direct the development of any technology, including all aspects of AI. Thus, the business education scheme affects the primary direction of AI technology (Acemoglu & Johnson, 2023). As institutions showing intellectual, civic, and societal responsibility, these higher education institutions promoting the Friedman doctrine need to assume some accountability for using AI and its derivates when providing education to their students.

We focus on professionalism, specifically in the context of AI and business education responsibilities. We ask what type of knowledge AI delivers here regarding the requirements for professional knowledge in the world of work as well as defined in the curricula in business education. Since we are interested in the academic setting where profit orientation is easily the dominant perspective in the use of technology, we need to discuss technology, especially AI, from this perspective. To address this topic, we first focus on AI and its dimensions regarding substituting for human labor and intellectual work to increase firm profits. This view is emphasized influentially by Daron Acemoglu and Simon Johnson (2023), who describe it as delivering knowledge that challenges autonomous human reasoning and decision-making and substitutes human labor for AI without significant productivity benefits. Since we consider the profit-oriented trajectory of AI technology to be somewhat problematic, we focus on an alternative perspective where AI technology is utilized with the help of responsible higher education institutions to complement human manual labor and intellectual work. This perspective highlights the role of higher education institutions in providing their students with relevant skills, competencies, and mindsets to utilize AI in their work in a responsible and ethically sound manner.

12.2   SUBSTITUTING NOT ONLY HUMAN LABOR BUT ALSO INTELLECTUAL WORK

AI applications based on a Large Language Model (LLM) are now easily capable of producing texts that are difficult to distinguish from those produced by humans. Despite the vast potential, serious concerns exist about the reliability of LLM-based technology used in knowledge production and the automation of human reasoning (see also Clark and Denman, Chapter 8 in this volume). It is suggested that AI will reduce "the cost of bullshit to zero" and that it is "great at mimicry and bad at facts" (Klein, 2023). Furthermore, Lindebaum and Fleming (2023) point out that AI (operating within its training data that may be false or badly trained) can't tell the difference between appearance and reality, and, therefore, does not deliver scientific knowledge. In addition, AI does not even aim for concrete contextual understanding and interpretation and is bad at understanding meanings (Lindebaum & Fleming, 2023).

Furthermore, Lindebaum and Fleming (2023) point out that AI is bounded by its training data, operates based on its high-probability decision logic, and cannot deliver significant new insights or present genuinely innovative thinking. Finally, since AI has no stakes in or commitment to the world (unlike humans), it is amoral intelligence operating without a genuine interest in truth and issues of right and wrong (Lindebaum & Fleming, 2023). However, these significant shortcomings of knowledge produced by LLMs do not mean that this technology cannot be used to substitute for human labor and critical thinking.

Digitalization, automation, and robotization are pictured as forces that profoundly impact the labor market by affecting the availability of waged work. As stated by the EU's Agency for the Development of Vocational Training – Cedefop (2022), future workforce and skills development is primarily connected to the hypothesis of "job polarization or routine-biased technological change." This hypothesis assumes that the digitalization of work will eradicate middle-skill, routine, or manual jobs, where human input is more expendable compared to the precision and cost-efficiency of robots or computerized machines. However, such developments are subject to political, economic, and social processes rather than technological ones (Avis, 2022). A significant implication of political choice affecting the primary direction of technology is presented by Darren Acemoglu and Simon Johnson (2023, 255) in their influential work *Power and Progress*. According to them, the USA from 1980 onwards is an example of a political economy where "digital technologies automated work, disadvantaged labor vis-à-vis capital, became the graveyard of shared prosperity, and where wage inequality surged." For them, this anti-labor redirection of digital technology affecting the direction of AI is deeply related to the Friedman doctrine promoted by business schools.

In Friedman's doctrine, maximizing profits represents the common good; it is seen as the basic principle for organizing the whole of society, and the task of business managers is to maximize shareholder value (Friedman, 1962; 1970). According to Acemoglu and Johnson (2023) this doctrine explains the anti-human tendency of digital technology in the US and beyond and the dominant ways of using AI. Supported by other influential economic theories, such as Michel Jensen's (Jensen & Meckling, 1976) agency theory, this doctrine made big businesses the promoters of the common good in society and gave their managers a clear target. It started the "shareholder value revolution" that "justified all sorts of efforts at moneymaking" and "altered the balance between managers and workers" so that good managers do not pay high wages (Acemoglu & Johnson 2023, 270–273).

This meant new things for business schools since the number of managers trained in them increased significantly, and these schools started to embrace and spread the doctrine (Khurana, 2010). Thus, according to Acemoglu and Johnson (2023, 273), business managers who "attended business schools started implementing the Friedman doctrine, especially when it came to wage setting. They stopped wage growth in their firms, compared to similar companies run by managers who did not attend business schools ... [and] they do increase shareholder value because they cut wages." Beyond wage setting, this same doctrine also offered business managers justification to fight against the labor movement since maximization of shareholder value represents the common good, and all the forces against profits undermine the common good (Acemoglu & Johnson, 2023; Acemoglu et al., 2022). The doctrine also increased the power of businesses against government regulations and offered large corporations major political powers, even though the doctrine is officially against the politicization of businesses (Lindman et al., 2023). Here, the ideas of another Chicago School Economist, George Stigler (Löppönen, 2017), who opposed anti-trust actions and saw them in the same light as other illegitimate government interventions in free markets, came to play a major role in leading to the competition policy where governments need to show the inefficiency of Big Tech in terms of price increases before they can use the anti-trust measures (Khan, 2017). Due to this approach, "[f]rom 1980 to today, concentration (market power of the largest firms) increased in more than three-quarters of US industries" (Acemoglu & Johnson, 2023, 276).

Thus, due to Friedman's doctrine, many American managers came to see labor as a cost that needed to be cut. To do so, business schools, major consulting companies, and the tech sector developed a new vision of reengineering the corporation. Software tools were used to downsize workforces and automate various office jobs, while robots were used to automate manual work and reduce the labor intensity of production. These technologies could have been used differently. However, the lack of a powerful labor movement in the US acting as a counterforce, US government tax policy favoring capital over labor, and lack of government technology leadership and funding (all related to the Friedman doctrine) gave the cost-cutting direction to technology in the US and globally (Acemoglu & Johnson, 2023, 284–288).

From that perspective, there is a considerable threat that generative artificial intelligence like ChatGPT and other LLMs will play out as a new technological tool for business school-educated managers to remake society, cut the costs of human labor, and substitute for human reasoning to increase profits. In this setting, the tech industry focuses on "extensive data collection and the automation of narrow tasks based on machine-learning techniques" (Acemoglu & Johnson, 2023, 263). However, the problem with this strategy, according to Acemoglu and Johnson (2023, 320), is that "humans are not as useless as sometimes presumed" and "machines are not as intelligent as typically assumed," leading to the displacement of humans with "little of the productivity gains." Thus, if AI is used to substitute for human intelligence, it simply "replaces humans in tasks for which we accumulated relevant skills over centuries" and which are a "mixture of routine and more complex activities that involve social communication, problem-solving, flexibility, and creativity. In such activities, humans draw on tacit knowledge and expertise that is context-dependent and situational" (Nonaka & Toyama, 2003, 3; Acemoglu & Johnson, 2023, 312).

It is important to remember that LLMs are predicting responses rather than knowing the meaning of these responses and that knowing and predicting are two different things (Hannigan et al., 2024). Some limitations of LLM-produced "knowledge" can be stated along the lines of Lindebaum and Fleming (2023). First, they focus on human reflexivity, which forms a significant part of critical thinking, as well as the human capacity to problem-solve and make (ethical) judgments. They point out that AI operates based on high-probability choices within the boundaries of its training data. However, human reflexivity often involves low-probability choices or ways of thinking that are novel within the boundaries of training data (innovative within the box) or even outside them (out-of-the-box innovation). The risk is that using wide high probability LLM systems may undermine human capacities for critical and creative thinking and the skills involved in making context-sensitive ethical judgments that demand moral imagination (Werhane, 2002).

For Acemoglu and Johnson (2023, 313) the most significant problem of AI undermining human "judgement" and "initiative" in production is that "human intelligence derives its strength from being situational and social." Thus, information used in human problem-solving "resides in the community," and to acquire it "implicit and explicit human communication" is needed. Furthermore, our reasoning is based on "social communication" and additional capabilities and skills humans gain from the "empathy" leading to shared objectives. However, the problem is that AI can't perform production tasks well "that involve social interaction, adaption, flexibility, and communication." This means that the substitution trajectory of AI leads to human losses without major productivity gains. Maybe there are alternatives without such dismal effects.

12.3   COMPLEMENTING HUMANS RESPONSIBLY

We must go beyond Friedman doctrine's political assumptions to prepare an alternative to substitution discussion where AI technology is used to complement human labor and critical thinking in higher education, especially in business education. Here, we can follow the propositions of Christopher Grey (2004), who writes that, at a minimum, it is clear that management education must explicitly recognize the political, ethical, and philosophical dimensions. While the critique that management education should focus on the practical aspects of management is significant, the solution should not only involve devising supposedly more effective techniques (see also Miller, Chapter 13 in this volume). Such an approach would further detach management from broader ethical values going beyond profit maximization.

Another important perspective relates to the nature of professional knowledge and the capability to create and utilize it. Professional knowledge has many different definitions, and there is no consensus on how to define professionalism and professionals (Alvesson, 2004; Buch & Jensen, 2018, 100). Lave and Wenger (1991) argue that creating professional knowledge by learning is not only an individual cognitive process but also a contextually situated social process through which newcomers become part of a community of practice and move toward full participation.

Williams and Rattray (2004) argue that management competence is always imperfect and exists only through mutual acceptance. It is always ephemeral – an agreed way of knowing and discussing management. This acceptance of a person's expertise can be changed unilaterally, in which case the expertise "disappears." This also leads us to discuss knowledge's social and contextual nature, especially professional knowledge.

Nonaka and Toyama (2003) define the creation of professional knowledge as a dialectical and contextual process in which various contradictions are synthesized through dynamic interactions among individuals, the organization, and the environment. According to Nonaka and Toyama, the interdependence between the agents and environment sets a framework for knowledge creation in this process. Further, in addition to structural interaction, dialectic knowledge creation occurs as the actors embrace their environment and synthesize tacit and explicit knowledge in social space. In knowledge creation, social, cultural, and historical contexts are important for individuals because such contexts give one the basis to interpret information to create meanings.

Following Rogoff (1994), learning is a change process through participation. People's/individuals' development depends on how their roles and understandings change in their activities. Rogoff rests here on John Dewey's (1859–1952) ideas, best formulated in the following citation: "The principle that development of experience comes about through interaction means that education is essentially a social process" (Dewey, 1938, 58) Rogoff's metaphor relates to apprenticeship, as she describes learning opportunities when novices learn a craft through observing and working with others as they contribute to the work (Rogoff, 1994). Thus, although we could argue that AI can learn, it cannot reflect the situational and contextual aspects of professional knowledge creation as humans do. In this case, there is a risk that using AI in decision-making fails to consider the relevant features of the operational context. This is relevant as knowledge can be regarded as one of the critical sources of sustainable competitive advantage (Nonaka, 1991; Nonaka & Toyama, 2003).

As mentioned, the classical liberalism of Friedman's doctrine aims for a market economy free from government regulations, free from egalitarian redistributive policies and related taxes, and free from organized labor, among other things. In addition, the alternative business school strategy needs a different theory of the business firm where the central task of businesses goes beyond profit maximization. After all, in the Acemoglu and Johnson argument, the Friedman doctrine explains the substitution direction of digital and AI technology.

To positively affect and transform this substitution tendency of AI, responsible business education needs to focus on delivering an alternative (to Friedman's classical liberal) variety of capitalism that could better complement human labor and thinking. Since Acamogly and Johnson (2023) do not focus much on this alternative perspective, we will briefly discuss these issues from the firm's political theory perspective in our final section.

The central idea of the complementation perspective is to focus on technology and the ways it empowers humans. Firstly, this can take place in tasks that people are already doing, and in this setting, the focus is on issues such as the "usability" of technology, "human-computer interaction," and "human-centered design," expanding "human skills" and "complementing human intelligence." Secondly, technology can create new tasks for people, as is done in personalized education with the help of digital technologies or in healthcare reforms where right kind of technology empowers professionals. Thirdly, creative human decision-making based on "drawing analogies" and "finding new combinations" can be helped by technologies that provide useful information and filter it accurately. Fourthly, technology can unite "people with different skills and endowments" (Acemoglu & Johnson, 2023, 327–330).

AI-produced knowledge is based on historical training data, and the quality and relevance of this data may vary. It is also essential to understand that AI does not consider the specific contexts of knowledge as humans do. Professionals must often operate in novel settings (within or out of the box) or changing operational environments. It is argued that in these types of situations, the best professionals are the ones who have a reflexive and reflective orientation to their work, i.e., experts are capable of evaluating and reflecting on their experiences and actions concerning the characteristics of their operational context. Argyris and Schön (1978) define this process as a double-loop learning.

To take these significant aspects of professional expert knowledge and its development seriously in business education, but also more broadly in the higher education sector, there is a need to ask a fundamental question: What kind of education must be provided (and how) to cope with the changes that especially AI will bring and how to learn to utilize it in an ethically sustainable manner? How do we ensure that curricula and pedagogical methods used in business education enhance human reflexivity, foster the professional growth and development of the individual, as well as communication among professionals, while simultaneously fulfilling the technological understanding of the role of a shrinking job description and productive efficiency? What kind of skills and expertise does the world of work expect? After all, in its fundamental nature, expertise is social and contextual, and the community defines who is an expert and what constitutes expertise. On the other hand, the constitutive starting point of the business schools' agenda, the managers, are individuals in their various roles and positions. Nevertheless, leadership is inherently social, and networks of close associates play an important role in leaders' learning and competence development (Aaltola et al., 2022).

The importance of social and cultural context is also highlighted by Siljander (2012), analyzing the thoughts of Johann Herbart (1776–1841), who asserts that the educatee's free will does not direct the process of self-formation. The Herbartian concept of Bildung emphasizes the pedagogical idealism that a learner can achieve self-formation and learning in a self-directed manner without external influence. This approach refutes the radical constructivist idea that an individual's subjective world and its meaning relationships can be freely constructed or adjusted without the objective structures of the sociocultural world. It is important to acknowledge that the sociocultural world's structures significantly impact the learner's subjective process of knowledge construction.

Knowledge is information that has been given meaning and has potential appropriability within the firm and its business environment. Quoting Davenport and Prusak (1998, 5), "Knowledge is a mix of framed experience, values, contextual information and expert insight that provides a framework for evaluating and incorporating new experiences and information." Therefore, it is important to focus in business education on practice- and context-based conceptions of knowledge, skills, and competence, studying the notion of professional "craftsmanship" among business students and assessing the potential for AI to enhance competency development in business "craftsmanship." Simultaneously, focusing on business teachers' conception of professionalism is important, exploring how AI may impact their pedagogy and didactics.

In addition, it is vital to see critical thinking as a significant human activity and be concerned about the potential pitfalls of aiming to outsource this activity to AI. This trend can lead to a lack of awareness of the social and cultural context in which thinking occurs, how elements relate, and how systems function. The critical question here is how relevant knowledge related to business practice is created and understood in the era of AI. We acknowledge that knowledge construction is an active and situational learning process, essentially a form of pragmatic craftsmanship that combines theoretical and practical knowledge dimensions. This notion also holds in the context of business education and business students. In this setting, the central issue is the importance of context sensitivity, the human ability to adapt decision-making to specific social circumstances and yield positive outcomes even in situations lacking prior examples. This skill is closely tied to strategic iteration, intuition, and reflexivity – all vital components of critical thinking.

Furthermore, in business education that we would like to promote, significant emphasis is placed on theoretical knowledge, fostering critical thinking, and the practical application of concepts and knowledge in various working contexts and situations. What is needed here is a pedagogical approach that supports the dialogue between theory and practice, and fosters the development of practical skills, the cultivation of expertise, and a deep understanding of the profession, as well as enhancing the capabilities to apply skills and expertise in different contexts. Additionally, the significance of professional identity and ethics as a cornerstone for competence-based growth deserves further emphasis. This highlights the social dimension of higher education, i.e., the interconnectedness of learning, personal development, and the demands of expertise/skills in working life. The promotion of the (uncritical) use of generative AI in higher education would not only dehumanize our working life by undermining the human effort without significant productivity gains but, due to its deficiencies, also produce unintelligent solutions and subsequent outcomes, the long-lasting effects of which are no less than consequential.

12.4   BUSINESS EDUCATION AND SCHOOLS CONTRIBUTING TO A POSITIVE AI TRAJECTORY

Technology's direction is not separate from the theory of the firm, and the theory of the firm is not separate from political doctrines. For this reason, it is important that business education systematically explores different economic theory starting points and political backgrounds. Higher education institutions should produce knowledge and skills that are not only subject to calculative rationality. Knowledge is situational and social. Teaching in business education and, more generally, in higher education institutions should emphasize those forms of reasoning and learning that are not easily replaceable by generative AI. This applies also to the pedagogical approaches in higher education. AI should be used as a tool to support the teachers' work rather than replacing teachers. The most effective approach to using AI in teaching involves collaboration between AI and humans (Wilson & Daugherty, 2018; Kim et al., 2022; see also Martin and Williams, Chapter 2 in this volume).

One of the central tasks of responsible business education is to study and promote alternative varieties of capitalism with more positive AI trajectories than Friedman's doctrine. In this setting, one significant political tradition that could provide guidance is called high liberalism (Freeman, 2011). In it, the relatively strong institutions of the democratic state financed by taxes protect individual basic rights, promote political freedom and equality of opportunity, take care of distributive justice, and maintain the separation of business and politics (Rawls, 2001). Here, the scope for public structures in promoting political freedom and equality, and redistributing economic power over time, is more comprehensive than in classical liberalism.

Unlike Friedman's classical liberal limited government, the high liberal basic structure of society does not favor capital over labor, takes care of economic justice with the help of pre-distributive and re-distributive taxation and ownership structures, and focuses on shared prosperity. In this way, it supports human labor and reasoning institutionally in the labor markets. In a high liberal political setting, the conception of the business firm can also be changed from the narrow shareholder perspective to focus more on the firm's total economic value. Interestingly, the early developer of the dominant shareholder conception of the firm, Michael Jensen himself, has put forward some major elements of this alternative conception (2002). When developed further, this theory of the firm focuses on a company's long-run total economic value. It can consider all the firm's economic stakeholders, including labor. In it, the central task of a responsible manager is not to cut wages and fight against labor (movement) since they are the manager's major stakeholders.

In this high liberal setting, also the taxation authorities of the high liberal society can be seen as significant stakeholders of the firm (Kasanen et al., 2023). Thus, (instead of Friedmanian minimization of taxes) business managers' orientation changes so that high liberal government gets more economic resources via taxes to provide high-quality education and training for labor. This is needed since the development of technology and the changing nature of work continue to impact the skills required for the job. The development of AI will increase the speed of change, creating disruption and reorganization in every area of human experience. As the nature of work continues to change, so must the skills base needed to meet market demand and other pressures for change. As Cedefop (2022) notes, although digitalization evitably leads to some job losses, its impact will more likely result predominantly in task transformation in most jobs. The focus then will be on accommodating upskilling and reskilling needs. The demand for IT literacy and digital skills has arisen, as has been the case for some time in various professions. In the Finnish context, IT development is most clearly reflected in the renewal of job content within occupations. The occupational structure of the labor market change is more gradual, with entire job functions disappearing over time. The new jobs that replace them require higher skills (Ranki, 2023).

The projected shift in competencies and skills has been reflected by, among other actors, large international consulting firms like Mckinsey (Dondi et al., 2021), business journals like Forbes (Forbes, 2022), and academia (e.g., Voogt & Roblin, 2012). From the tradition of educational science, the proposed competencies are categorized under the umbrella of human capital. They are conceptualizations of the generic competencies of the enterprising, individualized, and self-responsible subject (Avis, 2022).

In this sense, from the impact of AI on the triad of the labour market, skills, and education, new issues have been raised for reflection, and old assumptions are being seriously reexamined. The rapid rise of AI has challenged researchers' and educational institutions' own assumptions about what the education sector has to offer and how it matches students' aspirations and employers' demands. The most pessimistic picture has been one of asking what kind of knowledge is needed, because all possible knowledge is found on smart devices, and, ultimately, AI will take care of the instantaneous need for knowledge. The other view is symbiotic; AI is a capable resource and at its best is a "supporting intelligence." It acts not as a substitute for human cognitive resources but as an extension of them. The keyword in this perspective of the use of AI is controlled, and the focus is, of course, on the individual's ability to manage and use AI productively. As said, the promotion of the (uncritical) use of generative AI in higher education would not only dehumanize our working life by undermining the human effort without significant productivity gains but, due to its deficiencies, also produce unintelligent solutions and subsequent outcomes, the long-lasting effects of which are no less than consequential.

REFERENCES

Aaltola, P., Lainema, K., Laajala, M., Hämäläinen, R., Manninen, A., & Koponen, S. (2022). Tiedosta tekoihin: Vuorovaikutus ja yhteisöllinen oppiminen johtajien koulutuksessa. *Amaatikasvatuksen aikakauskirja*, 24(1): 27–43.

Acemoglu, D., & Johnson, S. (2023). *Power and Progress*. New York: PublicAffairs.

Acemoglu, D., He, A., & le Maire, D. (2022). Eclipse of rent-sharing: the effects of managers' business education on wages and the labor share in the US and Denmark. NBER Working Paper Series. Working Paper 29874. http://www.nber.org/papers/w29874

Alvesson, M. (2004). *Knowledge Work and Knowledge-Intensive Firms*. Oxford: Oxford University Press.

Argyris, C., & Schön, D. (1978). *Organizational Learning: A Theory of Action Perspective*. Reading, MA: Addison-Wesley Publishing Co.

Avis, R. (2022). Thinking about the future: The Fourth Industrial Revolution, capitalism, waged labour and anti-work. In: Margaret Malloch, Len Cairns, Karen Evans, & Bridget N. O'Connor (Eds.), *The Sage Handbook of Learning and Work*. London: Sage Publications.

Buch, A., & Jensen, H. (2018). Professionalism, practice, and knowledge policy. In: Anders Buch & Theodore Schatzki (Eds.), *Questions of Practice in Philosophy and Social Theory*. New York: Routledge.

Cedefop (2022). *Challenging Digital Myths: First Findings from Cedefop's Second European Skills and Jobs Survey*. Policy brief. Luxembourg: Publications Office. http://data.europa.eu/doi/10.2801/818285

Davenport, T. H., & Prusak, L. (1998). *Working Knowledge*. Boston, MA: Harvard Business School Press.

Dewey, J. (1938). *Experience and Education*. New York: Collier Books.

Dondi, M., Klier, J., Panier, F., & Schubert, J. (2021). Defining the skills citizens will need in the future world of work. McKinsey & Company, June 25. https://www.mckinsey.com/industries/public - sector/our-insights/defining-the-skills-citizens-will-need-in-the-future-world-of-work

Forbes (2022). 15 skills employers seek in 2022 (and ways to gain them mid-career). https://www.forbes.com/sites/forbescoachescouncil/2022/08/11/15-skills-employers-seek- in-2022-and-ways-to-gain-them-midcareer

Freeman, S. (2011). Capitalism in the classical and high liberal traditions. *Social Philosophy and Policy*, 28(2): 19–55.

Friedman, M. (1962). *Capitalism and Freedom*. Chicago: University of Chicago Press.

Friedman, M. (1970). The social responsibility of business is to increase its profits. *New York Times Magazine*, September 13.

Grey, C. (2004). Reinventing business schools: The contribution of critical management education. *Academy of Management Learning & Education*, 3(2), 178–186.

Hannigan, T., McCarthy, I., & Spicer, A. (2024). Beware of botshit: How to manage the epistemic risks of generative chatbots. Forthcoming in *Business Horizons*.

Jensen, M. C. (2002). Value maximization, stakeholder theory, and the corporate objective function. *Business Ethics Quarterly*, 12(2): 235–256.

Jensen, M. C., & Meckling, W. H. (1976). Theory of the firm: Managerial behavior, agency costs and ownership structure. *Journal of Financial Economics*, 3(4): 305–360.

Kasanen, E., Kinnunen, J., & Mäkinen, J. (2023). Measuring company financial performance in enlarged stakeholder settings. Available at SSRN: https://ssrn.com/abstract =4602174 or http://dx.doi.org/10.2139/ssrn.4602174

Khan, L. M. (2017). Amazon's anti-trust paradox. *Yale Law Journal*, 126(3): 710–805.

Khurana, R. (2010). *From Higher Aims to Hired Hands: The Social Transformation of American Business Schools and the Unfulfilled Promise of Management as a Profession*. Princeton, NJ: Princeton University Press.

Kim, J., Lee, H., & Cho, Y. (2022). Learning design to support student-AI collaboration: Perspectives of leading teachers for AI in education. *Education and Information Technologies*, 27(5), 6069–6104.

Klein, N. (2023). AI machines aren't "hallucinating". But their makers are. *The Guardian*. https://www.theguardian.com/commentisfree/2023/may/08/ai-machines -hallucinating-naomi-klein

Lave, J. & Wenger, E. (1991). *Situated Learning: Legitimate Peripheral Participation*. Cambridge: University of Cambridge Press.

Lindebaum, D., & Fleming, P. (2023). ChatGPT undermines human reflexivity, scientific responsibility and responsible management research. *British Journal of Management*, 35(2): 566–575.

Lindman, J., Makinen, J., & Kasanen, E. (2023). Big Tech's power, political corporate social responsibility and regulation. *Journal of Information Technology*, 38(2): 144–159. https://doi.org/10.1177/02683962221113596.

Löppönen, P. (2017) *Vapauden markkinat: Uusliberalismin kertomus*. Tampere: Vastapaino.

Mäkinen, J., & Kourula, A. (2012). Pluralism in political corporate social responsibility. *Business Ethics Quarterly*, 22(4): 649–678.

Nonaka, I. (1991). The knowledge-creating company. *Harvard Business Review*, 96–104.

Nonaka, I., & Toyama, R. (2003). The knowledge-creating theory revisited: Knowledge creation as a synthesizing process. *Knowledge Management Research & Practice*, 1(1): 2–10.

Ranki, S. (2023). *HELP-katsaus: Työelämän muutosnäkymät*, Työterveyslaitos. https:// www.julkari.fi/handle/10024/145859

Rawls, J (2001). *Justice as Fairness: A Restatement*. Cambridge, MA: Harvard University Press.

Rogoff, B. (1994). Developing understanding of the idea of communities of learners. *Mind, Culture, and Activity*, 1(4): 209–229.

Siljander, P. (2012). Educability and *Bildung* in Herbart's theory of education. In: P. Siljander, A. Kivelä, & A. Sutinen (Eds.) *Theories of* Bildung *and Growth: Connections and Controversies Between Continental Educational Thinking and American Pragmatism*. Rotterdam: Sense Publishers.

Voogt, J. & Roblin, N. P. (2012). A comparative analysis of international frameworks for 21st century competences: Implications for national curriculum policies. *Journal of Curriculum Studies*, 44(3): 299–321.

Werhane, P. H. (2002). Moral imagination and systems thinking. *Journal of Business Ethics*, 38: 33–42.

Williams, R., & Rattray, R. (2004). Consultobabble's facilitatory role in process con-sultation. *Managerial Auditing Journal*, 19(2): 180–190. https://doi.org/10.1108/02686900410517812

Wilson, H., & Daugherty, P. (2018). Collaborative intelligence: Humans and AI are joining forces. *Harvard Business Review*, 114–123.

13. Generative AI as a challenge to faculty development: ugly advice at the dawn of generative AI

Michelle D. Miller

The rapid arrival of generative AI within higher education has triggered a flood of resources, guides, and other supports to help faculty cope. These efforts are well-intentioned, reflecting a sincere wish to get faculty off to a good start as they begin to incorporate AI into their teaching, and possibly in their research and other professional work as well.

Yet at this early stage, some of the guidance being offered to faculty ranges from frustratingly vague to actively unhelpful. Faculty may be receiving ominously worded warnings that their assignments, exams, and syllabi all need deep and immediate revision to avert rampant cheating. They may simultaneously be hearing exhortations to take advantage of all AI can supposedly do to enhance their teaching, or even, how it could take over some of their own time-consuming professional tasks (on time-impoverishment, see also Kerem, Chapter 6 in this volume). And finally, faculty are probably being told that they need to begin teaching their students how to use AI, lest future undergraduates end up woefully unprepared to succeed in the AI-driven workplaces of the future. But notably lacking in these communications may be specific statements about where to start, concrete examples of practice, or intriguing ideas to seed their creativity.

This is *ugly advice*: It's not bad, exactly, but in no way is it good.

One reason why it is not good is that it is not helping academic leaders accomplish what most of them are trying to do at this juncture: set the stage for the AI-aware teaching that needs to start taking root at institutions of higher learning. It is also contributing to the sense of overwhelm, bewilderment, or not knowing where to begin that is currently common among faculty (Stanford, 2023).

Those of us working in the field of faculty professional development can do better by informing and also inspiring faculty, sharing what they most need to know while also allaying fears to the best extent possible. Without effective supports for faculty, efforts to incorporate and manage impacts of AI will surely fall short. It's true that some faculty will take the initiative to come up with their own approaches even in the absence of extensive guidance, and some of these approaches will be impressive. However, these innovations will not be implemented consistently across a campus. Students will come away with AI-related experiences – be they policies, assignments, or opportunities to develop skills – that are scattered ineffectively across the curriculum.

Avoiding this fate, and ensuring a coherent and reasonably comprehensive exposure to AI for all students, requires that we share good advice with faculty. In other words, we need AI-informed faculty professional development, policies, and materials that go beyond vague urgings to address the issue, and instead offer faculty tangible action steps, examples, and inspirations that they can use, and will want to use.

I come to this topic from a particular positioning within higher education. I have been a faculty member for 25 years at a public, comprehensive institution of higher education in the western United States, where I've taught courses in psychological science at the undergraduate and graduate levels. I'm also trained as a researcher in the sub-discipline of cognitive psychology, which focuses on mental processes such as memory, attention, and the development of expertise. This disciplinary perspective has shaped my own work with faculty, something I have done through books, articles, workshops, and one-on-one consultations. From all of these experiences, I've learned that there are right ways and wrong ways to go about advising faculty as they seek to make deep changes to their pedagogy. I've also learned that those wrong ways, such as the ugly advice I'll discuss in this chapter, have pernicious effects throughout a campus, steadily eroding teaching quality and faculty morale.

It does not have to be this way, though. One faculty member seeing ideas that truly inspire them can put those ideas into practice right away, impacting dozens or even hundreds of students. Multiple faculty members working to put a coherent set of principles into practice can impact thousands. This kind of support isn't easy to create, but it is worth it, especially in a time when technological changes like the rise of AI demand a rapid and reasoned response.

13.1   WHO THIS CHAPTER IS FOR

This chapter is primarily geared to readers working in higher education. This includes degree-granting universities, colleges, and community colleges, but can also extend to other organizations that help train and develop skills among adults. There are lessons within the chapter that can apply to other professional settings, including secondary schools (high schools, in the United States context) or professional organizations that faculty might belong to as part of their disciplines or research programs.

I'll be referring in the chapter to "leadership" and "leaders" quite a bit as well. In the present context, these terms refer, first, to upper-level staff responsible for developing strategies, making policy decisions, and crafting institution-wide communications. This group includes the deans, vice presidents, and provosts whose words can change the course of an entire organization.

Leadership comprises some other important roles beyond just these high-profile ones. Faculty professional development staff, especially when situated within a dedicated office for teaching and learning, contribute powerfully to the teaching mission of a campus (Gyurko et al., 2016; Magna Publications, 2015). Directors of these centers are major players in advising faculty and thus influencing teaching practices. Instructional designers, as well, may not have the institutional profile or authority of those at dean status or above, but, because they frequently work one-on-one with faculty in designing courses, are important contributors to campus teaching practices involving AI and other technologies. Faculty without formal positions in faculty development may still be informal leaders, individuals whom others look to for advice on teaching and learning, and whose words carry special weight on a campus. Lastly, librarians and library leadership are another group poised to help direct AI policy and strategy.

Now, a word about the North American-centered perspective you may notice in this chapter. Because I've spent my professional career as a faculty member in the United States, this cultural context will necessarily infuse everything that I have to say. Readers from outside this context may be working within institutions that are organized differently than what I've described, and may face challenges – resource limitations, expectations from policymakers, access to technology – that aren't adequately addressed in this chapter. But even within the narrow confines of US higher education structures, there is a wide and varied spectrum of approaches, access to resources, and missions. While I can't guarantee that what I have to say will generalize across the entire global education community, my goal has been to offer guidance that is broadly inclusive of the kinds of systems and resources most common to any post-secondary institution that foregrounds teaching as an important part of its overall mission.

13.2   RECOGNIZING UGLY ADVICE

As critical thinkers and academics, we can probably spot advice that simply repeats industry talking points: the breathless (and frequently evidence-free) claims that generative AI tools will revolutionize workplaces, replacing whole classes of human information workers with chatbot equivalents. Or, less ominously, confident assertions of how today's professionals can just hop on AI to cut hours and hours of tedium out of their jobs, no matter what those jobs might actually entail (see also Mäkinen, Mattila, Tammilehto and Varsta, Chapter 12 in this volume).

Other forms of ugly advice are less obvious. Here are its most important defining characteristics, especially as they might manifest in communications to faculty. Ugly advice is:

- *Generic.* It attempts to address anyone, anywhere, teaching in any dis-cipline and at any level. Besides commingling important audiences and constituencies, it also conflates distinct issues within the overall topic of AI. Concerns about academic dishonesty are mixed in with new goals around preparing students to work effectively with AI, data privacy issues combine with the need to address media literacy in new ways, and so on.
- *Vague.* When advice tries to address a tangle of distinct issues all at once it becomes superficial, making it impossible for faculty to discern what they are supposed to do next. Faculty may come away with the impression they should be doing *something* to address this new AI development, but don't have a sense of exactly what that something is.
- *Anxiety-provoking.* Advice that emphasizes the speed and scope of the AI revolution, absent specific action steps faculty should be taking, is a perfect recipe for stoking worry and apprehension. Emphasizing the threat AI poses – to jobs, to academic integrity, even to the value of a college educa-tion – is unhelpful to faculty tasked with managing the change, regardless of whether the threats might have some grounding in reality.

Other red flags include:

- *Platitudes that state the obvious.* Examples include: AI is important, it is changing rapidly, faculty should consider its potential impacts on the work that they do. Faculty are probably well aware of these generalities already, and while articulating them might not be harmful, it's also not helpful.
- *Emphasis on larger, long-term dynamics that faculty lack the power to control.* These include national and international efforts to develop policies for managing and regulating AI. Passing along information about large-scale efforts to manage AI (for example, the OECED Recommendation of the Council on Artificial Intelligence [Organisation for Economic Co-operation and Development, n.d.] or the United Nations Internet Governance Principles [United Nations Advisory Body on Artificial Intelligence, 2023]) is a fine way to help faculty develop a general awareness of these efforts, and may help inspire a small number of them to get involved in these efforts themselves. But for the vast major-ity, this awareness won't directly aid their efforts to deal with generative AI in their day-to-day work.

– *Advice that over-weights the ethical and philosophical implications of AI, at the expense of practical ones.* Values surrounding any issue are an important basis for creating effective communications and supporting change, and in the long run, developing a coherent ethical stance on AI will also be necessary if its effects on humanity are to be in any way positive. However, it does a disservice to faculty to imply that pondering this enormous question is something they need to do *before* taking action to address AI in their own teaching.

Unhelpful advice to faculty has also taken one further form, one that perhaps made sense at the very outset of the generative AI revolution but no longer does. This is what I term the "wall of resources:" collections of links, pages, articles, and more, often presented in one lengthy web page. It is true that thoughtfully-designed resource collections are indeed helpful, and putting faculty in touch with the right tools and information is one way for leaders to offer useful support. But as a first-line strategy for bringing faculty up to speed, large, undifferentiated lists of potentially relevant materials are likely to backfire, intensifying a sense of overwhelm among already-stressed faculty.

To be clear: no one sets out to give overwhelming, vague, or counterproductive advice. Nor is creating better alternatives an easy endeavor. People charged with giving detailed, evidence-based guidance are right now in a near-impossible situation, for several reasons. At the time of writing, there isn't yet a deep reserve of scholarship on AI in higher education to draw on in crafting advice. And while a few practical frameworks have begun to emerge, they haven't had time to fully ripen into user-tested, refined, and revised systems that can be counted on to assure good results.

Rapid development of generative AI makes the development of best practices a moving target to say the least, and this speed of change is not something higher education is prepared to cope with (Swaak, 2024). Rapid adaptation is, if anything, an Achilles heel for higher education. Critics throughout modern history have observed that although higher education's culture and systems do some things well, they are massively weighted toward keeping existing practices in place (Rosenberg, 2023). Slow, deliberative processes that privilege consensus almost always crowd out nimble ones that privilege innovation. This is the challenging environment that advice-givers are operating in, and thus, the quality of what they have to say is even more important.

13.3   FIRST STEPS FOR CREATING GOOD ADVICE: BREAK DOWN THE PROBLEM

One of the things that makes approaching AI so overwhelming for newcomers to the topic is that there are so many distinct and sometimes competing implications for faculty work. Should you first tackle the issue of cheating, as many faculty are inclined to do? Or, should you be remaking your assignments with an AI component? Should you be forbidding it, embracing it, or somewhere in between? No single piece of advice, no one handy resource can possibly cover all of these questions, and trying to do so simply creates more confusion and overwhelm for faculty. Thus, it makes sense to start by separating and defining the different sides of the issue.

Here is one suggested scheme for doing so, starting with the piece that does tend to be foremost in mind among faculty just coming to the topic: the potential for rampant cheating and misrepresentation of student work.

13.3.1   Academic Dishonesty and Generative AI

Perhaps nothing has captured faculty energy like the issue of cheating with AI (Gecker, 2023; Massaro, 2023; Swaak, 2024). Tools like ChatGPT excel at drafting exam responses and term papers, as well as identifying the correct answers to multiple-choice questions. Especially in unsupervised settings like asynchronous online courses or homework sessions, professors may effectively have no way to know who or what generated the work submitted in their courses.

Defenses against unsanctioned uses of AI in student work are currently lacking. As faculty seek to come up with ways to cope, ideas for exposing AI-written material are flying fast and furious. One example involves planting "Trojan horse" instructions in assignments in a font that human users can't readily see, thus leading AI tools to incorporate specific, irrelevant words that are then used as proof that the student cheated (MondaysMadeEasy, 2023). Other faculty may rely on strongly worded policies laid out in syllabi forbidding the use of AI for course work. Neither approach – trapping students who use AI, or threatening sanctions – is likely to be effective over the long run. Students will inevitably learn to evade such traps, dragging faculty into a protracted arms race as they set up new ways to catch cheaters, students adapt, and so on in a never-ending cycle. Student-facing policy statements, while important, are also not reliable as mechanisms for guiding behavior, especially given ongoing difficulty with getting students to read and abide by syllabi in the first place (Zamudio-Suarez, 2016).

AI detection tools, which echo the concept and design of popular plagiarism detection software products, evoked early interest among faculty, but soon came under criticism for the high false alarm and miss rates (Coffey, 2024; Weber-Wulff et al., 2023). More disturbingly, these detectors may be predisposed to flag text written by non-native speakers, putting these learners at increased risk of false accusation and punishment (Liang et al., 2023). Perhaps future technological developments will make reliable detection a possibility, but even if so, their use (presumably to catch and punish cheaters) should be only one component of an overall deterrence and prevention strategy. Currently, it is important to stress to faculty just how flawed AI detection tools are (and likely always will be), and the considerable risks of relying on automated detection, up to and including the risk of legal action on the part of students accused of using AI dishonestly.

All of these key facts – that AI can complete many assignments quite competently, that detectors have major limitations, and that policy statements won't make the problem go away – can form the basis for thoughtful guidance to faculty. Here are some ways to begin building on and expanding these core truths.

First, faculty should be assured that they do not have to craft their own AI-related policy statements from scratch. Databases of examples have sprung up, for example, the influential open document "Syllabus Policies for Generative AI" maintained by educator and instructional designer Lance Eaton (Eaton, 2023). At the same time as they are encouraging faculty to use existing examples as starting points, leaders can also discourage them from relying entirely on detection and punishment as AI strategies (although it may be appropriate to also assure them that the institution will back them up in substantiated cases of misconduct).

Some assignments may become, if not AI-proof, significantly more difficult to cheat on with a few changes to the design. Asking students to specifically reference a classroom discussion, or their own prior work on other assignments, tends to trip up AI tools (which can't easily reference something that went on in a real-world environment). Video-presented class content is also more difficult (but not impossible) for AI tools to process, compared to text-based content. Faculty could even consider real-time verbal assessments, such as oral examinations or presentations, as alternatives that make cheating with AI less enticing to students (Young, 2023).

That idea of reducing motivations to cheat, and not just catching students when they do, is the basis for another set of productive conversations leaders can open up with faculty. Emphasizing transparency in assignments, that is, giving explicit explanations of both the purpose and how to succeed, is a research-tested pedagogical strategy (Winkelmes, 2023) that may also help deter cheating by highlighting what students stand to gain through completing the work. Faculty may also want to consider alternatives to rigid grading structures and deadlines (Miller, 2022). This kind of inflexibility (e.g., no late work accepted for any reason, no opportunities to re-do failing work) may be well-intended as a way to achieve rigor and encourage better time management. However, it also makes course work a high-stakes, high-stress endeavor, a condition under which cheating flourishes and that makes otherwise honest students feel that they have little choice but to cheat (Lang, 2013).

Airtight, perfectly equitable, and easy-to-implement AI cheating prevention strategies currently do not, and may never, exist. However, concrete examples geared to specific disciplines and types of courses are part of what leaders can provide to faculty who are struggling to cope with this anxiety-provoking aspect of AI in education. These examples, coupled with encouragement to re-examine course policies for transparency and flexibility, can inspire faculty to move forward in productive ways.

13.3.2   Using AI in Teaching

Balancing out worries involving cheating are the first glimmers of excitement about using AI in teaching. Faculty development leaders can capitalize on this budding enthusiasm to both engage faculty in AI generally and to surface new ideas for accelerating learning and supporting student success. In doing so, leaders can build on a long line of work on incorporating educational technology generally. Much of this work emphasizes starting with the goals of instruction – learning objectives, skills students need to develop, and so on – and using that to guide the selection and design of technology-based activities (Miller, 2019). This contrasts with the first impulse of newcomers to using technology in teaching, which is to seize on a particular tool first then look for ways to use it. Given that we are focusing on a specific technology (generative AI), we may have to let go of this ideal to some extent. That said, this long-standing principle of starting with the goal, then finding the right technology tool, remains an important guide to faculty, one that will save them (and their students) from wasted time and effort. Similarly, identifying the most difficult concepts, or "pinch points" where students repeatedly stumble, can reveal places where technology will offer the biggest return on time invested (Miller, 2019).

Creating good faculty guidance on AI in teaching involves hitting a particular sweet spot between being too general and too focused on the tool itself. This can be accomplished by starting with the goals as they relate to student experience, then offering examples of how the goal could be accomplished using AI. Faculty may or may not adopt those exact examples in their own teaching, but even if not, they will likely use them as a springboard for their own ideas, adapting and changing them to fit style, discipline, and preferences.

For faculty developers tasked with promoting AI in teaching, this raises the question of where to find good ideas and examples. As with other technologies (Miller, 2009, 2019), principles drawn from learning science offer a good starting point. Learning new facts, for example, is facilitated through retrieval practice (actively working to pull information out of memory, as in a practice quiz), spaced practice (spreading study sessions over time rather than cramming), and deep processing (grappling with material in a meaningful, effortful way) (Miller, 2009, 2014, 2022). Developing the ability to engage in sophisticated reasoning and transfer knowledge to new settings – in other words, thinking skills – is facilitated through having students work through multiple challenging problems involving common underlying principles or skills, and by practicing the application of knowledge in reasonably realistic scenarios or situations (Miller, 2014). Starting with these key cognitive processes – developing knowledge, practicing thinking skills – can help faculty identify areas where AI could have the greatest impact.

From there, AI-specific examples can be offered to match the goals. Fortunately, there are currently in circulation several high-quality frameworks that incorporate AI-specific examples geared to college teaching, and more will surely come. The most prominent among these so far are the works produced by Ethan and Lilach Mollick, which offer verbatim prompts aligned to a range of teaching-related goals and approaches (Mollick & Mollick 2023a, 2023b). "Using AI to implement effective teaching strategies in classrooms: Five strategies, including prompts" highlights AI's capacity to help faculty produce (1) examples, (2) explanations, (3) low-stakes quizzes to promote knowledge development, (4) assessment of knowledge gaps that instructors should be addressing, and (5) distributed or spaced practice (Mollick & Mollick, 2023a). "Assigning AI: Seven approaches for students with prompts" takes a different approach, focusing more on different ways of interacting with AI, and the strengths and potential pitfalls to avoid. Roles include AI as tutor, coach, mentor, teammate, tool, simulator, and student, with the last role enabling students to benefit from teaching someone else as a way to solidify one's own knowledge (Mollick & Mollick, 2023b; see also Hendriksen, Chapter 5 in this volume). Notably, these frameworks include verbatim prompt examples that illustrate how AI tools both accomplish the intended goals and serve as materials that faculty can begin using and adapting right away.

Other current standouts among AI teaching frameworks include Daniel Stanford's "Incorporating AI in teaching: Practical examples for busy instructors" and the associated "One useful thing" Substack (Stanford, 2023). Stanford synthesizes work from across different disciplines to create categories of assignment types, including critiquing AI-produced work for accuracy or bias, brainstorming ideas for creative writing projects, and preparing presentations based on a student's own original content.

The future is likely to bring additional ideas for AI-aided teaching, especially those ideas which are discipline- or area-specific. As these resources become more tailored to given areas, it will become easier for developers to connect faculty to those that are likeliest to inspire them, with a minimum of confusion and wasted effort along the way. Regardless of the discipline, however, the best frameworks will have in common an orientation toward the goals the instructor wishes to address, actual prompt language that faculty can use as a starting point, and a connection to principles of how people learn, with particular emphasis on active engagement, realistic practice of skills, spaced practice, and retrieval practice.

13.4   NEXT STEPS: DEVELOPING FACULTY SKILLS IN USING GENERATIVE AI

One of the commonest features of ugly advice is some type of dictate to faculty that they are now responsible for preparing students to work with AI in their careers after graduation. This nebulous vision of future workplaces becomes especially anxiety-provoking when coupled with the fact that few faculty currently have foundational skills, let alone expertise, in using AI for workplace tasks themselves. It is no wonder, then, if they feel particularly adrift when it comes to this aspect of AI.

Given this, the first impulse among leaders may be to offer trainings: workshops and tutorials about different generative AI tools and how to use them. These can be a good start, but won't in themselves provide the one thing that faculty most need, which is well-practiced, field-specific, genuinely useful professional skills. These skills will come, instead, when faculty begin to use AI themselves frequently and organically as part of their own day-to-day work.

One benefit of actual usage is that it rapidly exposes what commercially available AI tools are actually capable of doing, while filtering out company-generated hype (Abril, 2024). For example, some applications are currently touted as being able to create visually appealing, well-structured slide decks that will effectively convey any kind of content the user wishes, at the press of a button or two. Currently, however, slide-making applications fall well short of their promise (in the experience of this author, at least). This disparity between promise and reality will surely change, as will the ease of use and capabilities of all other classes of AI tools. But again, the fastest and most reliable way to know whether this has happened is through experience.

Experience also helps shape that nebulous vision of how AI will be a part of students' future working lives into concrete tasks that faculty can picture and, in turn, teach to their students. Whatever the future of AI in workplaces is, it will surely look different across different sectors: business, healthcare, education, the arts. No one prescription can fit all of these, so good guidance involves having faculty themselves become authentic experts on what it means to use AI effectively and appropriately within a given field. Good leaders will provide the basic working knowledge that gets them started on doing so.

There is one caveat to this facet of good advice, and that is that professional fields themselves are still sorting out what is and is not appropriate use. Even within the relatively small and homogenous field of scientific publishing, for example, there are still a range of different policies and expectations for what constitutes appropriate use of generative AI (Hoover, 2023). There will also no doubt be intense debates about professional practice standards and potential impacts on students as AI-aided grading tools become widely available to faculty (Kumar, 2023; Ma et al., 2024). It's not possible for any instructor, no matter how skilled, to confidently teach what isn't yet known or doesn't exist. But this fact reveals one last important piece of guidance for faculty, which is that they need to stay apprised of these evolving standards within their own professional fields. They likely won't engage in this difficult work just because an institution says they ought to, but they might for the sake of their own research, creative endeavors, or even routine administrative tasks. It will then become a natural next step for them to pass these benefits along to students.

13.5   CONCLUSIONS: CRAFTING BEAUTIFUL ADVICE

Ugly advice can be avoided, and beautiful advice created, with a few working guidelines. First, academic dishonesty and positive uses of AI should be addressed as separate and distinct issues. Then, within the category of positive uses, advice should tightly focus on ideas that are not only specific to educators (as opposed to businesspeople, media creators and so on), but also geared to particular disciplines. This discipline-focused frame, within which educators envision how AI will be used in their own fields, can cut through irrelevant information and reveal the kinds of AI-aided teaching activities that faculty will be genuinely excited to use, revealing ways of using AI that faculty can confidently share with students.

Foregrounding learning science principles, as educational technology experts have long advised doing, can also be a catalyst for new ideas. Lastly, like other academic planning, generative AI benefits from a goal-oriented approach, with an eye to how the tools will be used in students' future work within that field.

But the most important source of ideas is one that is easily overlooked: faculty-to-faculty sharing. Once faculty develop the curiosity and the basic working knowledge to start exploring for themselves, leaders need to provide natural and readily available mechanisms to make faculty discoveries visible throughout a campus. This means affirming and supporting forward-thinking faculty who have stepped up to the AI challenge, encouraging faculty to teach one another, and helping them share the uses of AI that have worked well for them. Taken together, this can help leaders sidestep the bad and the ugly, and elevate the good, as they work to help their campuses adapt to the age of generative AI.

REFERENCES

Abril, D. (2024, February 26). I used AI work tools to do my job. Here's how it went. *The Washington Post*. https://www.washingtonpost.com/technology/2024/02/26/work-ai-copilot-gemini-test/

Coffey, L. (2024, February 9). Professors cautious of tools to detect AI-generated writing. *Inside Higher Ed*. https://www.insidehighered.com/news/tech-innovation/artificial-intelligence/2024/02/09/professors-proceed-caution-using-ai

Eaton, L. (2023). Syllabus policies for generative AI. *Google Docs*. https://docs.google.com/spreadsheets/d/1lM6g4yveQMyWeUbEwBM6FZVxEWCLfvWDh1aWUErWWbQ/edit#gid=0

Gecker, J. (2023, August 10). Paper exams, chatbot bans: Colleges seek to 'ChatGPT-proof' assignments. *Associated Press*. https://apnews.com/article/chatgpt-cheating-ai-college-1b654b44de2d0dfa4e50bf0186137fc1

Gyurko, J., MacCormack, P., Bless, M. M., & Jodl, J. (2016). Why colleges and universities need to invest in quality teaching more than ever: Faculty development, evidence-based teaching practices, and student success [White paper]. *Association of College and University Educators*. https://acue.org/wp-content/uploads/2018/07/ACUE-White-Paper1.pdf

Hoover, A. (2023, August 17). Use of AI is seeping into academic journals – And it's proving difficult to detect. *Wired*. https://www.wired.com/story/use-of-ai-is-seeping-into-academic-journals-and-its-proving-difficult-to-detect/

Kumar, R. (2023). Faculty members' use of artificial intelligence to grade student papers: A case of implications. *International Journal for Educational Integrity*, *19*(1), 1–10. https://doi.org/10.1007/s40979-023-00130-7

Lang, J. M. (2013). Cheating lessons: Learning from academic dishonesty. Harvard University Press.

Liang, W., Yuksekgonul, M., Mao, Y., Wu, E., & Zou, J. (2023). GPT detectors are biased against non-native English writers. *Patterns*, *4*(7), 100779. https://doi.org/10.1016/j.patter.2023.100779

Ma, J., Wang, Y., Zhu, J., & Han, T. (2024). Grading by AI makes me feel fairer? How different evaluators affect college students' perception of fairness. *Frontiers in Psychology*, (February). https://doi.org/10.3389/fpsyg.2024.1221177

Magna Publications (2015). Administrator leadership and faculty support: Best practices for supporting faculty [White paper].

Massaro, M. (2023, August 23). AI cheating has hopelessly, irreparably corrupted US higher education. *The Hill*. https://thehill.com/opinion/education/4162766-ai-cheating-has-hopelessly-irreparably-corrupted-us-higher-education/

Miller, M. D. (2009). What the science of cognition tells us about instructional technology. *Change: The Magazine of Higher Learning*, *41*, 71–74.

Miller, M. D. (2014). *Minds online: Teaching effectively with technology*. Harvard University Press.

Miller, M. D. (2019, August 23). How to make smart choices about tech for your course. *The Chronicle of Higher Education*.

Miller, M. D. (2022, August 2). Ungrading Light: 4 simple ways to ease the spotlight off points. *The Chronicle of Higher Education*.

Mollick, E. R., & Mollick, L. (2023a). Using AI to implement effective teaching strategies in classrooms: Five strategies, including prompts. *SSRN Electronic Journal*. https://doi.org/10.2139/ssrn.4391243

Mollick, E. R., & Mollick, L. (2023b). Assigning AI: Seven approaches for students, with prompts. *SSRN Electronic Journal*, 1–46. https://doi.org/10.2139/ssrn.4475995

MondaysMadeEasy. (2023, November 23). [Here's some advice for using this teacher hack] [Video]. TikTok. https://www.tiktok.com/@mondaysmadeeasy/video/7304804982673476870?lang=en

Organisation for Economic Co-operation and Development (n.d.). OECD legal instruments [Database]. https://legalinstruments.oecd.org/en/instruments/OECD-LEGAL-0449

Rosenberg, B. (2023). *Whatever it is, I'm against it: Resistance to change in higher education.* Harvard Education Press.

Stanford, D. (2023). Incorporating AI in teaching: Practical examples for busy instructors. https://danielstanford.substack.com/p/incorporating-ai-in-teaching-practical

Swaak, T. (2024, February 26). AI will shake up higher ed: Are colleges ready? *The Chronicle of Higher Education.* https://www.chronicle.com/article/ai-will-shake-up-higher-ed-are-colleges-ready

United Nations Advisory Body on Artificial Intelligence (2023). Interim report: Governing AI for humanity. https://www.un.org/en/ai-advisory-body

Weber-Wulff, D., Anohina-Naumeca, A., Bjelobaba, S., Foltýnek, T., Guerrero-Dib, J., Popoola, O., Šigut, P., & Waddington, L. (2023). Testing of detection tools for AI-generated text. *International Journal for Educational Integrity*, *19*(1). https://doi.org/10.1007/s40979-023-00146-z

Winkelmes, M. (2023). Introduction to transparency in learning and teaching. Perspectives In Learning, 20(1). https://csuepress.columbusstate.edu/pil/vol20/iss1/2

Young, J. R. (2023, October 5). As AI chatbots rise, more educators look to oral exams — With high-tech twist. *EdSurge.* https://www.edsurge.com/news/2023-10-05-as-ai-chatbots-rise-more-educators-look-to-oral-exams-with-high-tech-twist

Zamudio-Suarez, F. (2016, August 31). Is anybody reading the syllabus? To find out, some professors bury "hidden gems". *The Chronicle of Higher Education.* https://www.chronicle.com/article/is-anybody-reading-the-syllabus-to-find-out-some-professors-bury-hidden-gems

Index